NATIONALISM ON THE WORLD STAGE

Cultural Performance at the Olympic Games

Philip A. D'Agati

University Press of America,® Inc.
Lanham · Boulder · New York · Toronto · Plymouth, UK

Copyright © 2011 by
University Press of America,® Inc.
4501 Forbes Boulevard
, Suite 200
Lanham, Maryland 20706
UPA Acquisitions Department (301) 459-3366

Estover Road
Plymouth PL6 7PY
United Kingdom

Library of Congress Control Number: 2011920222
ISBN: 978-0-7618-5451-7 (paperback : alk. paper)
eISBN: 978-0-7618-5452-4

CONTENTS

ACKNOWLEDGEMENTS

This book would not have been possible had it rested solely on my shoulders. In reflecting on this project as it went from idea to rough draft to the book you are now reading, several individuals and institutions regularly come to mind. First, I wish to acknowledge two academics, Amilcar Antonio Barreto and William D. Kay, for their support, considerations, and review of the original manuscript. Their guidance proved invaluable in the vision for this study. Richard Pound, a current member and former vice president of the International Olympic Committee from Canada, was also of great help through consultation and review of the original manuscript. Finally, Holly Jordan was an invaluable resource as editor of the final manuscript and a welcomed commentary on my occasionally interesting use of the English language.

On a personal level, this study is the direct result of a group of individuals who maintained my focus (and my sanity) while conducting the research and the writing. I would like to start by thanking my immediate family, including my father Anthony D'Agati, my mother Shirley D'Agati, and my sister Deborah Helfrich for believing in my work and in me as I undertook my collegiate degrees and subsequent research.

As for my friends, there is simply too many who have contributed to my life during the composition of the pages that follow. As I have learned over the years that any attempt to list everyone by name results in both a boring experience for the reader and the guarantee that you forget at least one person, I will spare us both the pain. Instead, I wish to extend my gratitude to my closest circle of friends whose support, care, and patience has been with me for some time. Though each of us came from different pasts and seeks different futures, the brotherhood that develops from true friendship is a rare thing and a contributing factor to every part of our lives.

I would also like to thank my larger circle of friends, including my colleagues at NU and the students/alumni on my Model UN and Model Arab League team, my music ministry at St. Augustine's in Andover, and my friends from Northeastern University, Merrimack College, and Central Catholic. Lastly, I would also like to thank a group of undaunted friends who have been at my side no matter the challenge that lay ahead and whose dedication and diligence to each other have had lasting impressions on all our lives.

Before finishing, I would also like to extend my appreciation to the International Olympic Committee and every city that had the inspiration to host the games. When one strips away the multiple political and economic layers of the Olympic movement, we find a very real and perhaps simple commitment to peace and the growth of humanity at its simplest and most fundamental levels. This study hoped to reach into that spirit and show how identity, ethnicity, and the politics that result from it can shape society instead of destroy it.

ABBREVIATIONS AND ACRONYMS

ACOG: Atlanta Committee to Organize the Games
AAFLA: Amateur Athletics Foundation of Los Angeles
COJO: (Albertville) Comite *Organization* Jeux Olympiques
COOB'92: Organizing Committee of the 1992 Barcelona Summer
   Olympics
FIFA: Fédération Internationale de Football Association (International
   Federation of the Soccer Association)
FIG: Fédération Internationale de Gymnastics (International Federation of
   Gymnastics)
IAAF: International Assocation of Athletics Federations
IF: International Federation
IOC: International Olympic Committee
LAOOC: Los Angeles Olympic Organizing Committee
LOOC: Lillehammer Olympic Organizing Committee
NOC: National Olympic Committee
OCO'88: Organizing Committee of the 1988 Calgary Winter Games
OCOG: Organizing Committee of the Games
OCOG-80: Organizing Committee of the Olympic Games – Moscow 1980
URSS: Union des Republiques Socialistes Sovietiques (Union of Soviet
   Socialist Republics)
USOC: United States Olympic Committee
SLOC: Salt Lake City Organizing Committee
SOCOG: Sydney Organizing Committee of the Olympic Games
SLOOC: Seoul Olympic Organizing Committee

INTRODUCTION

> In the ethnic arsenal you can partially forget what you know if others do
> not notice or do not mind. You can add things if exact knowledge is not
> available. You can choose a suitable variant if different theories exist . . .
> Almost anything and everything are possible, as long as no falsehoods are
> told that are too obviously refuted by common knowledge and as long as
> the adversary is not too strong. (Roosens 1989: 161)

Nationalism is concerned with the grouping of human beings on the basis of
a pre-determined collection of traits the all members of said group are
believed to possess. Frederick Barth (1969) posited that there was the
process of creating an *Us* as a unique category that distinguished its
members from *Them*. *Them,* as a means of referring to those people not
within the culture specified as *us,* simply referred to everyone else. The
process didn't merely involve stipulating a list of traits. It was more
complicated, involving processes of objectification, hegemony, and other
political tools. One of these processes, which has a critical role in
nationalism in the Olympics, involves display. The very essence of display is
cultural performance, which is at the very heart of this study of identity
formation in the Olympics. For the purposes of this study, cultural
performance will be defined as the artistic display of elements of a national
or sub-national identity done so with a planned (deliberate) use of those
elements of culture, icons, narrative, etc. for some purpose.

The goal, therefore, is to discover precisely how cultural performance is
constructed. First, it involves understanding how decision-makers arrive at
their choices and then realizing how those choices are made artistically.
Second, given the expressed set(s) of goals the designer of the message has,

it requires recognizing how these displays are strategically crafted in order to attain said goal. Third, it necessitates discerning in what manner are these goals categorized; the benefit of which is to have a broader understanding of cultural performance in general and specifically in the examples presented in this study. Finally, it concludes with an overall understanding of cultural performance as a facet of an international festival, specifically the Olympic games.

Cultural performance, while always present in the Olympic games, has expanded in scope and function in more recent games. This is, in part, due to a changing understanding of what the Olympics are and their cultural value. This background sets the stage for decades of dynamic change and controversy that never sees a culmination. The Olympics, for whatever reason and for whatever value, are ever-changing and consistent only in that the interpretation of the potential gain, as participating states defines it, from inclusion in them changes as often as the sphere of international relations within which they are nestled.

In 1894, Pierre de Coubertin established the International Olympic Committee [IOC], awarded the Games to Athens and orchestrated a Greek president of the IOC. De Coubertin began a tradition that has lasted for over a century and does not appear to be fading. Quite the contrary, the Olympic movement has grown to include every sovereign state in the world in addition to territories, non-sovereign entities, and nations. Also, the prestige of the games has grown from a mere side show at a World's Fair, as it was in 1900 and 1904, into two major quadrennial events that draw audiences in the billions and revenues just as impressive. In addition to growth in audiences and revenues, the IOC has seen a surge in the number of cities bidding to host the games.

In their infancy, the IOC, at an official session, would offer the duty of hosting the summer games to a city or a state and the planning of the games would grow from that agreement. The procedure would later grow into a nomination process in which IOC members could suggest locations, but the IOC continued, until after World War II, to select the host country from an internally created list and to offer the games to a city the majority of IOC members voted for. Currently, the system has grown in complexity mainly to ensure fairness in a competition that involves cities competing actively with each other to win IOC support. The competition for the 2012 Summer Games had nine cities bidding, which was then reduced to five cities expending extensive city resources to win the right to host.

It is understandable that cities and states have sought the games with such enthusiasm. Hosting the Olympics provides many important opportunities. First and foremost, the economic and infrastructural benefits are undeniable. Peter Ueberroth, the organizer of the 1984 Los Angeles Summer Olympics, proved that the games could be profitable by making over 200 million USD, primarily through implementing cost-reducing plans that required modifying existing structures, utilizing already-built city infrastructures, and pursuing corporate sponsorship and donations of other needs. There is little point elaborating extensively the economic benefits of hosting the Olympics, beyond the fact that careful planning can result in revenues for the city, and as Seoul and Nagano demonstrated, can lead to new trade opportunities as well. However, benefits to Seoul, Nagano and the failed Osaka bid, require some explanation since they are not as readily apparent.

Seoul capitalized on the games by opening political and economic relations with countries that, prior to the Olympics, South Korea had very little or no relations. Nagano used hosting as a means of expanding Japanese industry, including from Central and Southern Japan to northern parts of the archipelago. Finally, the proposed infrastructure changes that Osaka would have implemented had they won the right to host the 2008 summer games involved creating several new islands in the Harbor and supplying public transportation out to the new land. A whole new area of the city would have emerged out of the ocean had Osaka been chosen.

In short, cities have used the games for economic growth, revitalization, and expansion. Whole transportation systems have been built solely because the city had the funding for projects due to hosting the Olympics, or because the fixed deadline of the opening ceremonies offered adequate pressure to keep city and state officials from diverting funds from these projects to other interests. Beyond economical and physical changes to a city, there are many other benefits.

The Olympics have also been used as a form of political legitimization. Germany, a state in the beginning of its revitalization, sought the games for 1936 as a demonstration of their ascension back into European and world politics. This is of particular importance when one recalls that the Germans were not invited to the 1920 Antwerp Games, that the French refused German participation at the 1924 Paris and Charmonix Games, and that German inclusion at the 1928 Amsterdam Games was garnered only with strong lobbying on the part of Germany, Italy, and other European states.[1] This form of political legitimization is so effective and tempting that even the IOC has used it for their own political interests. For example, Antwerp, Belgium and London, United Kingdom were both selected to host the Games after a World War, partly as a symbol that the devastation Germany brought was a part of the past and that these [and other] states not only survived but were capable of hosting the Games in just a few years after being devastated. These examples of political legitimization, or in the case of Germany the reestablishment thereof, through the Games are also apparent in post-World War II politics.

Germany sought reinstatement as early as 1948; as did Japan[2]. Some states, particularly France, the U.K., and Norway, tried blocking the reinstatement of Axis states. Both sides of the debate were fully aware of the symbolic ramifications of German inclusion in the 1948 and 1952 summer and winter Games. Other examples of the political complications of recognizing new national Olympic Committees include the issues surrounding the Soviet Union and the two Chinas.

The Soviet Union first showed interest in the Games by making policy decisions that responded to Nazi organization of the Berlin games. Regardless of taking political positions on Olympic issues, the Soviet national Olympic committee did not gain recognition until 1951.[3] The delay was largely because the Soviet Union did not form a national Olympic committee while there remained unresolved issues between the USSR and the IOC. For both the USSR and the IOC, these issues were considered contingent on Russian membership. This was more complicated than one would think, because the IOC, while recognizing the potential headaches of Soviet involvement, saw benefits in it. Even non-sovereign entities such as Taiwan [now formally recognized by the IOC as Chinese Taipei, but previously as the Republic of China] and Palestine[4] fought for, and won, a form of international recognition they have yet to garner anywhere other than sports federations and the Olympic movement. This effect on politics would grow (some would argue, backfire) as the Olympics reached a new level of political power.

In the 1970s, it became painfully obvious that the Olympics were becoming easily exploited as a political weapon. The opportunities for political legitimization that are present in the Olympics were strong enough to bring bans, boycotts, and other political statements to the stage of the games. The IOC expelled South Africa as a formal protest to Apartheid and created the only compromise between China and Taiwan that resulted in the involvement the People's Republic of China while Chinese Taipei remained involved as well. Three Communist governments, Bulgaria, Soviet Union and Yugoslavia,[5] sought the right to host the games as a means of showing their political and economic systems were equal to or superior to Western systems of economics and governance. All sides of the Cold War used their success in the games as a demonstration of political superiority and civic pride, which simultaneously helped and hurt many states. In particular, it weighed harshly against states that were neutral in World War II and the Cold War. Only one neutral state, Switzerland in 1948, has been allowed to host the Olympics since the end of World War II.[6] The allure of the power the games possessed went beyond affecting states that had a history of involvement in the Olympics. The People's Republic of China tried joining the games but delayed it until after the Moscow games, most likely to avoid their ascension into the games being perceived as a 'communist bloc' event.

Before they considered competing, the Chinese demanded the extrication of Taiwan from the Olympic Movement. China finally became part of the movement and participated in the 1984 Summer Olympics in Los Angeles. China's understanding of the many benefits of hosting the games became quite evident during the Los Angeles Games, as they were already planning to have Beijing bid to host the games. (LAOOC. 1984b)

These examples show how governments have used the Olympics to legitimize themselves within the International Community, and arguably internally to their own people. The process, as explained above, usually affects the legitimacy of governance, which has ramification both internally and externally. However, to understand legitimizing effects of the Olympics on internal matters, one must go beyond the legitimacy of governance. To do this, one must consider other avenues of legitimization that have yet to be discussed herein, or even in the literature on the Olympics as a whole.

The Olympics, by their very nature as a festival, have cultural connotations and therefore cultural ramifications. In fact, the original plan of both the Ancient and Modern Olympics was to have competitions in the arts. Competitions in architecture, music, painting, dance, and other artistic forms of expression were conducted regularly at first, and then sporadically, until World War II. In the post-war period, arts exhibitions replaced competition but remained an integral part of the Games. In 1968, the IOC would actually endorse the use of the Olympics for expressions of nationalism when they amended the rules of exhibition to allow them to depict expressions of national culture instead of international perspectives during the Games.[7]

In its infancy, the IOC realized that the Olympics have great power to affect culture and, more importantly, cultural understanding both internally and externally beyond being just a political and economic event. When one thinks beyond the competitions of the sporting events, the Olympics are a stage—a stage with an international audience, upon which culture, history, heritage, legitimacy, and origin are carefully displayed. Beyond simply numbers, the Olympics have an intangible ability to assist in the process of re-identifying a society. In much the way that traditions are invented, to use Hobsbawm's (1983) terminology, they can be reinvented quickly and clearly in the festivities of the Olympics.

In 1931, Berlin had won the right to host the 1936 Games, by defeating Barcelona with a vote of 43 to 16.[8] At that time, the Weimar government was still in power and the Nazi regime was merely an obscure political party. By the time the games began, the Nazi party was in full control, and Hitler was given the authority, pursuant to the general protocol in the Olympic Charter on such occasions, to declare the games of the XI Olympiad officially open. German conceptions of its own identity, or more accurately Nazi conceptions thereof, were self-evident in the policies

Germany tried to force upon the IOC. Germany had announced restrictions on non-German, non-Aryan participants from Germany, delineating those individuals on the basis of a racial and religious profile, and further called for restrictions on athletes from other states. They argued that it was an insult to have "pure" and "impure" athletes competing together.

The racial policies of Nazi Germany were evident, as early as 1935, in their manipulations of the Olympics. Furthermore, German interest in the Olympics was clearly apathetic until Hitler saw what kind of opportunities a multi-racial, multi-ethnic, multi-cultural competition possessed for proving the superiority of the Aryan race. In an odd way, Germany had simply changed its goals for the games. Where Weimar Germany was seeking to demonstrate a vital and strong German state, Nazi Germany was seeking to demonstrate a vital and strong German nation, which transcended the official boundaries of the state of Germany. Future policies of annexing "German" parts of countries, is proof enough of the Ethnic/Cultural goals of the Nazi Games and the Nazi regime as a whole. The insidious nature of using the Olympics in this manner can be illustrated by the United Kingdom's response to the matter.

According to a March 7, 1936 letter from the British Olympic Association, "it would be nothing short of a calamity if . . . this country [UK] . . . were not fully represented at a gathering which will include athletes from almost every nation." (British Olympic Association 1936: 13.) The letter also stated, that "in sending a team to Berlin they are acting in the best interests of Sport." (ibid) Some states chose not to politicize the games and were then considered to either support the actions of the Host or to be nothing more than silent objectors. While questions of a possible boycott were raised, the U.K.'s response, followed by similar responses from Italy, and France, guaranteed the attendance of the United States and most of Europe regardless of their distain for current German policy. Put another way, Germany got its stage regardless of whether half the participating states liked it or not.

The Berlin Games remain the most memorable and by far the worst example of using the Olympics for an ethnic or racial stage and also of using the Olympics as an opportunity for reinventing a national identity. Since the Nazi games, the Olympic Movement and many states have condemned using the Olympics for such practices, but in fact the practice has continued unabated. Every host has, in some way, utilized the "world stage" to demonstrate their national identity. This demonstration has sometimes been straightforward, sometimes more subtle, and has been everything from a simple restating to a complete revisioning. Moreover, what has in the past been considered inappropriate, dangerous, even sinister, can be appropriate, well crafted, and beneficial.

The unfortunate reality is that perception very much drives opinions of such tactics. The Berlin example illustrates the currently standard viewpoint of the mingling of International events and nationalistic enterprises. Its demonization due to prior inauspicious uses has no bearing on the fact that nationalistic displays in the Olympics are not fascist and certainly not limited only to the popularly known example of 1936. This study will dismiss all notions that the processes articulated in this study are inherently bad. First, this study will establish the existence of many historical examples of the connection between nationalism and the Olympics. Second, it will indicate the many processes and strategies of conducting that relationship and demonstrating that they are objective processes that may be used for either beneficial or pernicious results.

When studied carefully, it becomes apparent that many hosts of the Olympics have used recognizable strategies to objectify, legitimize, alter, and/or display their national and/or sub-national identity(s). In some of the Games, particularly Atlanta and Barcelona, a regional identity can be reconstructed and sold to an international audience, usually in lieu of any display of national or supra-national identity. What has typically been looked down upon, as an inappropriate and damaging use of the Games, can be quite healthy for a society.

My goals are as follows. First, is to point out that processes affecting the concept of an ethnic or national identity can have an impact when conducted at the international level at an event such as the Olympics. The second goal is to dismiss notions that using the Olympics to further a national or sub-national identity is neither intrinsically good nor bad and to demonstrate it to be a process or set of tools that can be used for whatever goal the actor(s) seek. The third and most important goal is to discuss in what ways the Olympics have been used to influence interpretations of the host's national identity. This includes influencing individuals external to the identity entirely, individuals that the legitimizers would consider peripheral to the identity, and individuals that are fully encompassed by the identity. These categories of individuals are necessarily vague as they are meant to encompass all varieties of identities. In short, the categories are valid whether we are discussing a national identity, sub-national identity, or a supra-national identity.

In analyzing the processes of cultural performance in the Olympics, this study recognizes that the Olympics is not a source of nationalism. The Olympics offer only a stage through which a national identity is performed or displayed. In other words, the Olympics are a vehicle for nationalism with their own structures and strategies that affect the overall process by performing their identity on the Olympic Stage. The performance is a planned expression that is designed to meet the goals of the actor.

Additionally, performance of nationalism through the Olympics uses specific strategies, which attempt to accomplish certain nationalistic goals.

Depending on what type of individuals the actor intends to influence and also depending on what type of national identity is the "benefactor" of this effort, there are specific strategies in use to demonstrate and reform identity on the Olympic stage. The final goal driving this study involves an in-depth analysis of these methods and accounts for how these processes have affected politics of culture within the host nation as well as internationally. Taken together, the purpose of this study is to demonstrate that cultural performance of a national identity occurs by use of clearly identifiable and definable strategies that are utilized in order to attain specific goals, determined by the organizer. The choices actors made, while designing their iconic Cultural Displays are in fact deliberate attempts to redefine identity in ways convenient to the crafter.

In summary, this study will confirm several notions about cultural performance in the Olympics. First, that cultural performance and demonstration of a specific identity is a feasible undertaking in an international festival, such as the Olympics, and that these venues are not the sources of the identity but instead are processes that offer stages through which the demonstration is conducted. Second, that this process is constructed out of a collection of strategies intentionally selected by the actors, based their nationalism's circumstances and goals, which, when used effectively and efficiently, result in an alteration which either reemphasizes or alters the original perceptions of the identity. Finally, the process, as an objective reality, will be shown to have no intrinsic moral character but can result in whatever moral or immoral outcome that the actor conducting the process has set forth as his or her goals in the process.

NOTES

1. Letter of Count Benito Sorgano, President of the Italian National Olympic Committee, May 13, 1931.

2. In the post World War II period, states that were deconstructed due to invasion, being conquered, or losing the war, lost their national Olympic committees, often, in the case of Germany, this included the death of their IOC members. The result of that was their status as having recognized national Olympic committees ended and they needed to be re-admitted to the Games.

3. S. Sobolev, letter to IOC, Moscow, April 1951, in Avery Brundage Collection, No. 149, USOA NOC, 1947-69, p.2.

4. Athletes from Palestine began appearing in the Olympics as representatives of the Palestinian Liberation Organization [PLO]. Currently, the officially

recognized name of this NOC is the Palestinian Olympic Committee and they are recognized formally as Palestine.

5. The cities of Sofia, Moscow, and Sarajevo and Belgrade, respectively.

6. This is, of course, for no lack of trying. Switzerland, Sweden and Portugal have all failed, numerous times in the case of Sweden, to win the right to host either Winter and/or Summer games. St. Moritz was the only prior host of the Winter Olympics in Europe that was not occupied during the War.

7. From Susan Bandy's contribution in Segrave, Jeffrey O. and Donald Chu, *The Olympic Games in Transition,* (Champaign, IL: Human Kinetics Books, 1988), 167.

8. Outcomes of many IOC votes for host city selection have been archived by the website: http://www.gamesbids.com/.

CHAPTER 1
OLYMPIC HISTORY AND NATIONAL DISPLAYS

I. THE ANCIENT GAMES

The history of nationalism and the Olympics is a long history of inconsistency, vibrancy, and even dormancy. Through a brief history of the Olympics, both ancient and modern, one finds that displays of identity as rudimentary as city-state pride are an endemic part of "international" sports competition. This chapter will be a serviceable account of nationalism in the Olympics, as well as will illustrate in what ways it has become more prevalent in the Olympics. It then concludes with recent Olympiads, as a culmination of a process that now features nationalism as a constant part of the ceremonies of the Olympics.

Many of the political and cultural manifestations in the modern Olympics have their roots in, or at the very least their own equivalence in, the ancient Olympics. The ancient Olympics, which ran from 776 B.C. to 393 A.D.,[1] spanned nearly 1,200 years as a quadrennial festival open to all Greek men. City-states all across Greece were represented in these competitions. The current framework of nation-states competing in the modern Olympics is an artifact of this city-state tradition. Due to our rather broken history of the ancient Olympics, it is impossible to accurately gauge in what manner politics manifested itself in the ancient Olympics. While the process eludes us, certain observations on specific manifestations of politics in the ancient Olympics are both feasible and conducive to this study as those manifestations relate directly to the demonstration of political identity in the ancient Olympics.

Politics in the ancient Olympics often centered on matters of prestige and influence. As is the case with the modern Olympics, organizers of the ancient Olympics saw benefits to hosting and competing. However, unlike the modern games, the ancient Olympics did not move from location to location. They were always held at the Sanctuary of Zeus near the city of Elis. Elis played host to the games, provided all the judges, facilities, and equipment. Remembered in history for little else, the city of Elis took great pride in serving as the seat of the Olympic Games and flaunted that pride to other Greek city-states and foreign countries.

Leaving to one side the benefits—political, economic and social—that the city of Elis reaped from playing host, the other clear and perhaps most politically significant contribution of the ancient games was *ekecheiria*—the Olympic truce. Due to the awe and fear of the God of Thunder as well as the legal ramifications of violating it, the Olympic truce brought an end to all wars in Greece during the games. Beyond inciting the gods, city-states that violated the truce risked being banned from Olympic competition and were forced to pay fines to the Eleians; the only real enforcement of this protocol. Thucydides recorded that all athletes from a city-state or colony would be blocked from competition if their city-state violated this truce (1989: 344). This was true even though athletes were not seen as part of what we would designate today as a "national" team. Genealogical and political identities were used, not to coalesce a team, but to determine eligibility of athletes.[2]

Another political manifestation in the ancient Olympics was the simple role it played as host to diplomacy. The Olympic games were a rare occasion during which the leaders and notables of many city-states gathered together in one location. While impromptu diplomatic relations were by no means the reason these dignitaries attended, they were a side effect of the festival. In fact, most of the time leaders and their cohorts only attended the games if they had a citizen competing with a reasonable chance of winning a competition (Sinn 2000: 77). Alternatively, many attended because of something they wished to show or brag about to other leaders and notables (*Ibid.*). In short, the Olympics were both a source and a venue for civic pride—a rudimentary patriotism, perhaps—to be both nurtured and displayed.

One fact becomes apparent from this brief description. With the exception of the Olympic truce, politics in the ancient Olympics revolved around civic pride. Whether that was pride gleaned directly from competition or whether the Olympics were just a mere venue for boasting, the Olympics were a venue of city-state and individual prestige. Therefore, the Ancient Olympics can be seen as being deliberately used to foster community spirit.

There is not enough evidence at the moment to outright state that any city-state, with the possible exception of Elis, used the Olympics for any other direct political benefit. Since Elis was the constant host, political opportunity for all other Greek city-states rested solely on athletic performance

Only the Eleians could easily derive political benefits from hosting. Also, because the Olympics were conducted to pay homage to a deity and were also held on sacred ground, very few individuals were willing to risk any action that would desecrate the games. This relegated political uses of the Olympics to only the simplest of goals—mainly civic pride and diplomacy off to the side.

The presence of civic pride as a result of the competitions is far different from nationalism in the modern era, and a similar distinction in the Ancient Olympics was also prevalent. The Pindaric Olympic odes include many examples of praise of both athletes and city-states for their efforts and accomplishments.[3] There is limited evidence, in the Pindaric Odes and elsewhere, to suggest that the city-states were directly involved in promoting themselves to their citizens and to others through the Olympics. There is, however, indication that both athletes and city-states used the Ancient Olympics for what can be defined as tautopolism.

The term tautopolism, is taken from the Greek words *tautos*, which Aristotle used to describe identity in terms of "'being of the same blood' or 'of the same stock'"(Aristotle 1934: 1161b 1), and polis, the Greek word for 'city' (Crane 2005). Therefore, a literal translation would be the concept of 'city selfness.' In this sense, tautopolism is intended to suggest the concept of a shared city-state identity. Similar to nationalism, tautopolism was an elite-controlled concept that helped to define the people of a specific Greek city-state. Therefore, elite goals to foster nationalism through their competition in or hosting of the modern Olympic Games, can be seen as similar to elite goals to foster tautopolism through similar opportunities in the ancient Olympic Games.

All but one competition in the ancient games fielded individual athletes who supported themselves. In this sense, there is little connection to modern practices of choosing competitors through complicated qualifications and regulations. City-state involvement in eligibility was almost non-existent in the ancient Greece. Two thousand years ago, athletes decided to attend the games on their own and would travel to Elis for that purpose with approval of the city-state unnecessary. The only exception to this was the chariot races. Wealthy and prominent individuals and city-states fielded teams (Thucydides 1910: 6.16.2). For our study, the latter is the most important as it offers evidence that city-state elites saw value in the Olympic competitions such that they were willing to take upon the city the cost in fielding, in some cases, many teams (*Ibid.*).

It should not be presumed that, besides possessing the means to get to the game, anyone could compete. The aforementioned requirement of being Greek was an enforced regulation. Athletes were obliged to present proof of their Greek heritage. The ancient Olympics were a competition between

Greek-born citizens of the Greek city-states, and Greek colonies. It is reasonable to assume that the Greeks saw the Olympics as an opportunity for fostering pan-Hellenic pride. Gigliola Gori (1997) showed that 19th and 20th Century Italian sports policy was mainly interested in intra-state sports festivals for this purpose. Katharine Moore (1997: 72) suggested how the United Kingdom, in the same periods, saw the potential of sport in "strengthening the links within the empire."

Both examples show how states have used the games to consolidate authority within a state or empire. The British example may offer a keen insight into why athletes from Greek colonies were allowed to participate in the games, as it shows an effort to coalesce non-British subjects into a global empire. For the Greeks, this could have been a process of consolidating a pan-Hellenic sense of all Greek city-states and colonies. It should be noted that while athletes were required to establish themselves as being Greek, they did not have to establish their Hellenic ancestry as connected to a particular political or geographic entity. Many athletes, as is common today,[4] did accept incentives to claim they were from a specific city-state (Perrottet 2004: 50). Without the formal support of athletes by the city-states, there are very few links between athletes and polis interests. What is common, however, is that city-states took advantage of athletic victories by their citizens. These athletes were depicted in statues in their hometown and they were often immortalized in odes and songs (Pindar 1961).

The Pindaric odes include poems written to highlight and praise Olympian athletes. These celebrations of athletes included direct or subtle indications of the city-state of origin. However, they usually laud the athlete and his great feats instead of praising the city-state or its identity; but they do extol the athlete as the champion of that political entity. The odes offer minimal evidence of clear interpretations of the games for tautopolism, but do show a connection between the vibrancy of the city-state and a sense of accomplishment among Greek athletes.

In the modern games, these venues provide sufficient evidence of the Olympic-nationalism connection, but are by far not the most prolific or prominent examples of this relationship. The most common venue of nationalism in the Modern Olympics occurs during the opening and closing ceremonies, performed through the pageantry, the dress, and the deliberate display of national symbols throughout these events. A secondary type of this performance is victory ceremonies for medalists.[5]

The ancient Olympics did have a kind of opening ceremony. However, we have very little evidence regarding any deliberate presence of elements of political identity in those rituals. In the written histories of the times, particularly Thucydides and Herodotus, there are no references to such elements. Also, as athletes competed naked in the Ancient Olympics, there were no uniforms or outfits that could display city-state iconography. Unfortunately, other ceremonial aspects of the games are not a primary focus of ancient histories. These are detailed enough to indicate such descriptive facts as the color of the judges' robes. With such in-depth attention to detail, if city-state identity played a prominent role in the ceremonial aspect of the ancient Olympics, then it is reasonable to expect that this fact, or at least some evidence of it, would have been present in the recorded histories.

There is evidence that the Eleians did manipulate the games for their own pride and political identity. In 435 BC, Herodotus (1998: 160), recorded that a delegation from Elis visited Egypt to proclaim the greatness of their city and the Olympic games. For the Eleians, the games were the quintessential depiction of the life and times of their city. The Eleians' visit, more of a quest than a diplomatic excursion, sought the endorsement of the wisdom of Egypt on the fairness and organization of their games (*Ibid.*). From Herodotus's recordings, the Eleians discussed nothing else with the Egyptians.

The Eleian visit to Egypt offers adequate proof that the games were seen, at least by the Eleians, as possessing political advantage in the realm of tautopolic/civic pride. Taken together with the Pindaric odes and evidence of diplomatic opportunity within the ancient histories, there is reasonable evidence to support statements that athletes, city-states, and hosts of the ancient Olympic games used Olympic festivals to their own benefit and that of the city-state, if only marginally. Furthermore, recent studies on the ancient Olympics, particularly Sinn (1996), which discussed many cultural aspects of the Olympics in ancient sources such as Pausanias' travelogues, the Greek geographer Strabo, and Pindar, indicated the beginning of said relationships but did not offer compelling evidence of deliberate attempts at using the ancient Olympics to bolster the political and cultural aspects of the city-states.

Sinn (1996: 76) indicates that city-states sent "official festival legations" to festivals like the Olympic games. He also indicates that this was even more likely if one of their citizens was expected to win a competition. Sinn does not, however, indicate what tautopolic tendencies or accoutrements accompanied these legations. Again, we are only able to conclude that any such tendencies present were likely to be superficial at best. One exception to this is found in Herodotus's history.

In *The Histories*, written around 435 BC, Herodotus (1998: 311) justifies Macedonia and the Macedonians as Greek when he wrote "the officials in charge of the Greek games at Olympia have acknowledged that this is so." In a very interesting twist, the Olympic games were used to establish the presence of Greek identity instead of the games being used to either demonstrate or embellish that identity. In fact, the Olympic games appeared to have a transcendent importance above the welfare and wellbeing of the city-states. As war was being waged against all of Greece by the Persians, the Greeks "sent only an advanced guard" to hold the Persians at bay while everyone was at the games (*Ibid.*, 477). In a sense, therefore, we see a dichotomy in which the games held a very real and important position in Greek society and were revered to such a level that to make use of said position was only done with the utmost of care and respect.

It seems clear that the ancient Olympics held a very important and well-established role in the history of ancient Greece. It is further apparent that individuals and city-states exploited the games for their own goals, which resulted in tying city-state vibrancy and athletic success symbolically together. Such deliberate attempts at the extraction of political benefits from participation in the Ancient Games help to demonstrate that there is a legacy of fermenting political identity in the Modern Olympics, in the Ancient Olympics.

II. REBIRTH OF THE GAMES

After the ancient Olympics ceased, they remained an artifact of history for more than a millennium. While there were local manifestations of interest in such competitions, and were even well established—notably in England, Germany, and Greece in the 19th Century—these were ephemeral at best. It was not until Baron Pierre de Coubertin perceived political benefits in the Olympics that interest in the quadrennial event was rekindled. His interest was derived from French failures on the international scene, namely French failure to win the Franco-Prussian War due to the physical inferiority of French soldiers (Senn 1999: 20). While his interest in sport was vested in the physical wellbeing of youths, the objective of said interest was to maintain an able fighting force.

Coubertin's interest in sport was primarily vested in its ability to help build strong Frenchmen for war. This was, of course, very similar to the role sport played in Antiquity. After many years of research and practical experience, Coubertin started the Union des Sociétés Françaises de Sports Athlétiques, and two years later, in 1892, he decided to rekindle the Olympic Games. Initially, what was driven by vindictiveness directed towards the Prussians was now pushed forward by patriotism and peace. It is important to realize that the earliest manifestation of the modern games was, before they were even formulated, considered along national lines and configured to be contests between individuals that ultimately had utility for the nation-state.

Considering Coubertin's commitment to the roles of "nations" in the Olympics, the setup of the International Olympic Committee (IOC) was and remains quite opposite to Coubertin's vision of the benefits of the games for nation-states. Coubertin insisted that the IOC should be comprised of men who were ambassadors to their countries as opposed to having those men be ambassadors from their countries of origin to the Olympic Movement. Under this rubric, the IOC would chose the "representatives" of its member states. The result of this was the political independence of the Olympic movement from the intervention of the governments of the participating states.

A noteworthy side effect of this policy of not having direct representation of governments in the IOC was to make IOC membership more flexible than any other international organization. Because IOC members represented themselves, instead of a government, the IOC allowed non-sovereign entities to field competitors in the Olympic Games and were also able to solve controversial issues like China and Taiwan because IOC participation was not an *ipso facto* endorsement of legal sovereignty. The balance of national and individual interests in the movement helped to make the modern Olympic movement unique in the early years of its formation.

The early days of the Modern Olympics were driven by a commitment both to the nation and to individuals. This dichotomy continued into the 1896 Athens Olympics. The IOC members, chosen in part to guarantee the representation of many countries in the organization,[6] were specifically chosen to represent themselves and not their governments. Athletes represented their national Olympic committees (NOCs) at the opening ceremonies and in the competitions. Starting at the1896 Athens Games, winners had their flag of origin raised over the stadium in an awards ceremony. Athletes' uniforms for the competitions sported the logos of their countries of origin -- such as a red/white cross for Swiss track and field athletes. However, athletes broke down national barriers in many competitions, such as the joint Irish-German Tennis team that took first place in the pairs tennis final (Guttmann 1994: 19).

Beyond the placement of national symbols and the national pride that is endemic in any competition in which athletes represent their nations, there is relatively little more that can be added to the discussion of nationalism in the 1896 Olympics. Greek nationalism in the 1896 Olympics represents a marked exception. At first, Greek nationalism played a very minor role. Opening ceremonies were limited to formal proceedings and speeches. The pageant that is now the crown jewel of the opening ceremonies was not yet held. However, much along the lines of the current literature of nationalism and the Olympics, Greek national pride was fanned with every Greek victory, including the marathon (Guttmann 1994: 19).

With the first Olympiad behind them, the IOC continued its efforts to further solidify the Olympics recent manifestation into a permanent quadrennial event. For the purpose of this study, the most pertinent question in the Pre-World War I years was city selection. The process of bidding had not been created, so hosts were chosen by the direct invitation of the IOC. In this early period, very few people realized the potential benefits of hosting the Olympics. They were not even considered a possible avenue of financial gain. During this early period, cities such as Paris, Chicago, and Rome showed little interest in hosting the Olympics when they were approached with an offer. It was only with de Coubertin's hands-on politicking in France that convinced Paris to host the 1900 Games. Displaying a lack of enthusiasm for the games Chicago, the original host for the 1904 Summer Games, was replaced by St. Louis, which accepted them as a *sideshow* for their Louisiana Purchase Centennial Celebration (Guttmann 1994b: 25). Rome, the original host of the 1908 Games, also refused to host the Olympics,[7] which resulted in London agreeing to take on the responsibility.

The St. Louis Games were the first demonstration of the more pernicious side of nationalism in the Olympics. Partly due to a shortage of teams willing to travel across the Atlantic and half of America to get to St. Louis, and partly due to a pre-existing tone of racism, the St. Louis games had several racist demonstrations. Failures on the part of Asian and African competitors, who were not actually trained athletes but were instead taken from local sideshows, were attributed to the logical result of their race and not their lack of preparation. This began a negative trend that would last for several Olympiads. This form of nationalism in the Olympics would culminate in the 1936 Berlin Summer Games, but it took this form decisively, and by choice, in 1908.

London held a very successful and well-attended Olympic Games. Regardless of its success, the 4th Olympiad was marred with nationalist problems. Ireland, an integral part of the United Kingdom, was home to a significant independence movement. The British, who did allow some Irishmen on their team, kept their presence subdued and were reticent to include anything Irish in the ceremonies. The Americans, on the other hand, brought a team with a large Irish-American contingent, all of whom were more than willing to take the 1908 Summer Games as an opportunity to complain about the lack of Irish sovereignty.

London also saw the first demonstration of the tradition of not lowering the United States Flag in the presence of the monarch. By tradition, and out of deference to the reigning monarch, every national flag is lowered below the monarch's head as it passes his/her place in the stadium. The United States, out of an athletic tradition, and not due to any U.S. statutory regulation, refuses to lower its flag to any monarch. This insult, from the British perspective, was coupled by the brazen effort to keep the American flag at half-staff to protest Irish subjugation. Beyond a less than friendly atmosphere between the British and the Americans, this particular problem was limited to cheers and jeers by the crowd and accusations of misconduct by both sides.

At the London games, nationalism played yet another new role in the Olympics. In the early 20th century, Finland was occupied by Russian soldiers, and as a result was not considered a sovereign state. However, Finnish officials convinced the IOC to allow Finland to participate at the Olympics under the Finnish flag as opposed to the Russian flag. Early in the history of the games, there was a question as to what kind of entity could send teams to compete. Precedence was on the side of Finland, as Bohemian athletes competed under the flag of Bohemia at the 1900 Paris Olympics and even won a medal (*Olympic Games* 2000: 242). Further precedence was established with Canada's participation and victory at the St. Louis 1904 Games, which occurred prior to both Canadian independence (*Ibid.*, 246) and the formation of a national Olympic committee.

The IOC had no easy answer to these questions of state or non-state qualification for participation. In the early 20th Century, the concept of sovereignty was far more complicated than it is now. With colonies, nations under dominance by other empires, and even parts of the world that had no formal diplomatic relations with any Olympic-participating state, there was no easy means of determining who could or could not participate. While there are very few colonies left in the world, this problem persists with the myriad of nations currently without sovereignty (i.e., Catalonia in Spain, Quebec in Canada, Scotland in the United Kingdom, Sicily in Italy, etc.).

The British organizers of the London 1908 Olympics, led by Lord Desborough of Taplow, indicated the existence of the problem and offered a solution when the British Organizing Committee established the definition of "country" as "any territory[8] having separate representation on the International Olympic Committee" (Cook 1908: 29). As one can imagine, this was a less than helpful definition. This statement opened the door for participation by non-sovereign entities such as Canada, South Africa, Bohemia, and Finland. British officials welcomed the first two, while the last two were strongly objected to by the empires that ruled over them, the Hapsburg and the Russian empires, respectively. Regardless of their objections, Finland and Bohemia both attended the London games. Much to the surprise of many, the British even went so far as to allow Scotland, Ireland, and Wales to field individual teams in the Hockey competition (*Ibid.*, 197).

By the start of the 1912 Stockholm games, the situation became incredibly complicated and problematic. The International Olympic Committee was forced to recognize that it existed in a state-driven world. Finland lost its independent participation, having to settle for a token Finnish pennant atop the Russian Flag (Senn 1999: 30). The Czechs and Bohemians were also subjugated under the Austro-Hungarian Empire. Some non-sovereign polities were allowed to continue participating as separate entities -- notably Australia, Canada, New Zealand, and South Africa. In most cases, though, they participated with the permission of the government that controlled their territory

The 1908 London and 1912 Stockholm games are critical turning points in the history of nationalism and the Olympics. At these games, the broadening of inclusion[9] of non-sovereign entities gave these entities the chance to participate alongside sovereign states in an international event. The result was a sense of autonomy and even independence that some nations would eventually attain. Even now, states still hearken back to this early period as the beginning of their modern independence. For example, the Czech Republic, in its webpage on the Olympic website (International Olympic Committee 2005), and its predecessor Czechoslovakia, in many of its propaganda materials from the 1980s (i.e., Kossl 1988), refer to Czech and Czechoslovak participation in international sporting events beginning in 1899, more than two decades prior to its formal establishment as Czechoslovakia in the post World War I period.

Recognition as part of the international community is one of the most alluring aspects of the Olympics, which has very important nationalistic ramifications for the international community and the nations in question. The IOC, as a result of these decisions taken in the early years, set itself up for a series of very complicated situations involving the questions of states vs. nations and how to determine what should and what should not be considered nations viable for participation in the Olympics.

III. THE INTER-WAR PERIOD

The 1912 games were the last Olympics before World War I. The 1916 Games, which were slated to take place in Berlin, Germany, were cancelled due to hostilities. The result was an eight-year hiatus. The games returned to the international scene in 1920 when Antwerp, the center of Belgian resistance, hosted the event. The Antwerp Olympics signified an important change in the movement since Coubertin used these first post-war Olympics as the location to introduce an Olympic identity. The post-World War I period gave the Olympics a new symbol, oath, and motto. The new symbol and motto demonstrated that Coubertin had a keen understanding of the dichotomy of the Olympics: the local (national) and the international.

The motto represented the goals of the athletes of the Olympics. The motto in Latin is *Citius, Altius, Fortius*, which means "faster, higher, stronger." The meaning behind this is to call the athletes to strive even harder in order to be victorious. The Olympics, much like any sporting event, is about the individual, or team, seeking to become ever greater in their efforts, and in so doing, to surmount all others in their quest to be champions. The symbol of the Olympics, which can be found on the Olympic Flag and all other paraphernalia of the Olympic Movement, was five simple interlocking rings, each of a different color. Each color represented a geographic region of the world: Black for Africa, Blue for Australia and Oceania, Green for Europe, Red for the Americas and Yellow for Asia.

The symbol is one of peace, harmony, and equality. All of the rings are equal in size, and each color is no more or less vibrant than the others. Every polity that has ever and will ever field a time is represented by one of the five colors. These rings were a perfect symbol for Coubertin's view of the role of the Olympics on international relations. The rings represent harmony. The equality of the rings is obviously a symbol for the equality of all races, ethnicities, of all nations that are a part of the Olympic movement. In every means of interpretation, the rings represent peace. It is no surprise that this symbol was created and introduced in the post-World War I period, a time when the international community had accepted the arrival of a "lasting" peace, typified in the interlinking of many states together in the League of Nations

While he was initially unwilling to accept a formal role for states in the Olympic movement, Coubertin was clearly now willing to consider the athlete and their nation and/or state of origin as having interests in the games. It was a wise move on his part. The Olympics, through its own symbols, demonstrated that its mission is both to the welfare of the international world—the states—and to that of the athletes. The IOC could base its future decisions as supporting either one or the other, and not necessarily always to the exclusive interests of states or athletes. In addition to symbols created out of thin air, the Baron and future hosts slowly continued the Hellenization of the Olympics. The international sports festival appropriated more and more the symbols from the ancient Olympic Games. This was no doubt a process of further legitimizing the Olympics by making it appear more ancient. This process also had significant repercussions for the international dissemination of Greek identity.

Since the IOC's Olympics managed to survive the World War I, the games had a much stronger argument as the official and sole organizer of modern Olympiads. With the addition of new and ancient symbols, the next 16 years led to a complete legitimization of the IOC, the Olympics, and as a result, those entities formally attached to it. Specifically, the Olympics were already being effectively used to solidify the creation of International Federations and to further legitimize and recognize newly independent states, such as Czechoslovakia. Because of the survivability of what started out to be a tenuous celebration of sport, the end result was also a sanctification of the Baron, the rest of the IOC and of its decisions from that point on.

While the post-World War One history of the Olympics represented a period of revitalization and growth, this was also a period of exclusion and retribution. The end of the war did not see an opportunity at reconciliation immediately; formal reconciliation of all European States into the Olympics did not happen right away. As a result of their military actions, Germany was excluded from the 1920 Games. It was no secret that Antwerp was selected because it made a political statement about the war and its only temporary effects on Belgium.

The war effectively did temporarily eliminate the overt presence of nationalism in the Olympics. The Belgians had only roughly one and a half years to organize the Olympics. In that time, they managed a simple and austere event. Adding to this was the inclusion of the Baron's new symbols and traditions. In short, the Antwerp games did not provide Belgians the opportunity to play games with nationalism. However, the very fact that they were granted the chance to host the Games as a symbol of their "triumph" over Germany indicates, regardless of the lack of presence of nationalism in the event, that the whole event itself was a sign of resurgence in Belgian pride, independence, and identity.

The Antwerp Summer Olympics were followed by both Winter and Summer Olympics in France. In 1924, the International Olympic Committee decided to institute a winter competition for the first time. Paris had been selected the host of the 1924 Olympics as a means of commemorating the 30th anniversary of the IOC and Coubertin, who announced his retirement prior to the selection. France, as host of the summer games, was given the right to select the host of the Winter Olympics. They chose the Alpine resort of Chamonix.

From these games onward to Berlin, the Olympics continued through a series of internal changes. The games lost their founder and the IOC elected Count Henri de Baillet-Latour of Belgium as the new President of the IOC. The IOC also addressed questions of amateurism, the inclusion of women in new sporting events, the arrival of new sports, and the restructuring of the winter festival in a successful quadrennial event.

The changes to the Olympic Movement did not end with Antwerp. Paris saw the official debut of the aforementioned Olympic motto, and St. Moritz played host to the first Olympic winter games under that title.[10] The Amsterdam Games saw the beginning of the tradition of Greece leading the Parade of Nations while the host team ended the parade. The incorporation of these and other traditions was perhaps the most important aspect of the Inter-War Games. While this was a period of growing symbolism and increasing traditions for the Olympics, this was also a period of increasing nationalistic tendencies in the official ceremonies of the games.

As already mentioned, there was a change in the parade of nations; the host country was given a position of distinction as the last team to enter the opening ceremonies. The torch relay, instituted at the Berlin Games, allowed the Olympics to be brought to every corner of the host country, symbolically incorporating the whole nation in the event. At the 1932 Los Angeles Games, a victory stand was added to raise the national flag of the winner.

This latter gesture ended any question as to the primacy of the nation in the Olympic Games and the opportunities for nationalism and patriotism in the quadrennial event. Beyond these observations, very little else has been well researched and written about the inter-war games other than the 1936 German Olympics.

What historians would praise as a Golden Age of the modern Olympics (See Guttmann 1994b & Senn 1999) has been the least studied aspect of Olympic history. If anything typified this period, it would be growth, great competition, and a sense of spectacle that slowly reinvigorated the games. These games are rarely discussed in depth due entirely to their timing. Occurring between World War I and the infamous Nazi Olympics, these games are usually remembered only superficially for their relative simplicity and lack of controversy. As for studies of nationalism, most histories of the Olympics either superficially or do not comment on any presence of nationalism in the Olympics prior to the Nazi Olympics.

While the degree of nationalism exhibited by the host was somewhat limited, the exact opposite was true about nationalities that were seeking recognition on the international scene. Guttmann (1994) indicated that nationalism posed new problems because many groups, including the Czechs and the Poles achieved independence and sought international recognition through the games. The Czechs and the Poles were allowed entrance, but not the Hungarians because they were on the losing side of the war. The Irish and the Armenians were also denied entry due to the lack of independence (Guttmann, 1994b: 38). These events mark a period of an increasing presence of nationalism based issues in the Olympics.

Taken together, the resurgence of nationalism and the incorporation of Olympic symbols and traditions that led to the prominent placement of national symbols set the stage for the next 80 years of nationalism in the Olympics. The only detractor on the placement of nationalism in the Olympics was the ramifications and perceptions of the concept that resulted from the Nazi Olympics.

IV. DEUTSCHLAND ÜBER ALLES

In 1936, the IOC turned its attention to the first German games. Berlin, which lost its first chance to host due to World War I, now had a chance to recapture it. In addition to the Summer Olympics, the Germans had the Winter Olympics in Garmisch-Partenkirchen. Together, the two German Olympics represent the penultimate expression of nationalism in the Olympics. What had been a slow growing process since 1896 resulted in two things: first, the ascension of the Olympics into the preeminent international sports competition and, second, the now unquestionable role nationalism played in the Olympics.

The Weimer Republic was still the official government of Germany in 1931 when Berlin was awarded the 1936 Olympics, and its leadership was looking forward to the opportunity to demonstrate a rebuilt, revitalized, and peaceful German state. The war had been very destructive for Germany. Years of warfare were followed by economic isolation that fueled the slow disintegration of the German state. By the time the Olympics were approaching, the Weimer Republic had collapsed under Hitler's Nazi regime. Initially, the Hitler government was disinterested in its duty to host the Olympics (Senn 1999: 50-52). However, Hitler rapidly changed his mind when he realized that Weimar Germany was not simply being shortsighted when it sought the chance to host.

What was initially supposed to be an opportunity to demonstrate the ascension of a strong and vibrant German state would remain fully intact, but with a different message. The Nazi Olympics, as they are now referred to by many historians, were now aimed at demonstrating the power of a reconstructed German state and the supremacy of the German–Aryan people. The new goals of the German Olympics immediately caused problems for the Olympic movement. By the time the Los Angeles Olympics ended, the Olympic movement had divested itself of a history of discrimination. While there were no written policies on discrimination, the Olympics raised the issue of who could or could not compete. For example women had not been allowed to compete at all in the Athens Games. The number of women competitors increased by 400% from the Antwerp to Berlin (Senn 1999: 41).

Racial discrimination in the international Olympic movement was very rare; incidents such as the aforementioned ones in St. Louis were exceptions. Typically, racism in the Olympic movement manifested itself primarily via National Olympic Committees rather than by the IOC or by a host nation. However, as illustrated in the previous section, punitive measures against the losing parties in World War I resulted in banning Germans from competition. Regardless of the intentions, restrictions on the participation of specific individuals, whether it was due to gender or politics, had all but evaporated by the time the Olympic movement was preparing for the 1936 Olympics.

The entire direction of the Olympics with regard to discrimination formally ended as a result of two occurrences. First, was the imposition of Nazis racist policies on the Berlin Games, which became increasingly more blatant. Second, and much to the credit of the IOC, Olympic and government leaders in several states, heretofore silent objectors on this issue, ceased to remain silent as Nazi policies of ostracizing people on the basis of race and religion became obvious.

By 1935, Berlin officials wanted to reject all black and Jewish athletes from competition. This met with the opposition of the IOC and several countries, particularly the United States. Calls for a boycott of the Berlin games rose in response to these German demands. Complaints over Nazis policies even generated calls for either boycotting or moving the 1936 Olympics elsewhere. These complaints even came from the Soviet Union, a country with until that time no formal relations with the Olympic Movement.

For several reasons, mostly related to logistical matters, the boycotts were averted.[11] Those that threatened a boycott were not completely chagrined, since German officials were forced to back away from most of their discriminatory policies. The Germans were open to backing off from some of their own racist policies, specifically because Hitler was well aware that hosting an Olympics free of boycott and other such political turmoil was better than hosting an Olympics whose message was lost among the protests. Hitler's goals for the Olympics were to trumpet the greatness of the German nation. Regardless of all other benefits, Hitler saw the 1936 Olympics as a chance to display German and Nazi national preeminence through innovation, architecture, precision, and physical fitness.

There is overwhelming evidence that the Nazi regime accepted the Olympics onto their own soil for purely political and nationalist reasons. The best example of this is found in a quote from Joseph Goebbels, the German Minister of Propaganda, in which he is recorded as stating that the Olympics are both *Sportwettkampf*, a sports competition, and *Wettkampf des Geistes,* a competition of the spirit (Senn 1999: 52). Yet another example appears in numerous reports of *Kölner Zeitung*, a state-controlled German newspaper, which indicated that the Olympics where a chance for the "youth of the world [to] gather in a festival of friendship and learn the 'truth' about the New Germany"(Senn 1999: 55). From this last statement, it is perfectly clear that German officials, through a state-run press agency, were defining the role the games would play in demonstrating the newly "revised" Germany. This would provide a global forum to rewrite the concept of all that was German, new and old.

With these ambitious goals in mind, Hitler had to concede on the race issue, allowing token representation of Jews on the German team and remaining completely neutral on the selection of individual delegations from other countries, lest his grand demonstration of the superiority of the German people be displayed to empty seats and its athletes garnering victories only over other Germans. Hitler even went so far as to willingly remove anti-Semitic signs, declaring the winter games host city of Garmisch-Partenkirchen off limits to Jews (Holmes 1971). In fact, Goebbels was unyielding on his insistence that the athletics be free of Nazi propaganda. He stated, on August 3, 1936, that "the racial point of view should not in any form be a part of the discussion of the athletic results. Special care should be exercised not to offend Negro athletes" (Guttmann 1994: 68). Hitler made a strategic choice. Twenty-eight countries attended the Winter Olympics and forty-nine countries participated in the Summer Olympics. Every national Olympic committee recognized by the IOC was in attendance in Berlin. For the Germans, the Winter and Summer Olympics were nothing short of an unqualified success.

The Berlin games were truly a spectacle. While Nazi propaganda was necessarily low key and, in many cases, non-existent, the German government still saw the games as a success. To understand why, one must be reminded of the goal of the Berlin Games. The regime's primary goal was to demonstrate the revitalization of Germany and, in so doing, show its strength, precision, pride, etc. The Nazi Olympics were meant to present a new Germany, and the result was a propaganda machine. Every attempt, whether it was subtle, silent, or blatant, was made to remind the world of the new nationalistic tendencies of Germany and the "fact" of Aryan supremacy. These involved complicated manifestations, such as choreographed music, dance, and light displays at the Opening and Closing Ceremonies, as well as more simplistic and subtle attempts, like the "Aryan-looking" statues of over-muscled men that were used to symbolize Greek athleticism.

What would the Germans have gained by being overly racist in their coverage of their own Olympics? Germany, according to Goebbels and Hitler, had to put a good foot forward in order to avoid further criticism in the international Community. An apparent anti-racist stance was the best way for the Germans to alleviate international concerns and pressures on the Nazi domestic and international policies. Then IOC President, Comte Henri de Baillet-Latour of Belgium, future IOC President, Avery Brundage of the United States, and Former IOC President Baron Pierre de Coubertin of France, all praised the Nazi Olympics as fitting tributes to the Olympic ideals. They were, of course, far more interested in the austere glory that could describe the German spectacle than the propaganda, racism, and warmongering that underscored the event.

Certainly, the goal of the German organizers was to cement Nazi policy and legitimacy internationally. In summation, while the Nazis put on an excellent show, they took the opportunities of the grandest International sports festival and used it to their own nefarious ends. In fact, when one shelves the message and the political motivations of the Nazi Games, very little can be held against them. Berlin held great games, set standards far higher than previous hosts, and in the process served as a model for future hosts.

Finally, before moving on, it is worth noting precisely what the Germans did to contribute to the concept of Olympism and an Olympic global identity. The Nazi regime, oddly enough, was committed to the notion that the Olympics were a festival of peace. They also accepted that the Olympics were an effort to bring people of many nations together in a competition that highlighted the body and the soul. Recalling statements by Goebbels, quoted earlier, the spirit of Olympism—minus of course Nazi positions that wanted "inferior" races completely excluded from competition—was not entirely antithetical to fascist ideology.[12]

With the exception of Nazi policies on race and religion, Nazi manipulation of the Olympics was no more excessive than any other prior host. In many cases, their policies were actually compatible with Olympism. Since the Nazis were willing to forego their ideology on Aryan supremacy, at least publicly during the Olympic Games, it was feasible to expect only a limited number of problems during the Berlin Games. What was completely unexpected, however, was the degree to which the Nazis sought to add to the myth of Olympism. First and foremost, the Berlin organizers introduced the torch relay. An Olympic torch was first present at the Amsterdam Summer Olympics of 1928, but the concept of a relay from Olympia, Greece to the site of the Games did not previously occur in modern times.

The Germans, no doubt in an effort to even further legitimize both themselves and the modern Olympics, had the flame of the Olympic torch lit by the sun on Mount Olympus and then ran from Greece to Berlin. It was the start of a tradition that continues to this day. Another, often forgotten German contribution, was the introduction of the statement *"Ich rufe die Jugend der Welt"*—I summon the Youth of the World. The parade of nations, which is now a mainstay of every Olympic opening ceremony, often starts with a symbolic "summoning" of the athletes.

Finally, the German ceremonies that opened the Berlin Games, notably a festival of dance, music, and synchronization, is clearly the forerunner to the current opening ceremonies "pageant," in which the bulk of cultural displays are conducted. The Berlin organizers spent a great deal of time, and no doubt creative energy, further solidifying the myth of Olympism, and in so doing, formally introduced displays of nationalism as an official element of the Olympic Games.

V. Post World War II to the Age of Olympic Nationalism

The problems of the Nazi Olympics brought the inter-war period to a close. The 12th Olympiad of 1940 and the 13th of 1944 were sacrificed due to the onslaught of another world war. As was the case during World War I, the IOC and its members sat and waited for the war to end and for the Olympics to be reconvened. What was to come, however, was the next wave of politicization of the Olympics followed by a return to the questions of nation and state.

When the war ended, the IOC returned to its job of tending the Olympic movement. As was the case after World War I, the Olympics again became tool for the victors, but it was less brazen as neutral states were also included in the hosting of Games. St. Moritz, Switzerland (Winter) and London, United Kingdom (Summer) hosted the 1948 Games. Oslo, Norway (Winter) and Helsinki, Finland (Summer), hosted the 1952 Olympics, and Cortina D'Ampezzo, Italy (Winter) and Melbourne, Australia[13] (Summer) hosted the 1956 Olympics. World War II served as a lesson to be more forgiving in its policies against the losers of the war, and the Olympics were no exception. In the twelve years after the end of the Olympics, three allied cities, two neutral cities, one conquered city, and one axis city all hosted the Olympics.

In addition to hosting, the Axis states were slowly reincorporated into competition as well. While this took longer for Germany, mainly due to un-resolved questions involving the status of the two German states, Italy and other axis powers were quickly welcomed back into the fold. Also, as was the case with post World War I Olympiads, newly independent states sought recognition and legitimacy through the Olympics. The opposite situation was also true for the first time in the Olympics. Nations that were once inde-pendent, like Estonia, Latvia, and Lithuania, previously recognized competi-tors in the Olympics, were no longer sovereign. During the Cold War, their athletes competed under the Soviet hammer-and-sickle until 1992.

In a similar fashion to the Olympics in the Inter-War period, the primary issue of nationalism in the Olympics was one of membership, recognition, and participation. Other manifestations of nationalism in the Olympics were overshadowed due to these problems. Because of the political benefits of the Olympics, they became a source of contention in the Cold War. Other issues continued to plague the games as well.

In the late 1940s and into the early 1950s, new questions were raised as to what sports should be included in the games. Questions on the involve-ment of women, the contending definitions of amateurism under capitalism and socialism, and nagging questions like the two Chinas issue, the two Germanys issue, and decolonization, all created many distractions in the Olympic Movement. However, regardless of these issues, the Olympic movement continued growing and along with it grew the prominence of na-tionalism in that movement.

Nationalists—state and non-state actors—found the Olympics a sym-bolically rich terrain worthy of contention. The question of two Chinas, the authorities in Beijing and Taipei, and two Germanys, the governments in Bonn and East Berlin, had everything to do with which regime was the right-ful claimant to the national identity of China and of Germany. The Israeli issue and the resulting threats of boycott by Arab states was another chapter in this story. The early years of the Cold War were so rife with political is-sues that nationalism at the Olympics was necessarily limited in scope.

Avery Brundage became IOC president in 1952. From the start of his presidency onward, the IOC was plagued by complications due to the Cold

War. The bipolar international system featured regular occurrences of political grandstanding to highlight their political and economic systems. The Olympics were particularly susceptible to Cold War politics because they were inherently competitive, allowing for both sides to claim victories over each other. Analogies were drawn between victory on the field and the future ascendancy of the state's ideological framework. Cold War rivalries, there are other examples of states attempting to control the Olympics for their own political agendas. Examples of this include Soviet attempts to oust the fascist government in Spain by seeking Spanish expulsion from the games, attempts by Arab states to boycott the Olympics as a means of forcing Israel out of international sports competitions, and African threats of boycott to protest South African Apartheid policies.

While political games dominated the Olympics movement from the 1950s through the 1980s, the prominence of nationalism was never fully subverted. This was partly due to Avery Brundage. He was adamantly opposed to politics meddling in the Olympic movement. His aversion to governments was so intense that he was known for insisting that the Olympics did not deal with states but instead dealt with nations (Guttmann 1994b: 94). This would explain why the IOC under his leadership, as well as others, was adamantly opposed to admitting two German and two Chinese nations. Even though they were separate independent states, they constitute one nation and therefore one team, according to the IOC. The influence of Avery Brundage on the course of the Olympic Movement allowed for the burgeoning of a new era in the Olympics.

Brundage's presidency saw politics continue its intimate relationship with the Olympics. However, the weight of political influence of the Olympics was increasing in spite of Brundages warnings. Until this point, the history of the Olympics shows how the Olympics were used to further the political messages of many groups. After World War II, the Olympics grew enough in scope to be useful for more overtly political ends. It was this critical shift in the political weight of the Olympics that led to the change in the political atmosphere of the Olympics.

Nationalism always had its place in the Olympic Movement, however the prominence of the Olympics allowed for increasing displays. Before 1956, the Olympics and politics combined where the Olympic Movement and the people within it chose to politicize decisions or exploit the games to make political statements. The major exception was the manipulation of the 1936 Olympics.

From 1948 through 1960, the Olympic Movement began to shift from being just a political actor to being both a political actor and a political tool for others. This transitional period ended, culminating in 1958, when states began using the Olympics as a platform, a tool, sometimes a weapon, and always as an opportunity to make a statement.[14]

While the 1950s and 1960s were a tumultuous time in the Olympic Community, the continued growth of nationalism in the Olympics was becoming more apparent. Initially, hosts and governments that sought better avenues for international influence played these symbolic "games." However, it did not take long for individuals to see the potential power and seek to wield it. This began in the athletic competitions but swiftly spread to other aspects of the Olympics.

A prime example of the spread of politics into the sports arena is the water polo match at the 1956 Melbourne Summer Games. This semi-final match pitted the Soviet Union against Hungary, a state the Soviet army invaded to quell an uprising against the Soviet-installed and supported Communist government. The match quickly turned bloody, literally, as angered Hungarian players responded to their Soviet adversaries as they wished they could back home against Soviet soldiers and tanks. What was supposed to be only a match quickly turned into a battle for Hungarian national identity and independence against their would-be conquerors.

Outside of the actual sports competitions, athletes and spectators dragged nationalism into the Olympics by other means. Where most prior political manipulations of the Olympics specifically targeted governments in the hope of altering some form of policy of one or more states, these newer forms of nationalism were unique in that they targeted the citizens of those states as well. The two most prominent examples come at the end of this period in the growth in the Olympic Movement. First, is the famous black power salute by two victorious American athletes at the 1968 Mexico City Summer Olympics.

During the official playing of the United States national anthem and the raising of the U.S. flag, as part of their victory ceremony, two African American athletes stared downward and held their fists in the air in a symbolic display of black power. This has been remembered as one of the most deliberate displays of ethnic/national identity at the Olympics. Instead of accepting their national identity and heritage as American, they chose to demonstrate themselves as being part of a sub-national identity within the concept of American Nationalism.

A second example is the act of terrorism at the 1972 Munich Summer Games. Palestinian gunmen infiltrated the Olympic Village and took 11 Israeli athletes hostage. By the end of the hostage situation, all 11 athletes died along with a German police officer. Since terrorists often seek the most visible possible stage to commit their crimes, the Olympics have become a tempting venue. The incident at the Munich Games demonstrated that the Olympics could be a venue for armed nationalistic movements. For good or for bad, the Olympics were, by 1972, solidified as a stage for political protest, national identity, and cultural displays.

Finally, cultural displays were the final step towards the complete incorporation of nationalism into the Olympic movement. Cultural displays were originally a part of the competitions in the early days of the Olympics. When they returned to the Olympic Movement, it was relegated to artistic presentations only. Artistic competitions have yet to be rekindled. From 1912-1948, the Olympics had artistic competitions. These events, which were rewarded with medals just like the athletic events, included architecture, literature, music, painting, and sculpture (Stanton 2001). These would, however, be short-lived competitions as the Olympics moved away from these and other events in favor of *pure* athletic competition.[15]

While the artistic competitions have not returned, the elements of those competitions would. The IOC has endorsed artistic, cultural, exhibitions as a formal part of the Olympic Cultural Programme (IOC 2003: 80). The IOC made it clear that these "festivals" were not a precursor to the return of the competitions. They were, instead, only opportunities for the host city to share its own culture, and art with the athletes, officials, and spectators of the Olympic Games. Their return signified two important facts for nationalism in the Olympics. First, it signified an endorsement of cultural displays in the Olympics. Second, it signified that the National Olympic Committees, or at least those hosting the Olympics, were ready for a formal and legitimizing endorsement of the link between culture and the games.

This study will focus its analysis to the Olympic Games since 1980 for both political and structural reasons. First, this work does not suggest that information cannot be drawn from an earlier Olympiad, as examples in this chapter from Berlin, and Antwerp clearly demonstrate. There have been politically driven nationalistic tendencies in the Olympics since its inception; but they were surrounded by a wealth of circumstances and complicated issues which drew attention away from nationalism. Because of these distractions, and since nationalism in the Olympics was clearly different in the early years of the games, compared to the Post World War I period, and compared to the Post World War II period, and compared to the decolonization period, it makes more sense to restrict analysis to recent Olympiads and winter Olympic games.

Decolonization is an important factor in influencing the scope of this study. The end of the decolonization period represents a slowdown in the continued increase in the number of National Olympic Committees until the disintegration of the Soviet and Yugoslav federations in the early 1990s. This represents the end of the last significant trend in Olympism before the ascendancy of contemporary nationalism in the Olympic movement.

A second explanation has to do with the structure of Olympic Ceremonies. The structure and the style of Olympic Ceremonies have changed over time. These changes have moved the Olympic Games towards a more structurally-compatible system for displays of nationalism. Montserrat Llinés (1996) made it clear that the 1964 Tokyo Ceremonies were a critical turning point in the evolution of ceremonies. Titling her section on Tokyo "The Ceremonies as Host City Cultural Expression and Promotion" (Llinés 1996: 75), she identified these games as the starting point of a new style and method of Olympic Ceremonies. Llinés (1996: 76) also highlighted how culture began playing a deeper role in Olympic Ceremonies during the 1968 Mexico City Games. Moving forward to the Montreal Games, we have a decisive demonstration in the Opening Ceremonies of nationalistic demonstration. Llinés writes, "this was the first time ever that two people had simultaneously lit the Olympic Flame in the Stadium... Together, in their coordinated run, they represented the two founding peoples of Canada, the two cultures living side by side in the Canadian State" (*Ibid.,* 77). Similarly, the closing ceremonies involved a historical/cultural display by incorporating 500 Native Americans for cultural purposes (*Ibid.*).

The processes Llinés recognized are particularly important for setting the appropriate scope of analysis of this study. Further structural matters on this analysis are found in Otto Schantz's (1996) study on ceremonies. Schantz studied the process by which Olympic opening ceremonies went from ritual to spectacle. During the period from 1960–1973, he documented seven changes in the style and structure of Olympic Ceremonies. Most critical among them is his second hypothesis that "ritual 'as lived' is losing ground to things visual because of the influence of television and the nature of the formal rite is losing ground to the spectacle, the festival" (*Ibid.,* 135). He also noted, during this time period, that ceremonies were becoming more "emancipative" (*Ibid.*) as it incorporated multiple elements of society.

While I agree with many of Schantz's (1996: 135) points, I believe he is mistaken when he claims "national symbols are losing strength in favour of international symbols." His notion needs careful reconsideration in light of growing globalization (see also King 1997a, 1997b, and Hall 1997). He is right however, when he sees this, and other hypotheses on the shifting context and structure of opening ceremonies, due to the influence of television (Shantz 1996: 139). Chappelet (1996: 154) reinforced this concept when he noted "the same transition towards a television spectacle." He concludes that "we may confirm that over the last fifteen years [1980-1995], the Olympic Ceremonies have grown considerably, both in quantity and quality, in parallel with the growth of the Olympic Movement" (*Ibid.,* 156).

In considering these observations by Llinés, Schantz, and Chappelet, we find that the transition of the olympic ceremonies structure and content occurred predominantly during the period of 1964 through 1976. One is then able to see that the process of growth and change in these ceremonies began in 1980. Considering both Olympic history and the analysis of these studies, this study on nationalism in the Olympics Games will begin its study with the Winter and Summer Olympics of 1980 and progress forward to current Olympiads.

NOTES

1. While the date of the final Olympics is clearly recorded, the date of the first Olympics is not as clear. Perrottet (2004: 39), Sinn, (2000: 5), Spivey (2004: xxi), and others have accepted archaeological evidence that 776 B.C. is the appropriate, or at least the safest, guess at the official starting year.

2. It is interesting to note that the current basis of eligibility does not significantly vary from the ancient rules.

3. Examples are found in many of the Pindaric Olympic Odes. A few examples include: "Psaumis, who exalted they city, Camarina, that fostereth its people, at the greatest festival of the gods." *Olympian V: For Psaumis of Camarina (Pindar 1961: 49)*; "Now mark how the tide of song is floweth, is washing the rolling pebbles ashore! Mark how we shall pay our debt as a welcome boon in our praise of the victor's home!" *(Ibid., 111)*, and "I, the while, who am eagerly lending a hand of help, have taken to my heart the famous tribe of the Locrians, while I besprinkle with honey a city of noble sons." *(Ibid., 119) Olympian X: For Hâgêsidâmus of Locri Epizephyrii* (Pindar 1961). Other examples may be found in other areas of these poems and in *Olympian IX: For Epharmostus of Opus* (Pindar 1961).

4. Athletes must actually claim a nationality that would "tie" them to the state they represent in the modern olympics. While attempts to purchase athletes do occur, there does have to be some sense of justifiable claim for the athlete to compete for the buying state.

5. Certainly, the ceremony is rife with symbolism as the flag of the gold medalist is raised higher than all others and only its accompanying national anthem is performed.

6. Most of the early members of the IOC were selected because their economic or political clout would allow them the necessary influence to help get the Olympics of the ground; but they were also independent enough of their governments to guarantee that the games were not going to be controlled by a state.

7. While the Italians opted to blame an eruption of Mount Vesuvius, it was no secret that the Rome officials were more interested in a national event than an international event (Gori 1997).

8. The terminology, while ultimately successful in solving some of these problems for the London Games, was inaccurate as no territorial dependency had representation on the IOC.

9. Australia and New Zealand competed separately from the Great Britain in 1896, which is the official start of the inclusion of non-sovereign states in the Olympics.

10. The Chamonix Games were originally titled the International Sports Week. Owing to their success, the IOC opted to change its name to the 1st Olympic Winter Games. St. Moritz was therefore the first Winter Olympics so titled at the ceremonies.

11. The threatened boycotts against Berlin were averted for several reasons, including extraordinary efforts on the part of Avery Brundage. See Guttmann 1994a or Senn 1999 for an account of this history.

12. Arnd Krüger (1999), a noted historian on sports and politics, studied in depth the compatibility of fascism and sports. While fascism objected to the mingling of *inferior* races with *superior* ones, it did see the benefits of athleticism and sports for those who deserved to compete. Sport, in fact, was considered one of the best means of indoctrinating youth into the fascist ideology that drove Nazi Germany, Fascist Italy, and Franco's Spain.

13. It should be noted that Australian law did not allow for the importation of horses without strict periods of quarantine. This resulted in the relocation of all equestrian events to Stockholm, Sweden.

14. 1958 marks the period when the South Africa Apartheid issue spurred many states, particularly African countries, to further politicize the games because it was the only effective means of protest they had.

15. Stanton's (2001) work is an excellent source of information for Olympic art competitions.

CHAPTER 2
THOUGHTS ON NATIONALISM, PERFORMANCE, AND THE ROLE OF SPORTS

National identity is a description of a community, in which all members of the group are said to possess the same list of traits and project that identity onto each other. These shared conceptions are rooted in a definition that is systematically constructed out of many icons during the process of invention or myth making. As part of this effort, demonstration plays a key role in either indoctrinating an existing ideology or in socializing the general population into new ideologies in the process of formation or revision. Beyond patriotic moments, these are deeply cultural, often times spiritual, processes that result in a stronger and more vibrant concept of *us*. While many authors have notated these processes, discussed their demonstration, and observed the ramifications of both the process and the show, very few have broadened this concept to an international stage or a sports stage. Demonstrating a specific identity is not only feasible in an international festival but is also productive. While the degree of productivity inherent in this relationship is of some interest, primary focus in this study rests in how the Olympics serve as a venue for this demonstration and on what methods or strategies are used in this process.

In the study of identity performance at the Olympics, the political benefits of hosting the Olympics are expanded beyond simple economics and political legitimacy, inter-state conflict, and diplomacy. Rather, by looking at how the Olympics can be used to further goals rooted in national identity of a host, this study will link a series of previously disconnected ideas in the areas of nationalism and Olympic politic. This kind of merger has the potential of offering new avenues of research in both fields and therefore is of relevance to both.

I. NATIONALISM AND PERFORMANCE

We begin by establishing some common understandings of nationalism as a kind of foundation for our discussion of this topic. This study works with the basic premise that national identities are artifacts of human design, whose crafters take deliberate and calculated steps to accomplish specific goals. As identity is constructed, there is no pure example of a national identity that exists as a biological or teleological truth about humanity. Therefore, we are discussing a concept that is literally created by elites. This invention or imagining of a shared community has its root in the analysis of Hobsbawm and Ranger's *Invention of Tradition* and Anderson's *Imagined Communities*.

Traditionally, members of a particular populace who knew one another shared a sense of communal belonging. For Anderson (1983), the concept of a unified national community exists more in our shared understanding than in any real fact. Through various forms of popular media, particularly print media in local vernaculars, individuals developed a sense of belonging to a new and large community united by a common language. Anderson recognized that the concept of the nation was an artificial one. Older sociopolitical myths were based on incontestable dogmas such as sacred beliefs and liturgical language, the divine right of monarchs, and an ancient cosmology. As these notions slowly weakened, new ideas of the community, fostered by media and print capitalism, took hold and created a new identity.

What is beneficial, and very interesting when considering Anderson's work through the lens of the Olympic games, is that Olympic performance actually supplies a means for communal and identity creation. Instead of protracted commentary through the written word, the Olympics offer a visual depiction of community that does not require the people of a nation to be literate. National performance through the Olympics becomes the means of reinforcing previously existing written or oral narratives of national identity or as a channel through which particular chronicles are revised. Since community is the sharing of a set of qualities, identity demonstration in the Olympics can be seen as a process of selecting, demonstrating, and confirming the elements of the imagined community. The Olympics can offer the opportunity to reinforce or redo the community-creation process.

The factual truth behind the concept of a national identity is often times stretched or even completely fabricated. Whether we are talking about grand mythologies such as the basis for many faiths or simplistic ones such as the legend behind the founding of a particular people, careful analysis can reap many interesting and beneficial truths about a society. Anderson demonstrates that these ideas, regardless of factual truth, hold weight and influence among a population. Eric Hobsbawm and Terrence Ranger also elaborated on this concept; but they did so by questioning the process of myth creation.

Hobsbawm and Ranger's (1983) work is at the center of revising/creating official history as part of establishing national identity. In long-established communities, custom sets the parameters for beliefs and behavior. But custom is not a static concept. It changes with the ebb and flow of time and external influences. In contrast, traditions are artificial constructs; they lock customs into a particular time and place designating a locus and era as correct and authentic. By borrowing selectively from history, they argue, groups are able to construct for themselves a vivid historic narrative and institutionalize cultural traditions that form a unique identity that all members of the community can collectively share. Hugh Trevor-Roper (1983) demonstrated, for example, how borrowing from Irish history and manufacturing a highland Scottish dress, the short kilt, and other symbols, Scottish elites cleverly created key elements of a pan-Scottish identity.

Inventing traditions is a process that incorporates cultural and ethnic traits and historic narratives into a new myth. However, sometimes this can be done as a means of promoting specific ideas or beliefs pertinent to the society under the process of self-definition. For example, in the United States, the use of ancient Greek architecture on government buildings is designed to recall ancient Greece, the locus of early democracy (Harris 1999). The invention of tradition, therefore, involves not just the incorporation of historical moments, whether true or doctored, but also the use of icons, artistry, and the sense of a common or shared past.

Patrick Geary (2002) noted that modern European national identities could not have derived from ancient political identities. Still, modern national mythmakers refute such claims in favor of a myth of historic continuity. Geary (2002: 157) noted that "by constructing a continuous, linear story of these peoples in Europe, [historians] validate the attempts of military commanders and political leaders to claim that they did indeed incorporate ancient traditions of people." Therefore, by accepting historically driven myths that claim modern nations are legacies of an ancient past, we further disseminate and institutionalize these claims.

Regardless of the traits that are eventually woven into the elite's nationalist narrative, this select grouping aspires to institutionalize their newly crafted myth. Simply stating that a nationalist or ethnic identity is made up of a certain set of traits is not enough. Indeed, Barth (1969) highlighted that social parameters survive changes in the traits used to define group boundaries. Cultures, abstract notions by nature, do not possess a solid or tangible form. A key facet of identity articulation is making concrete that which has no physical form. Cultures "can only be specified in terms of the particular points of view of those who create and act culture, and these points of view are various and constantly changing" (Handler 1984: 63).

Performance will always be a two-factor concept for studies of nationalism. First, there are the qualities (real or imagined) that are injected into performance in order to have a "show" laden with nationalistic enterprises. Second are the actual means of performance—the nuts and bolts of a display that manifests ideas that are not often times wholly tangible. Cultural objectification, as Handler (1984: 56) intends it to mean, is the process of imbuing human identity into cultural artifacts such that they becoming embodiments of that identity. Objectification, therefore, is a process that involves taking intangible traits and making them physical realities that people can interact with and utilize as a demonstration of their identity. This process creates, out of the necessity of having a shared understanding of identity, "an object which is inherently inauthentic" (*Ibid*, 64) and is inherently creative in its depiction of identity.

The process of objectification can demonstrate the uniqueness of an identity and legitimize those traits through employment of physically real symbols. Instead of a complex ideology, members of a community have tangible evidence of what their identity represents. These symbols possess a specific meaning, delineated by elites through objectification, which are incontestable artifacts of a nationality. Also, objectification, by drawing connections between intangible ideas and physical symbols, defines and therefore makes readily apparent the specific meaning of an identity to people inside and outside the ethnic or national group. In short, nationalistic performance must weave these "concepts" into physical realities that have audio and visual storytelling tools.

The role of objectifying the intangible is a potent element of this study. Since ethnic and national identities are not physically real, objectification becomes critical as elites ascribe a meaning to tangible cultural elements and in the process gives symbolic importance in terms of group identity. The Olympics offer a means of displaying, reinterpreting, and even altering such traits.

Organizers utilize the opportunity to host the Olympics as an opportunity to promote a strategically advantageous objectification. At the Olympics, objectifiers have an opportunity to employ a host of different tools. In the opening ceremonies alone, the host can incorporate architecture, history, music, dance, dress, icons, etc. in one large expression of identity. Also, the Olympics have a legitimizing effect. What took the full course of the French Revolution and cost thousands of lives, according to Weber (1976) and Lefebvre (1979), could be accomplished in a safer and quicker process that emphasizes cultural performance opportunities as the nexus of a formation or alteration of a national identity.

What role the Olympics as a venue play in the cultural objectification process still remains an insufficiently studied avenue of research. The nature of cultural performance, as intertwining many symbols and pageantry, can diminish the creation of hegemonic symbols, as referenced by Florencia Mallon (1995). Once the main stream of a society as an axiom accepts an idea, we can begin talking about that idea becoming a hegemonic notion.

Hegemony, according to Gramsci (1971: 12-13), is a system of domination of the masses by the ruling group in society, which contains within it the state ideology and the process by which the masses willfully adhere. Hegemony therefore offers a definition of social and political hierarchy which guarantees the continuation of elite authority and which is the fundamental result of societal notions that culminate in a sort of cultural domination of society. For Gramsci, cultural domination is founded on the basis of cognitive ability and is vested in a specific phylum of society: the intellectuals. Instead of giving one symbol overwhelming clout within a national identity, its prominence is diffused among the entire performance; its status as a hegemonic symbol is therefore never full attained.

According to Mallon (1995), hegemony is the ascendancy of an icon to such a level that that particular icon itself becomes a *de facto* expression of an idea. By looking at the interplay of political, cultural, and social approaches to studying the past from below in Mexico and Peru, Mallon identifies trends in continued contestations of power by groups of people defining their identifiable commonalities. By the incorporation of the peasantry in the process of nation-state formation, the elements of identity formation were incorporated at all levels of society and resulted in incontestable myths.

As an example of identity formation we can examine the formation of French national ideal. Eugene Weber (1976), Jeremy D. Popkin (1990), and Georges Lefebvre (1979) focused on the process by which a group of people was brought under a unifying political and national identity. Lefebvre demonstrates how the revolution involved a process of creating the identity of the revolution, and therefore of France, that involved the violent replacement of French aristocratic symbols with new French national symbols that were then indoctrinated in a process that is reminiscent of Mallon's analysis. The story, as he tells it, is segmented into actions and reactions on the basis of social and economic class: First, the nobles, then the bourgeoisie, the urban population, and finally the peasantry.

Various portions of French society had divergent understandings of themselves and this scenario culminated in open revolt. Arguably, this can be interpreted to show that a French national identity formed as result of class divisions united to fight absolutism in France. Lefebvre's work further can be interpreted to show how a lack of unity within each class group, as well as disunity among the differing classes, led to the bulk of the hyperviolent nature of the revolution.

Jeremy Popkin (1990) demonstrated the important role the revolutionary press played in French national identity formation. Criticizing prior works on French history, Popkin contends that many of the unprecedented changes in France were fomented by the press. During the different stages of the Revolution, different concepts of *us* and *them* became paramount. Popkin and Lefebvre's understanding was that this process was carried out primarily through the written press, and the iconographic symbols used to identify members of the revolution—most notably, the Tri-Color. Recalling Handler, Weber, and Lefebvre, the intended effect of Olympic objectification is to broaden the popular base of a larger expression of identity by way of objectified symbols.

Identity construction and objectification are processes by which specific cultural traits are selected to define the extent of an identity. Amílcar Barreto (2001a, 2001b) drew attention to the elite actors that engineered a new national identity by carefully objectifying those cultural traits that best suited their group interests. His studies on Puerto Rican identity showed how elites prioritized specific traits that would maintain their power while also establishing themselves as a distinct group. First, elites seek to define their national identity in a manner that excludes outsiders. As Eriksen (1993) and Barth (1969) would see it, game organizers are driven to represent the host's identity as a unique one. The elite's next goal is to ensure that objectified traits are not found among outsiders. This may help to explain why religion has played such a limited role in the performing national identities during the Olympics. Lastly, elites divide the list of traits that establish their unique identity into those traits that are beneficial to the maintenance of their power and those that are not.

Elites manipulate the identity construction process by incorporating the elements that are most beneficial to them. First, the selected traits should encompass the breadth of the group's constituents. Second, the traits selected should be ones that maintain their group's equality or superiority vis-à-vis non-group members. Third, cultural objectification should preserve the elites' privileged status within their own group. Gramscian notions of hegemony apply as a recollection over the total goal: the maintenance of authority of the elite. Identity, regardless of how it is created or presented, is about maintenance of or the creation of the authority of its definers.

Understanding nationalism in this study involves two separate paths. The aforementioned dialogue illustrates the basic assumptions on nationalism that are at work in this study. The following dialogue explores two key factors at work in performance; specifically performance on an international stage. First is to consider the dichotomy of the us vs. them relationship as performance of identity at the Olympics involves both communities. Later involves that actual concept of display and how it can function.

Since the Olympics are a global gathering, there are usually hundreds of cultural identities being displayed, albeit subtly, in addition to the identity of the regime or nation playing host. Eriksen (1993) noted that the purpose of a nationalist identity is to demonstrate that the people ascribing to their identity are noticeably different from everyone else. Eriksen framed ethnicity as a system that uses culturally demarcated boundaries to facilitate ethnic categorization. The concept, as he described it, provides a socially accepted framework in which interactions between members of the same group and between members of different groups are maintained.

Eriksen looked at the role language played in stratifying society in Mauritius and Trinidad; he studied their power relations in terms of cultural difference within the population of both island states. This process was used to establish the unique quality of an identity in contrast to other state and regional concepts of nationalism. The traits that are selected for objectification, therefore, are cultural elements that attempt to portray an identity as unique.

Take, for instance, the development of a distinct Quebecois identity. Far beyond mere geography, the most apparent current difference between Quebecois and Anglo-Canadian identity is language. Speaking French is so intricately connected to Quebecois identity that it delineates, even by street in Montreal, between English and French Canadian. The Quebecois hosts were limited in using French as a part of their identity at the Olympics because audience members were just as likely to draw connections between French, as an official language of the Olympics, and Olympism instead of French and Quebecois identity unless the language was backed up by significant use of other Quebecois symbols. With French a mandated language at the games, this facet of the identity would be seen as a *de facto* presentation of Olympic identity.[1] The Quebecois needed to use other methods to represent themselves, forcing the organizers to abandon use of the hegemonic symbol of Quebecois identity.

Returning to notions of *us* vs. *them*, Fredrik Barth (1969) elaborated on the process by discussing the importance of boundaries maintenance. Barth noted that the importance in an identity is not found within a collection of all objectified traits that label an individual as being from one specific and unique group. Instead, the focus of analysis should be on which traits the actor(s) themselves regard as the most important. The establishment of an "us" and a "them" is defined in terms of those seminal traits that separate identities from each other and simultaneously hold a degree of importance for the members of that identity group. Furthermore, the qualities of any specific identity are not continuous. The importance herein is that the boundaries of an identity will persevere longer than the specific traits within them. As the world surrounding an identity group changes, the internal definitions of "us" will modify to maintain the boundary and therefore guarantee the continuation of that group as distinct. The concept of boundaries is particularly important in issues of cultural performance on an international stage. During the Olympic ceremonies, the boundaries between *us* and *them* are more pronounced. Host organizers have a limited amount of time in which to make their point. This limitation forces identity demonstration to focus more narrowly on the core pieces of that identity.

Typically, the core identity remains the focus; it is the one most clearly on display. But peripheral identities are often times strongly demonstrated in the games as well. This culminates in a very strange dichotomy in the Olympics, one in which core and peripheral identities are either in competition for or share the spotlight with the Olympics. This is partly due to the fact that the Olympics provide an excellent opportunity for a society to symbolically heal by reintegrating once-peripheralized elements. For example, the incorporation of Aboriginal identity during the Sydney Games was an attempt at reconciliation between two very different cultures. In addition, the Olympics have in the past been hosted by cities that are centers of a regional culture, and the goals of the host can easily shift the focus to a regional identity as opposed to a national identity; such was the case in Barcelona and Atlanta.

Thus far, we have focused on various ideas on nationalism and how identities are defined, constructed, and objectified. Connected to all of this, and the very basis of this study, is the concept of identity demonstration or performance. Here, performance and demonstration will be interchangeable terms that share a common meaning of displaying one's identity through its icons and symbols that have been vested a deeper meaning in terms of their identities.

David Guss (2000) studied how identity is reinterpreted through the staging of festivals in Venezuela. He makes several observations that lay some groundwork for my dissertation. In particular, he notes that identity "was something created with each performance, and to understand it meant comprehending the entire context in which it was produced" (*Ibid.*, 7) While I agree theoretically with this assertion, I disagree with him when he further explains, "it also [means] recognizing that this context was continually changing and that festivals were being readily deployed to meet these changes" (*Ibid.*). He is correct if one assumes that the festival itself is part of the identity. With that in mind, the festival is not just a language through which the identity is explained it is actually an integral part of the identity. If the festival is transient, its expression of identity is likewise transient.

Guss suggests using the term "cultural performance." Still, this term implies two things. First, it implies that culture can be performed in some manner as an expression of said identity. In this study on the Olympics the focus of this expression will be in the opening and closing ceremonies. Second, it implies that the intrinsic nature of the performance itself is a part of the identity.

Guss (2000: 7) borrowed from Milton Singer, the mid-20th century authority on Indian cultures, to explain his terminology. These are excellent examples of how culture, in and of it self, exists as performance. This is not, however, applicable to this study, because the "festival" through which the performance is being conducted is an international, rather than national, cultural artifact. The two-tiered concept of cultural performance, while useful for domestic analysis, has limitations for an international study.

Regardless of whether the festival is domestic or international, it has its own symbols, rituals, etc. In the domestic event, the symbols and the rituals are under the control of local elites and possibly by the state. In international events, the situation is more complex. There are international symbols such as the Olympic rings, the flame, its anthem and motto. There are also rituals such as the torch relay and the structure of the opening ceremonies. These are controlled by an international order and are therefore not subject to the control and cultural specifications of the host state. Two separate identities are therefore present: a global one and a domestic one. Tying Anderson (1983) into this argument briefly, the international culture that is endemic to the regularly occurring Olympic festivals is a mechanism through which an identity is shown. The association of locally organized ceremonies such as the opening and closing ceremonies during the Olympics also bestows upon these rituals a considerable degree of international legitimacy. This would suggest that international festivals are an underestimated avenue for identity formation, demonstration, and revision.

One final issue with Guss' work is the degree of specificity of cultural performance. Guss (2000: 9) argues, "cultural performances will remain both contentious and ambiguous, and while the basic structure of the event may be repeated, enough change will be implemented so that its meaning is redirected." In the case of an annual, domestic event in which the performance participants are not restricted to selected "actors" but include "the audience," Guss may well be correct. However, in a staged "cultural performance" event, like a pageant, the subject matter is by necessity specific, as opposed to ambiguous, and the message is only continually changing if the event occurs on a regular interval.

In a domestic event that is possible, but in an international event it is not, simply because the location of the "festival" changes thus not allowing for an analysis of the reinterpretation of identity through changes in the context and contents of performance.[2] In many ways, Guss was identifying methods of domestic consolidation of the nation-state through cultural demonstration of identity. Instead of focusing on Guss' notation of the ever-changing concept of Venezuelan culture, through domestic festival, we need to focus on how he and others explained the nature and methodology of cultural performance.

A rather fruitful source of information on this question actually comes from a study of museums. Museums offer a public venue for continued socialization of people through their carefully designed and scripted displays. Timothy Luke (2002) went so far as to suggest that museum exhibitions help to formalize our understandings of historical events and icons and thus places them into a perspective that is shared among all visitors to the museum.

Historical displays are venues for elites to define and then demonstrate elements of "our shared" existence. This further implies that these artifacts of history are being vested with specific interpretations that are not just culturally determined. Luke also shows some of the benefits and problems of the increasing entertainment-like feel of museums. He contends that "entertainment values have so saturated museums that one cannot assume that the theme parks provide only amusement while museums generate only enlightenment" (*Ibid.*, 219). Thus, the "entertainment" portions of the opening and closing ceremonies of the Olympic games are not mere entertainment; they are, in fact, episodes of cultural enlightenment. Thus, performance, as Guss and Luke see it, is simultaneously cultural enlightenment or indoctrination and entertainment. To finalize our understanding of culture performance, a quick look at film and how directors capture (whether through fictional motion picture entertainment or through documentary) icons of culture and therefore contribute to the establishment or reinforcement of identity traits.

As an art form, films and movies can simultaneously capture actual and artificial depictions of society. Sumiko Higashi (1995) explained that the success of episodes of historical revision through film exist only when the attempt to modification is close enough to reality such that viewers do not question its validity. Higashi's study of postmodernist and illusionist narratives of film shows that a historical or cultural depiction of society fails when the history is too far removed from truth. For example, the reconstruction of the past in the film *Mississippi Burning* failed because audiences were more wrapped up in debates over its authenticity than accepting its alterations as an accurate depiction of Mississippi's society in the 1960's. While caught up mainly in the interplay of historiography and film, Higashi does give us a framework for understanding the limitations of cultural displays as described by Guss and Luke.

John Mraz (1995) expands our understandings, and therefore limitations, given to us by Higashi by placing a condition on the discussion. By looking at Latin American cinema, Mraz indicates the power of cultural performance, through film, in transforming a society. He agrees with Higashi's conclusion on limitations of stretching truth, but argues it is more successful when society itself is in the process of a paradigm shift. While society has one foot in the past and one foot in the future (Rosenstone 1995b: 107), perceptions of the self are more open to change. He explains that "the use of realist[3] techniques . . . encourage identification" (Rosenstone 1995b: 107). Therefore, bringing Roosens (1989) into this discussion, when an identity is in flux, due to the process of construction, performance and display can take more liberties with truth to accentuate the efforts of the elites constructing the new identity. Robert Rosenstone adds a critical explanation to tie this all together.

Rosenstone looks at the strategies and interpretations necessary to construct a postmodernist history through film. While his contributing chapter to his anthology is very much an effort in successful historical revision, it is beneficial to this study when applied to nationalism. Rosenstone explains that the process of revision is not merely rewriting a history. He explains that you must first take traditional historical tasks and tie them with new ways to visualize societies current connection to its past. Then, you must present this process with historically true elements that are already accepted by the audience. In our terms, the process of objectification a new version of identity lacks legitimacy if it does not incorporate elements of the current definition, which are already accepted by the population.

As a final note on film and identity, the role of cinematics in combating racism has been a topic of some note in studies on film and culture. Robert Stam and Louise Spence (1983) showed that oppressed groups, specifically colonially dominated cultures and women, have been using film techniques to undermine hegemonic concepts. This is more or less an example of the fundamental concepts of this study in reverse. Instead of utilizing performance to entrench new concepts into a society's identity, cultural performance is instead used to systematically dissect assumptions and then discard elements that are no longer tenable as part of a modern identity.

While Stam and Spence are arguing specifically about a combat between hegemonic images that upheld and legitimized colonial domination, the concept can be expanded to take on clear nationalistic or ethnic discourses in the same manner. While the text of their article is occupied with what they call third world cinema and competing understanding of various avenues of depiction, their notion becomes useful for this study when we strip it of its film art aspect and take it in the light of cultural performance.

Stam and Spence broadened their discussion to answer an important question: To what extent are audience perceptions influencing their interpretations? They explain that cultural and ideological assumptions frame their understanding and therefore influence how they view films. For us, this is a strong reminder of the success of objectification and identity construction, which builds off of people's current understanding. What remains somewhat uncertain at this point is whether such demonstrations through any medium, not just film, can undermine hegemonic symbols and notions, as the authors appear to claim.

Certainly, there is potential in understanding the interesting role that performance can play, regardless of type, in deconstructing hegemonic concepts. Brian Winston (1995) effectively demonstrated the role performance, again through film, could play in giving voice to individuals and their cultures that are held below hegemonic symbols. By pointing out that anthropological and ethnographical film gave voice to peripheralized[4] individuals. Winston (1995: 195) was arguing about the changes necessary for the documentary film industry due to digitalization.

By pointing out that the digital age has destroyed photography's ability to authenticate the past, Winston (1995) asserts that the film will quickly fall victim to the same trend. He argues that documentary must cease claiming they present reality, because skepticism in its authenticity will cause audiences to cease to accept it as such. While I personally believe Winston is overreacting, he does make a worthwhile point for this study.

Cultural performance, whether through film, pageantry at the Olympics, local festivals, or museums, has limitations to the extent it can subversively change perceptions of the audience. Nevertheless, they provide avenues for identity demonstration, alteration, and creation. It is also clear that cultural performance and the Olympics can, and in fact regularly do, walk hand-in-hand as a process of nationalism. Furthermore, this process is not arbitrary, as the decision-making literature will quickly indicate. Whether we are discussing performance, objectification, or mythmaking, the process of performing nationalism in the Olympics is a deliberate one. As such, this study will find it necessary to root itself in concepts of rational decision-making.

Beyond the theories already present, there are studies that have sought to systematize public events by categorizing them into models. Two specific studies, that of MacAloon (1996) and Handelman (1990), are worthy of note in this review. John J. MacAloon (1996: 36) attempted to argue that the entire realm of recent Olympic ceremonies organization can be summed up into three models: impresario, the cultural experts, and the auteur. Instead of being based on content of a ceremony, these three models are defined in terms of their designer. The impresario model involves hiring a Hollywood showman or other similar performer whose experience is deeply imbedded in the world of spectacle. The impresario then is tasked with three things: managing individuals capable of getting the spectacle off the ground feasibly, managing individuals with experience and skill in handling the protocol and logistics of an official ceremony, assuring that the artistry of the show reflects a vibrant and independent artistic world and not just the elements of the impresario's world of spectacle (MacAloon 1996: 36).

MacAloon's cultural experts model requires a team of experts on the national culture and its traditions. Under this model, the ceremonies are constructed for their ritualistic purposes and meaning instead of for mere entertainment (MacAloon 1996: 36-37). The final model is the auteur model. Taken from the French Cinema, this term explains that a director has a specific style, typically a list of traits that typify his filmmaking. The traits of auteurs, according to this concept of film theory and criticism, are present in the bulk, if not all, films made by the director. MacAloon (1996: 37) chose this term for his third model to suggest that the designer of the ceremonies is selected because of his vision of a specific, typically avant-garde, feel to all elements of the ceremonies, granting it a clearly artistic feel to it.

MacAloon's three models are useful to conceptualize different types of ceremonies in terms of their stylistic creators. However, MacAloon errs in his assumptions, when he contends that the cultural experts model is distinct from the other two for its use of cultural icons. MacAloon's explanation establishes the second model as a bureaucratic one, intended on playing to a whole list of necessary interests in forming a ceremonial display. He holds up Los Angeles as an example of the impresario model, Seoul as the example of the cultural experts model, and Albertville as the example of the auteur model. All three ceremonies outlined by MacAloon hold the potential for displays of national identities.

It is possible that MacAloon might not completely appreciate the deeply embedded nature of nationalism in Olympic ceremonies. He explains "...again, the key thing is to grasp that there is nothing homogenously "Korean," or "Spanish-Catalan," or "American" about these artistic and organizational choices" (MacAloon 1996: 38). He further argues that "to speak of "American culture," or "French Culture," or "Korean Culture" as monolithic wholes in this or any other context is sheer and very dangerous and very nationalistic romanticism (*Ibid.*, 37-38).

Another study that attempted to establish models of performance is Don Handelman's (1990) *Model and Mirrors: Towards an Anthropology of Public Events*. His research design looks more at the effort of the display than categorizing the artistic style of the display. Handelman established three types of public events: events that model, present, or re-present the lived-in world. Events that model the lived-in world seek to demonstrate the possibilities of change for what is being demonstrated. The event that models presents a microcosm of the world. It is a simplified, closed system within which opportunities for change can be both tested and demonstrated (Handelman 1990: 27). Events that present or represent the lived-in world do not, however, show change. They are, from the title of his book, the "mirrors" of his study.

Handelman (1990: 41) notes that the hallmarks of events that present something include statements, mirror-images, and reflections. He establishes that "events that model are scarce. But events of presentation are the dominant forms of occasion that publicly enunciate and index lineaments of statehood, nationhood, and civic collectivity" (*Ibid.*, 42). It is interesting to note that Handelman does not use the term nationalism or other similar terminology. This study argues that nationalism is fluid. What can be presented will flux with the goals and decisions of the objectifier. In this sense, modeling and presentation should go hand-in-hand, although Handelman does not appear to argue this.

Handelman (1990: 48) states, "the event of modeling makes transformation happen that directly affects wide social orders. The events of presentation hold up a mirror to social order, selectively reflecting versions of the latter that largely are known." Where events that present are direct presentations of society, events that re-present do so in an indirect manner (Puijk 1999: 100). Handelman's third model is one of comparison; it contrasts itself with other social realities. While Handelman does not use this terminology, he is essentially arguing that the re-presentation "mirror" is the process of establishing identity along Barth (1969) and Eriksen's (1993) concepts of us vs. them. While Handelman's three models were not intended for a discussion of nationalism, it is clear that the two concepts are easily interconnected.

Handelman makes one final, and incredibly useful, observation. He notes that these three models are not typically established in isolation of each other. In fact, he offers a diagram of a triangle as a means of explaining the relationship between the three (Handelman 1990: 61). Two corners of the isosceles triangle are close together, representing presentation and re-presentation. They are connected by a dashed line, which indicates that that border is permeable and therefore non-specified. The third corner, which is drawn away from the other two and narrower, represents modeling, which is both limited in scope and usage. Any demonstration of the "lived-in world" can easily involve elements of modeling, presentation and re-presentation. In making this observation, he notes that this process can be highly complex, but that this complexity has no correlation "between the organizational complexity of a public event and of the complexity or resonance of meaning it produces" (*Ibid.*, 62).

II. PREVIOUS GROUNDWORK IN STUDIES OF THE OLYMPICS AND NATIONALISM

The discussion of sports politics, with reference to patriotism and nationalism, has already seen significant consideration by many others that have offered insightful and useful groundwork for this work. However, while many consider previous scholarship adequate in its considerations, I disagree. In short, there is, as I see it, significant discussion of the relationship of sports and nationalism and in the beneficial impacts of sports' role in nation building. There is not, however, extensive and successful analysis of how sport and sport festivals are used to construct identity strategically.

The bulk of scholarly discourse on this topic consists mostly of unpublished works or books that just glance at the relationship of nationalism and the Olympics, or sport in general. Jong-Young Lee (1990) is an adequate example of this. Most examples of this literature do not take into account the literature or theories of nationalism to any great degree. Rather, they tend to look at the interrelation of sports and nationalism as the interplay of politics, competition, and national pride. In fact, many works, such as Lee (1990), do not look at the relationship between sports and nationalism but instead look at how sport can affect nationalism or, more accurately, the nation-state.[5]

To establish, for the reader, the ground already laid for this study, we can consider three broad areas of contribution: sport and state well-being, sport and nation-state building, and sport and identity construction. Patriotism, specifically pride or devotion to the country or ethnic group that an individual is a part of, permeates all three. It is most common in the first two, where promotions of civic pride are the underlying goal (Moore (1997), Gori (1997), Roche (2000), and others).

The role of sports in state wellness argues the manner in which sport affects the vitality of the state's citizenry. For example, Lee (1990) explains that the Czech, Germans, and Greeks in the early 18th century used sports as a means to train youths to be physically and psychologically ready for war (*Ibid.*, 54) Lee also cites authors, such as D. B. Kanin who made the very same point but about Spartan athletes in relation to sport programs for the ancient Games in the 4th century (Lee 1990: 51). Lee and Kanin's works, to name a few, are examples of sports and nationalism or sports and politics literatures that makes the assumption that the relationship between nationalism and sport is limited to sport being used to bolster the state. In short, whereas this work uses sport and nationalism to study the restructuring of identity, objectification, and international display, Young chose instead to focus on a more political aspect. The games were a tool for the objectives of states and nationalism; they were merely the means to that end. This should not be confused with elite action and nationalism.

This is not in the same manner as described by Barreto (2001a) and others. In those cases, identity creation saw to the best interests of the survival of the elites creating the identity. In Young and others' suggestions, using sports to serve the ends of the state usually meant surges in national pride. According to Lee (1990), by framing exercise and fitness as the groundwork for representing the state in athletic competition, the goal of national pride and the goal of a physically fit and capable population—mostly to guarantee a healthy source of soldiers—share the same means of attainment. This is a common problem in examples of this topic in scholarly work, which has been avoided by only a few authors.

Katharine Moore (1997) argued that part of the reason for British apathy toward the Olympic movement was due to the great surge of nationalistic celebrations that culminated and then continued after Queen Victoria's Diamond Jubilee in 1897 (Naul 1997: 79). In short, the celebrations of the Queen, the British Empire, and the wealth of expos hosted in Great Britain at this time left no need for international sport to foster national pride. Sport was providing the important task of fostering citizen pride and awareness in their state's process of nation building The British self-confidence had no need for the kind of boost sports competitions could provide, but a continued connection between elites drafting the identity of the Britain and its citizens was still necessary.

By limiting the list of benefits the Olympics can provide a state to pride and duty, Moore is able to conclude that England had no use for the Olympics. Her arguments are well taken, and back in the pre-World War I Olympics, is a distinct possibility. But as she does not question the status of nationalism, beyond pride, within England and the empire at large, she makes few conclusions as to whether there was a role the Olympics could have played in the identity of the English or the Empire at large. Moore does indicate a certain interest in the Olympics, in terms of the formation of an Empire team. This could suggest that nationalism might have been quietly playing a role as a part of several attempts at consolidating the Empire. However, her research does not indicate if this was the case, but it does indicate that national pride and perhaps nationalism could exist at the domestic level, as well as the international.

Maurice Roche (2000: 234) noted that mega-events, such as World Expos and Olympic games, provided transient "bridges" between elites and people. The popularity of said events, he notes, is partially explained by the opportunities of defending and exercising concepts of identity. (*Ibid.*, 220-225). Roche is providing us with two key elements of the relationship of sport and nationalism. First, he is demonstrating that "mega-events," as he defines them, are in fact vehicles upon which post-industrialist reformations of identity are made popular. Second, in his detailed analysis of how and why states create these events, he has provided a necessary legitimization of any discourse on the interplay of sport and identity.

Another example, reported by Gigliola Gori (1997) pointed out how this phenomenon does occur in domestic sports. Gori's research demonstrated that the Italians saw a connection between nationalism and sport. In an article published in *Il Regno*, Italian officials felt that the opportunity to host the 1908 Olympics in Rome was an excellent idea, but the offer was refused because they felt Rome and Italy would benefit more from a national competition than an international one (*Ibid.*, 40). A point like this is both interesting and relevant, as it offers a possible explanation as to why Italy did not host the Olympics until 1960 and thus could validate a statement that the cultural benefits of the Olympics weigh far more heavily into the decisions to host than previously indicated by scholars.[6]

Both Gori and Moore studied the same question, but in two different states. Instead of looking at sport as a means of creating, objectifying, or explaining a national identity, Gori and Moore showed how sport is used to foster pride in the nation. In fact, much of sports and nationalism literature examines the role of sport in fostering national pride and patriotism as a support mechanism for national identity instead of studying sport as a means of fermenting its creation and definition; in other words, sport is being displayed as merely propaganda aimed at citizens and nothing more. Victor Peppard and James Riordan (1993) further demonstrated how this relationship exists through their study of Soviet sports policy, providing a clearer and more deliberate example of official state-use of sport and sport festival.

Peppard and Riordan (1993) showed that the Soviet Union, from the 1920s through the 1950s, only competed in international sports competitions in which they were guaranteed a victory. They quoted Nikoli Romanov, Chairman of the Soviet Committee on Physical Culture and Sport, who wrote "once we decided to take part in foreign competitions, we were forced to guarantee victory . . . To gain permission to go to international tournaments, I had to send a special note to Stalin guaranteeing victory" (Peppard & Riordan 1993: 63).

Peppard and Riordan have some of the most telling evidence of the mutual roles sports, policy, and pride can play. They looked at Soviet sports policy for a period of roughly seventy years, during which they found consistent examples of how Soviet decisions on sports competitions were governed by domestic and international policies aimed at bolstering the image of the Soviet system as better than the capitalist system. While not merely an issue of national pride, Soviet sports policy is clearly working with the desire to look good to both the international community and to their domestic population. This is no different from Gori and Moore's arguments in that sport is being used for national pride and nothing more. In the Soviet case, however, the Soviet officials were seeking respect from the international community instead of pride from the peoples of the Union of Soviet Socialist Republics (U.S.S.R.). The assumption that sport excellence also meant excellence of their political and economic system appears in several examples of this literature from the Cold War period.

Along similar lines, Jean M. Leiper (1988) defined sports nationalism as an understanding that the total reputation of a country can be enhanced through sport (Segrave & Chu 1988: 331). Expanding on this, Leiper further noted that all athletes recognize themselves as national representatives and seek to excel to bring pride and honor to their country. In fact, Leiper went so far as to insist that nationalism was a prerequisite of any inter-state sports competition. I believe Leiper is wrong in this assertion.

Leiper is dealing with civic pride, not nationalism. In fact, Leiper does not even address whether an athlete is fighting for multiple levels of a society—city, state, nation—but simply asserts it is nationalism. She looks at the boycotts of 1980 and 1984 and notates that they are a result of almost a century of sports being indoctrinated into human endeavor. She then explains how governments have exploited athletic victory and sports opportunity for their sports-policy aims. Leiper explains, "nationalism might well be explained as the attitude that the total reputation of a country can be enhanced through sport success because citizen's pride is heightened" (Segrave & Chu 1988: 331).

Several authors deal with sports in this manner, often interchanging terms like patriotism, nationalism, culture, and society without realizing there are key differences among them. By making the assumption that the concepts are interchangeable, they fail to clarify that their conclusions are about how sports influences pride by encouraging displays of national unity. In fact, all of these authors, specifically Leiper (1984), Peppard and Riordan (1993), Gori (1997), and Moore (1997), are looking at how performance in sport can affect a nation.

Roche (2000) makes the same argument but expands it to point out that these events provide agency for continuity and change within a social structure; therefore within a concept of state and global identities, Roche looks at the opportunity of identity formation, though does not study in detail the strategies of that process. The authors listed above, along with Roche, emphasize the effects of the outcome of sport and festival itself, placing broad evidence of accomplishments as the vehicle for fostering state pride and loyalty. This study dismisses the latter as a second step of identity formation.

As I see it, there are two grand steps to realize and understand. The first step is to create a well-crafted definition of identity, done so through strategy. The second step is to then supply a stage upon which that identity is both displayed and energized. By energized, I mean to invoke pride and support for the state's official identity within the citizens and the audience. Several of the aforementioned authors dealt only with this latter step, predominantly along the Soviet lines of promoting athletic victories as metaphors for the greatness of the Soviet people. Moore was more in line with my subjects of study in that she looked at the festival as well as the sport itself. However, she is still considering things from a perspective of fostering pride instead of any other possible affects on nationalism. Other authors have taken these concepts even further and sought uses for sports and politics as a relationship that goes beyond national pride but also towards nation building.

To a degree, Roche, Moore, Leiper, and others are suggesting that sports can play a pivotal role in political socialization. Martin Barry Vinokur (1988) drew several interesting conclusions on the interplay of nationalism, nation building, civic-pride, and sport, in an effort to demonstrate the role sport played in socialist states. There are important two core themes of his book. One, "The stronger the national identification of participants and spectators in sports in a country, the more the national integration of that country will be furthered" (Vinokur 1988: 18). Sport is, therefore, a tool of nation-building and political integration of people. Two, he further argued that the "significance and conduct of a national sports system reflects the political system of that country rather than individual effort" (*Ibid.*, 18).

By drawing on examples in Romania and East Germany, Vinokur concludes that his initial assertions, among others, were correct and that sports are a strong tool of political socialization. Of his first theme presented here, I agree in that he is witnessing the final step of the process of utilizing sport as a tool for nationalism and the integration of a state's population into that myth. I disagree with his second assertion, quoted above, and believe his conclusions are based on poor selection of case studies. He concludes that sport, as a tool of nationalism and political consolidation, is a process of the government only. This conclusion, while understandable, is highly limiting due to what states he studied.

Naturally, he would come to a conclusion that the process is government controlled only, because he limited his study to two socialist states that have integrated their sports programs into their governments. If Vinokur had considered other events, especially the Los Angeles summer Olympics in 1984,[7] he may have come to a contradictory conclusion. Regardless, he offered a look at the end result and not the process of sports and nationalism integration. While giving us a stronger sense of the interplay between nationalism and sports, this focus the end process still restricts his study into a national pride example.

Again, like other authors, Vinokur is actually conducting a study based on how sport can affect a community of people.[8] While I believe Vinokur has made an excellent argument for why states, particularly socialist states, expend so much money and energy into international sports, I feel he has not adequately paid attention to the cultural connotations of the games. In short, for all that he sees sports doing for a state, he is still limiting that benefit on the act of winning the competition and nothing more.

A critical facet of nation-building, as described by several authors above, is consolidation. In the post-identity construction phase, the job of entrenching that identity into the newly defined society involves taking a diverse group of interests and identities and pulling them together into a single group. This can be discussed at the national and the international level, which has been accomplished by a few critical scholars, particularly Alan Bairner (2001), Giglio Gori (1997), and Hay (1998).

Bairner's (2001) study focused on the role sports played in both nationalism and in globalization. He noted "through sport, nationalism and nationalities have successfully resisted globalization unless we adopt a very weak definition of the latter" (*Ibid.*, 177). Bairner's study focused primarily on the concept of national sports and how people can incorporate their sense of nationalist identity through their connection to sport while still being incorporated into a broader sense of global identity. Thus, "for most sports fans, the nation that deserves their support is a given and in following their national teams, they underline their sense of identity while simultaneously reflecting its complex character" (*Ibid.*, 167).

Roche (2000) offers similar ideas in noting a duality between national and global identities, in terms of multi-national mega-events and their continuing international appeal. (2000: 235). Bairner's and Roche's points are important for this study on two levels. First, they are a reminder that audience, national and international, are attuned to international sport for the purpose of supporting their national identity. This may be through mere patriotism or, and more in line with this study, through acknowledging oneself as part of their community and identity, by supporting it.

Beyond how audience, sports fans as he puts it, interact with the Olympics, we can find a second valuable point for this strategy in how Bairner sees the relationship between sport and globalization. Bairner (2001: 162) believes that globalization and nationalism can exist along side of each other. If we accept this notion, then we can easily see sport as being a venue for that shared existence. Furthermore, we can also see international performance, and international festival, as being venues for that demonstration together. Bairner (2001: 17) focuses mainly on the concept of sport itself and not on demonstration through and surrounding sport. His work does, however, emphasize the decisions actors have made to merge sports and national interests. Along similar lines, Gigliola Gori (1997) studied the role sports played in the consolidation of Italy.

Gigliola Gori (1997) studied the role competitive sports played in the consolidation of Italy. Instead of an argument about fostering a national identity, she demonstrates how Italy used sport to consolidate the concept of a unified Italy, which, in turn, fostered a concept of unity in all areas of the Italian peninsula. She argued about inter-province gymnastics competition by asking, "Could there be any better occasion to strengthen ties among the regions whose distance was more historical than geographical . . . and to instill in the Italian people the awareness of their own worth" (Naul 1997: 25). While she mainly focused on the process of consolidation of the Italian state, we can see in her study a shift away from mere national pride and towards a broader understanding of nationalism and the Olympics.

Brian Petrie (1975), in his chapter sports and politics, takes the understanding of consolidation a step further, arguing that aggressive nationalism can be transferred to sports competitions as a forum for competition between competing identities and ideologies. This takes consolidation a step further towards the Barthian *Us vs Them* argument by establishing [sport] conflict as a means to consolidate identity when it encounters an alien identity. While this is still a national pride issue, it is also indicating concepts of group and identity survival, success, and vitality all of which weave together true concepts of nationalism with national pride. Along a similar vein, Vayrynen (1984) illustrated how sport is simultaneously a reflection of social contradictions and social unification. He explained, "sports provides linguistic symbolism and a kind of social dream by which people can be socialized into the dominant culture" (Ilmarinen 1984: 64).

The socialization into the dominant culture has its opposite argument in the survival of a peripheral identity through sport. Roy Hay (1998: 61) showed that Croatian identity was able to remain cohesive while the Croatian-Australian community was absorbed into the dominant national culture, because of sports clubs that emphasized pride in its peripheral identity. In other words, national consolidation efforts were alongside communal ethnic consolidation through sports enterprises.

While Vayrynen and Hay are identifying a strand of nationalism, along the lines of my analysis, they are still vesting much of their ideas into national pride. On several occasions he reminds us that the games are a cultural or ritualistic struggle between national communities and success is determined in terms of athletic victory. He does assert that sports in a non-unified social setting can develop a unified sports culture. He even indicates the roles sports can play in consolidation of a new state. Hay, in his discussion of Croatians in Australia, is clearly presenting a national pride argument, in that sports does not provide a vehicle for altering concepts of Croatian identity—merely a venue to continue their exercise. This is the critical difference between consolidation and construction. Construction is always about the creation and selling of definitions of identity. Consolidation is always about taking these established elements of nationalism and continually fermenting their prevalence in society.

But a sport is the unifying force and provides itself as a national symbol. It is not, as this study argues, a venue for such efforts which would use national symbols as the means of identity creation and not the sporting event itself. Therefore, while he does open the door further to the concepts in this dissertation, he is still limiting nationalism and sports to the sport competition itself being the sole source of national identity and its consolidation. As other authors have identified the roles of sports and national pride, Vayrynen is doing so as well because the sport gives the people a rallying point to build pride in their identity. It still does not create or define identity. To use his own words, "Competitive sports has primarily a symbolic value vis-à-vis other members of the international community" (Ilmarinen 1984: 70).

Gori and Petrie represent for us a transitional stage in which national pride is not seen strictly as the relationship between identity and sports but also begins to accept a much broader understanding, and therefore implication, for the role of nationalism in the Olympics and in sports in general. Those few monographs, taken together with these previous two examples, introduce us to the concept of sport and identity construction.. While most of these examples, mainly S. W. Pope (1997), Mark Dyreson (1998), Arne Martin Klausen (1999), and John Hargreaves (2000), include elements of national pride, patriotism, and state well-being, they only incorporate these elements into the main understandings of the interplay between nationalism, identity construction, and sports.

S.W. Pope (1997) is a comfortable starting point, as he is fixated on the idea of identity formation. The difference in Pope's study, compared to almost all others in this book, is that Pope is concerned with the creation of an American sports identity, not an American national identity. Noting that the modern Olympic games "provided a forum for cultural performance at both the national and international levels," (1997: 58) Pope offers another strong foundation for this and other studies on identity construction through sports and festivals. Where this study, and others (Hargreaves (2000). Klausen (1999), Guss (2000), etc.) establish a national identity on that foundation; Pope is content to establish American sports identity as a vibrant element within American culture.

Pope goes so far as to suggestion that a unique American identity was somewhat vacuous in the early 20th century, and that sports identity formed the basis for collective engagement and consolidation of the American nation. (1997: 158) To establish that, Pope's study demonstrates how sports, amateurism, professionalism, and collegiate athletics were manipulated by sports moguls and political elites into an expression of a unified American spirit. In short, baseball, basketball, the St. Louis Olympics, and other sports venues were the stage to create this new "nationalism."

Mark Dyreson (1998) is similar in Popes interests, in that a sports republic, after its creation, can be used to unite a state. To a degree, this is another consolidation argument. However, a more careful read demonstrates two processes occurring. First is the creation of the sports republic, an endeavor not significantly dissimilar from Pope's suggestions. Second is the use of the sports republic's playing fields "as the civic forum in the drive to construct a national culture." (Dyreson 1998: 124) In the spirit of many authors discussed in this chapter, Dyreson turns to an argument of patriotism as he reminds his readers of sport's duty to establish the dominance of a nation, in comparison to others. (*Ibid.*, 131-132)

Pope (1997) and Dyreson (1998) both establish the dual constructionist tendencies in sports: a sports nation and a nationalism. Whether the former is a prerequisite of the latter will remain an interesting question for others to ponder. Cronin and Mayall's (1998) edited volume on the study of sporting nationalisms looks specifically at the role modern sport enterprises can and have played in construction and consolidation of a state. Without reservation, they clearly establish early in their introduction that sports and its events are a vehicle for identity construction. (Cronin and Mayall, 1998: 1-2) Sporting events thus provide an opportunity for either construction or consolidation of identity. Cronin and Mayall (*Ibid.*) are one of a few examples in which studies of sports and nationalism are indelibly constructionist in their use of modern theories and concepts of nationalism. Further examples, can be found in Pope (1997), Dyreson (1998), Klausen (1999), and Hargreaves (2000).

Arne Martin Klausen (1999) offered an anthropological study of how the Olympics are used to promote a country. While the study is not expressly one on nationalism, its premise and overall approach to the question is quite interesting and germane to this work. The book examined the various aspects of the Olympics as they pertain to display. Klausen and the other authors spend most of their time looking at displays of economy, culture, landscape and humanity. Klausen shows that in the Olympics, the identity of the host is not the only set of traditions being displayed. Therefore Norway, instead of trying to reinvent itself, attempted to use the opportunity to host the winter games to reinvent Olympic traditions. The torch relay, which since its inception in 1936 has always begun with the ceremonial lighting in Greece, was one of the traditions Norway targeted for "reinvention." Norway believes the heart of the winter Olympics that being skiing, was born in Mørgedal, Norway. Therefore, the Norwegians attempted to have a torch lit and run from there as well as from Greece. As one can imagine, the Greeks objected. The point to be made is that any effective work on nationalism and the Olympics will need to discern between traditions that are inherent in the Olympic ritual and those that are not. Klausen's collection of articles is an excellent example of drawing that line within a study of the Lillehammer Winter Olympics of 1994.

Found within Klausen's collection of articles is a study of the production side of the Norwegian cultural display at the Lillehammer Olympics. Roel Puijk's (1999) study weaves together description of the types of displays suggested or planned with a discussion of the goals of the Lillehammer Organizers. Puijk's chapter, and most of Klausen's book, is one of the closest examples of the kind of analysis of Olympic displays of nationalism that this study offers. By discussing the particular elements of the ceremonies and their purpose, Puijk offers keen insights into a framework that begins to tie nationalistic goals of the actor and the resulting cultural performance.

Where Klausen (1999) and Puijk (1999) excel in indicating the organizer's purpose in designing the pageantry of the ceremonies, they both fall short of a hardcore analysis of the opening ceremonies from a perspective of nationalism theory. The extent of their analysis delves into Handelman's (1990) and MacAloon's (1996) studies on models of performance, including cultural performance. John Hargreaves (2000) embeds his study in the goals of both the Catalan and Spanish organizers for the Barcelona games, but his study focuses more on the politics behind the event than on the performance at the event. Therefore, his study represents an interesting tangent to this type of literature.

John Hargreaves focused specifically on an example of nationalism and sports as more than just civic pride. His study is one of the only examples of a study that combines nationalism and the Olympics as the premise of the book. Hargreaves studied the uses of the Olympics to further Catalan identity as his contribution to Olympics and nationalism studies. His work questions the potential of an independent Catalonia and simultaneously studies how hosting the Olympics was a beneficial step in that direction. He does not spend adequate time relating the processes of the Barcelona organizers or the Spanish Olympic Committee to the relevant theoretical frameworks of nationalism studies. Second, his conclusions, while appropriate for a study on Barcelona, are not necessarily accurate for a nationalism study of the Sydney, Nagano, or Atlanta games. He concludes that "the Barcelona games demonstrated unequivocally that far from any tendency for the Games to exert a homogenizing effect, in fact the very opposite occurred" (Hargreaves 2000: 60). His presumption is based on a case study that involved the host city being the capital of a region with its own language, culture, and strong independence-minded organizers. In this scenario, homogenization may be unlikely, if not impossible, but there are other scenarios where the results could be homogenization, heterogenization, or neither—the status quo. This study intends on finding the various ways that the Olympics have affected nationalism and will do so with examples from several Olympiads, instead of just one.

III. CONCLUSION

A general overview of prior attempts to analyze the relationships of this enterprise has turned up a few consistent problems. The most prominent of those problems is the surprising inter-changeable nature that many scholars have given to the terms *nationalism* and *patriotism*. In some cases, this has been due to a lack of grounding in solid theories of nationalism. In other cases, it has been due to their only tertiary use. To avoid this problem, we will seek to attach the main theoretical notions presented herein to the current body of theory of identity, nationalism, and demonstration of these concepts. Vesting these principles with a solid methodology in political science will provide further grounding for the principles discussed. As part of this effort, the next chapter will delineate a cognitive theoretical approach that roots this study in the fundamentals of rational choice and structural theoretical understandings.

In an attempt to contribute to a growing field of research, this book will focus on sports and sports festivals as tools for nationalist-minded hosts. Instead of seeing the sporting event as the interplay of nationalism, the outcome of which either strengthens or weakens a state due to success or failure, we will instead see how hosts can use opportunities to participate in and/or host these events. The result of this goal will be to more or less dismiss the precepts of patriotism from a prominent role in this analysis. Unlike previous works, the emphasis of this study is on the stages of identity-establishment in sports events prior to overt statements of patriotism and nation building. Nationalism in sports and cultural events is a two-step process. Step one is the establishment of a common definition of identity. Step two is the celebration of that identity as an effort of loyalty building. This book is absorbed primarily with step one, however it is not possible to dismiss the presence of the spirit of step two throughout the entire process. Roche (2000) and Hay (1998), without going into the facets of step one, establish its existence as well as to showcase patriotism, nation building and state pride as cogent elements of the entire event.

The following chapters serve a few purposes and, as such, can be clustered together to serve that end. The next chapter will build off concepts developed in this chapter to formulate a working understand of nationalism and its plasticity. Chapters four through six establish processes of altering national identity with specific strategic qualities. These chapters establish commonalities in several opening ceremonies as the basis for constructing typical expressions of a national identity through specific types of tools. Chapter seven then introduces concepts of identity demonstration in cleaved states and provides a simple yet necessary introduction to the remainder of the book. The following two chapters, eight and nine, look instead at specific goals of organizers: exalting the core or the periphery. In these two chapters we see compelling evidence of how the tools described in previous chapters are utilized to attain a specific series of goals for their respective identities.

The final chapter of this book sums up the general outcome of this study's main points. In establishing a more coherent understanding of displays of national identity, it offers keen insights into the use of processes to alter official state identities and points out future directions in research and understanding of identity as it can be performed.

NOTES

1. Interestingly enough, this means that the difference between *us* and *them* is not one founded just on ethnic identities but on the identities of international organizations such as the Olympics as well.

2. Unless, of course, the "identity" that is being reinterpreted is an international identity or is actually the identity of the festival itself; in the case of the Olympics, this would be the Olympic culture and its stack of symbols.

3. In this sense, *realist* is used with its film definition, which calls for the presentation of images in the most accurate, or realistic, manner possible. Conventions of art, and style, are minimized to create the illusion that what is filmed really happened or could have really happened.

4. Winston uses "native" here, but for our discussion, it is more useful to use peripheral as I intend to expand this notion to include any sub or regional identity held up against a core identity.

5. I choose to use the term "nation-state," even though "state" is the most accurate explanation of what is being discussed because I wish to emphasize that the "states" in question are simultaneously bolstering the strength of the state and civic "national" pride and because, for this to be effective, athletes must buy into some vision of what they are fighting for.

6. This is even more likely when one considers that Italy had decided to host the winter Olympics in the 1940's, at the height of the consolidation of a national Italian identity. These games, which were to have been in Cortina D'Ampezzo, were cancelled due to World War II.

7. Several works on Peter Ueberroth and the 1984 Los Angeles games, especially Ken Reich's *Making It Happen: Peter Ueberroth and the 1984 Summer*

Games, argued sport is most effective in the hands of businessmen and not government officials.

8. I hesitate to use the term 'nation' as I am not convinced Vinokur is implying any form of homogenization of people's identity. Considering the fact that Romania and East Germany are made of more than ethnic Romanians and Germans, respectively, and that sport in these countries must be coalescing people under a "pride" of the state, instead of anything else.

CHAPTER 3
TOWARDS A THEORETICAL UNDERSTANDING OF NATIONALISM IN THE OLYMPICS

I. OLYMPIC-NATIONALISM PROPOSITIONS

The root cause of the relationship of between nationalism and the Olympics is vested in the fact that actors, particularly political actors (state and non-state), have used the games as an opportunity to attain specific nationalistic goals. This study will use the term actor to indicate an individual or set of individuals that are in control of the decision process of the nationalistic displays at the Olympics. In terms of a stage or file actor, the term "actor" will either be qualified with specific reference to type of actor: Hollywood, Stage, etc., or be substituted with the term "performer." Regardless of their goals, all demonstrations of identity in the Olympics function under a specific set of conceptual and theoretical notions. As a result, two key statements about this relationship can be made.

Guss' (2000) observation about domestic festivals holds true at the international level. He argued that domestic festivals in Venezuela offered opportunities to create and then regularly recreate identity on stage. This provided the objectifiers an opportunity to regularly demonstrate and reassess their identity as a part of reoccurring festivals. International events can provide an excellent and underestimated avenue for identity formation and performance. Whereas previous studies on identity performance have looked primarily at domestic demonstrations, this study contends that this manifestation also occurs at international festivals. While this is international in its scope, it is still a process targeted at audience members on both the domestic and international level.

Highlighting the existence of nationalism formation and demonstration at the international level is only half the issue at hand. The second half is to explain how the relationship functions. Displays of nationalism in the Olympics are a deliberate process that use multiple strategies to attain the specific goals. A paramount goal is establishing the uniqueness and legitimacy of the identity being performed. Nationalistic displays in the Olympics are a deliberate attempt by the organizers to demonstrate specific facets of an identity. Therefore, the organizers are goal-seeking individuals, or groups of individuals, who construct the performance of identity in a manner that they expect will delineate their national identity in a manner that suits their short-term and/or long-term interests.

The festival nature of the opening and closing ceremonies provide the organizer an opportunity to articulate their carefully planned performance of nationalism through recognizable processes. These processes, which are strategic plans designed to assist actors in attaining their nationalistic goals, are manifested in several ways. In analyzing performances of nationalism in the Olympics, this study will focus on seven key manifestations: historical revision & creation, indoctrination of ideology, custodians of culture, core, periphery and regional, racial/ethnic & native/immigrant, religion and mythology, and globalization.

Because the interplay of nationalism and the Olympics has been defined and categorized in terms of processes that actors use, it becomes obvious that ascribing a moral alignment to this relationship is untenable. As a result of the 1936 Berlin games, in large measure, the use of the Olympics for nationalistic goals is either cautioned as dangerous or outright demonized as an authoritarian tactic. A principle outcome of the theoretical framework of this study will be the complete dismissal of this notion.

II. THE THEORETICAL FRAMEWORK

Within the realm of political science inquiry, intellectual discourse centers on debates over the explanatory power of three major theoretical frameworks: rational choice, structuralism, and political culture. Political culture argues that political phenomena are governed by culture itself. The course of events in a given situation is the result of culturally endemic qualities in a society and these attributes are independent variables explaining the outcome of events. Thus, as Almond and Verba (1980) see it, politics is the dependent variable and culture is the independent. Adherents to this school of thought maintain that political systems are determined by the course of socialization within that society (Chilcote 1984: 182).

Too often culturalists have concluded that nationalism is culturally determined. If this is true, the processes of constructing identity and inventing tradition become completely irrelevant. Nationalism would result from inherent qualities of culture rather than the choices of elites that objectified components of national identity. I accept Clifford Geertz's (1973a: 89) definition of culture as "an historically transmitted pattern of meaning embodied in symbols, a system of inherited conceptions expressed in symbolic forms by means of which men communicate, perpetuate, and develop their knowledge about and attitudes towards life." It is interesting to note that, in terms of nationalism, every element of the Geertz definition of culture contains concepts that this study describes as deliberately constructed to attempt to develop an individual's understanding of their own existence.

As Ross (1999: 42) explained, culture has two relevant factors to comparative political inquiry: "First, culture is a system of meaning that people use to manage their daily worlds, large and small; second, culture is the basis of social and political identity that affects how people line up and how they act on a wide range of matters." He concedes that it is necessary to place a cultural approach within a framework of inquiry that assesses "how the impact of culture interacts with interests and institutions" (*Ibid.*). While description of pageantry will play a major role, this study seeks not to conclude that these elements were *ipso facto* culturally determined and were objectively accurate but rather were instead the result of calculated plans. Chilcote (1984: 184) pointed out most analyses employing a political culture approach rely on "descriptive rather than analytical criteria." As Lichbach (1999: 6) said, this approach lacks "the ability to generalize to abstract categories and the ability to provide explanations that apply to more than the case at hand." Therefore, instead of focusing on the particular elements of nationalism, which may or may not be derivatives of cultural "truths" about a society, this study accepts cultural aspects at face value and seeks to make more meaningful conclusions on how individuals construct a goal-seeking performance of their identity within the opportunity of hosting the Olympics.

Second, this section turns to the structural theoretical framework. Structuralism posits that political phenomena are a result of the structures within which they occur. In short, "social life and action ... is shaped by processes" (Katznelson 1999: 83). Beyond merely shaping outcomes, structuralism orients an actor towards attaining their goals by regulating their expenditure of energy (Parsons 1961: 37).

Parsons dealt with systems theory, focusing a bulk of his work on interaction of individuals within networks. Parsons (1951: 5-6) noted that actors make decisions based on their mutual interactions and that these interactions are mediated by a culturally constructed and shared system. The system provides constraints as well as motivation. "Parsons see the actor as motivated to spend energy in reaching a desirable goal or end, as defined by the cultural system" (Wallace 1999: 29). Systems theory often extends outside of the realm of individual action and culture. In certain situations, that extension could warrant a broader consideration of the role of the system itself; in other words, a look at the structures that have bearing on the question.

Structuralism's main assumption, in terms of world systems theory, is that "analysts must at some point decipher the pervasive structural context within which all behavior is conducted" (Thompson 1983: 9). Fred Spier (1996: 5) noted: "a regime is an interdependency constellation of all people who conform more or less to a certain social order." He went on to explain: "Human regimes are constellations of more or less institutionalized behavior" (*Ibid.*). Pulling together Parsonian notions with Thompson, Spier, and others, one can establish the main goal of a structural theoretical framework; structuralists "...emphasize the formal organizations of governments; some . . . class relations; some . . . political parties and interests" (Lichbach 1999: 6).

Institutions form a major point of interest for structuralist studies. Kathleen Thelen and Sven Steinmo (1998:2) indicated that definitions of institutions by historical institutionalists emphasize both formal organizations and informal rules and procedures. Therefore, a structural-institutional approach recognizes that the structure of institutions, as well as their rules and procedures, "Constrain and refract politics" and as a result, influences the outcome of actions taken within them (*Ibid.*). Margaret Weir (1998) noted the importance of the role of the organization of political institutions in framing domestic policy within a state. The basis of her analysis emphasized the role of institutions in steering the development of ideas and interests (*Ibid.*, 195). Weir concludes that institutions greatly influenced policy outcomes (*Ibid.*, 210-211) and thus reinforced her objective to guide attention towards diverse linkages between ideas, political institutions, political actors, networks of experts, and social interests (*Ibid.*, 192).

In terms of analysis of state action, the structuralist position holds that "activities of the state are determined by the structures of society rather than by persons in positions of state power" (Chilcote 1984: 305). It is this latter statement that will limitedly influence the theoretical framework of this study. If by recognizing that institutions affect the system, then structuralism must play a minor role in the framework of this study. Specifically, in our analysis one will see how structures within the Olympic system influence actors by constraining they choices they are able to make.

The limit of a structural approach for this study rests directly in the fact that by focusing on institutions the study is too restricted in its methodology.

To take a structuralist framework would require focus of the study on the institutions of the International Olympic Committee (IOC), the organizing committee of the games (OCOG), and the governments with jurisdiction over the host city. In an attempt to find generalizations on the relationship between nationalistic goals and the Olympics, research at the OCOG and government level would produce results that are case-specific and therefore unlikely to provide broader understandings of the phenomena. One could focus on the structures of the IOC, but without looking through the structural issues to the actual goals and choices of actors, conducting this study with the intention of finding processes for nationalism displays at the Olympics simply falls apart. The structuralist approach would be most useful would in a study where the strategies and choices of actors of a single Olympiad are studied with an emphasis on structures and institutions in order to establish what effect, if any, they have on the relationship analyzed herein.

Third, and most pertinent to this study, is the rational choice framework. Niccolo Machiavelli (1992: 75-77, 94-95) presented individuals as goal seeking when he noted that a prince must seek to be clement, not cruel, and feared but not hated. The decision to avoid hatred is rational in that it is a deliberate attempt by the sovereign to maintain power. Machiavelli is a good starting point for this discussion, because he presents several paths for the sovereign to take and points out the dangers of each.

When a ruler acts, with the goal of maintaining his power, he must choose the path that is most likely to secure the continuance of his authority. This analysis is strengthened by La Rochfoucauld's (1959: 39) 15th *maxim* where he stated "The clemency of princes is often nothing but policy to gain popular affection." In short, leaders are rational in choosing to be clement because they expect that such an action will gain the love of the masses and therefore, at least as Machiavelli argues, guarantees the continuation of their tenure in office. Theories employing a rational choice approach attempt to explain the actions of individuals by interpreting them in terms of actions being attempts at attaining goals.

Rational choice, as Levi (1999: 23) explains, places emphasis "on rational and strategic individuals who make choices within constraints to obtain their desired ends, whose decisions rest on their assessment of the probable actions of others..." Frank Zagare (1987) broke the concept into two camps: procedural and instrumental. The latter is the most pertinent to this analysis. The instrumentalist approach to rationality simply states that "a rational actor is one who makes a decision based upon goals as he or she defines them and selects a strategy from among a set of options as he or she perceives them" (*Ibid.*, 9).

One of the main criticisms of instrumental rationality is that it attempts to explain why some individuals make sub-optimal choices. For example, classic Downsian analyses start with the premise that politicians in democratic polities are vote maximizers. George Tsebelis (1992) was perplexed by cases where political actors clearly endorsed unpopular policies. Tsebelis explained this problem by noting that buried within a game can be any number of 'nested' games. By taking what appears to be a sub-optimal choice, according to Tsebelis, actors may actually be deliberately seeking an outcome that alters another game. Therefore the sub-optimal choice is actually a step along the way towards attaining the main goal, as defined by the actor.

Ronald Chilcote (1984: 190) draws attention to Marxist-rational choice, which also grounds itself in rational choice theory as "a normative theory and assumes that all individuals can be rational." He explains that the Marxist variant of the rational choice approach "focuses on the utility of individual choice in attaining goals and on the principle that all people act rationally to achieve their preferences" (*Ibid.*, 191).

As valuable as a primer on the general scope of rational choice may be for both the author and the reader, this discussion requires a foray into the current trends of rational choice in nationalism, in order to provide the clearest introduction to the theoretics of this study. The most convincing argument of this indicates that elite preference is rational when one accepts George Tsebelis' concept of nested games (Barreto 2001b). Tsebelis' (1992) concept basically suggests that there are games buried within games, and therefore, choices that may seem suboptimal may actually be a deliberate attempt to affect another game and therefore are actually rational. Barreto applied this concept to his Puerto Rican nationalism study.

In *Politics of Language in Puerto Rico,* Barreto (2001b) demonstrated that elites chose to objectify the Spanish language instead of religion, even though religion would be a far stronger way to differentiate a predominantly Catholic Puerto Rican society as different from a predominantly protestant United States. The reason of the choice, he explains, is simply that the elites constructing Puerto Rican identity would more effectively hold on to power by objectifying Spanish because it meant that the secular intellectuals promoting early 20th century nationalism did not need to share power with Catholic clerics. Furthermore, the highest ranking of these Rome-appointed prelates in Puerto Rico were Americans.

Turning from a generic analysis of rational choice to a keener understanding of the theoretical framework of this study, a few statements on rational choice must be made. First, the rational choice approach assumes that an actor has choices, the actor sets goals for himself, and then deliberately takes actions he believes will result in the attainment of his self-defined goals. An actor's decisions are constrained by the structure of institutions within which decisions are made. For this study, an institution refers primarily to the IOC. On a limited basis, institution will include the organizing committees of the games and host governments. The approach this study will take is strengthened by Thelen & Steinmo's (1998: 7) note to the rational choice scholar to remember "institutions are important as features of a strategic context, imposing constraints on self-interested behavior."

In *The Intellectuals*, Gramsci outlines his concept of hegemony—a social engineering project that he limits to the ruling class. As he contends, hegemony refers to:

> The 'spontaneous' consent given by the great masses of the population to the general direction imposed on social life by the dominant fundamental group; this consent is "historically" caused by the prestige (and consequent confidence) which the dominant group enjoys because of its position and function in the world of production. (Gramsci 1971: 12)

Later, in his discourse on State and Civil Society, Gramsci (1971: 269) notes that "state/government ... should reflect back its prestige upon the class upon which it is based," and that "this phenomena is not something exceptional ... It can, it seems, be incorporated into the function of elites ... in relation to the class which they represent." Elites attempt to elevate traits specific to themselves as hegemonic. Elites then take deliberate actions to maintain their power. As Machiavelli (1992) explained in *The Prince*, all actions are taken in order to either gain or maintain power.

Given Machiavelli's assertion and Barreto's usage of actor's decision process, we can identity two primary elements of relevant decision-making. First is the actual decision to present nationalistic iconography within the framework of the Olympic games. Second is the decision process involved in selecting what element(s) to demonstrate through the Olympics. Political actors are rational in their attempt to demonstrate, accurately, a specific identity in the Olympics. By rational, I mean that actors are goal-seeking individuals who, after setting their goals, make choices on how to act based on the likelihood that those choices would result in the attainment of their goals. Thus the motivations of actors and decision makers in the Olympic movement play a key role in understanding political objectives in the games.

A few points should be reiterated on decision processes within Olympics and sports and Olympics and sports policies. There is a necessary point on elites and the Olympics, which brings to this review the literature on sports and decision-making. March L. Krotee applied Robert Michels's (1959) *iron law of oligarchy* to demonstrate that the Olympics are an elite-driven oligarchy. Michels indicated that elites present a kind of oligarchy--the structure of politics--which controls decision-processes and results in turning democracy into a kind of myth. This becomes particularly relevant for studies of the Olympics when one factors in Michels' assertion that political structure and the structure of pertinent institutions frames our understanding of decisions made through those structures.

Krotee (1988), by tying together the structural and oligarchic elements of Michels, inadvertently points out something peripherally relevant to this work. Krotee gives us a sociological understanding of the IOC and explains its formation and change up to the 1980s. From here, he applies Robert Michels' (1959) notions on leadership and oligarchy. Michels explains the inherent difficulty in maintaining democracy. By looking at political parties and the roles of elites therein, Michels demonstrates how easy it is, in fact even encouraged, for elected individuals to dominate the people that elected them.

The nature of political organization is that individuals with specific skills and knowledge rise to power in political parties and therefore political systems. These elites maintain their control, Michels argues, due to the human nature, the nature of political struggle, and the organization of political parties and systems. Therefore, Michels is offering a purely structuralist argument on the formation of oligarchy, which elites then present as democracy.

Michels' theory applies to all organizations, regardless of their level of idealism and therefore Krotee has a strong foundation to base his depiction of the Olympics. Krotee then further explains that the psychological aspects of the Games are based in both the elites and the public as the games continued for decades with a bleak financial outlook. Krotee concludes that the Olympic movement, because of significant challenges politically and economically, requires an oligarchic system with superior leadership. His final thoughts on his conclusion indicate a curiosity as to whether an oligarchic IOC structure can perceiver in an age of democratic spirit. Either way, what Krotee indicates for us is a clear and telling sign of the benefits of an institutional, structuralist analysis of the Games.

The notion that the structure of institutions has influence on the outcome of actions of the institutions opens a new avenue of research by looking at the institutions of the Olympics. Every Olympic host has a National Olympic Committee (NOC), and an Organizing Committee of the Olympic Games (OCOG). These organizations are created for the purpose of handling a nation's or state's involvement in the Olympics (NOC), and the handling of the actual plans of hosting (OCOG). NOCs and OCOGs are political and business organizations whose make-up can often influence the decisions that are made.

Richard Espy (1988) explained that the role of the Olympics in the international system was influenced by the organizational structure of the Olympic movement on the basis of national identification (Segrave & Chu 1988: 41). Most of this work focuses on the international aspect of the

Olympic structure, looking at the interaction of NOCs and the transnational status of the IOC. Espy references many key issues in the Olympics of the 20th Century, including the involvement of two Germanies, two Chinas, and other issues like Africa and the status of Rhodesia. Also referencing the east-west divide, Espy's essay chronicles how each of these major issues played out in the Olympics and thus demonstrates the role the Olympic movement can play in international issues.

In looking at transnational issues, Espy recognized that the interplay of politics and sport was rooted in both international and domestic politics. There is a very limited literature that actually focuses on the domestic side of Olympic structuralism, which is where a nationalism study of the Olympics must begin. Regardless of studying at the international or domestic level, Espy is correct when he asserts that dealing with ramifications of politics in sport is best handled by recognizing "that politics within this organizational framework was an integral part of sport" (Segrave & Chu 1988: 411).

Usage of Espy's understanding is a necessary part of this study's theoretical design only in those instances where the governing structures of the IOC actually influence the outcome of host city decisions. The main goal of this is to guarantee that the results of the study are not altered due to an aberration in the structural design of the NOC, OCOG, and other relevant organizations. The most relevant work is Laurence Chalip, Arthur Johnson, and Lisa Stachura's (1996) study of sports policies in seventeen countries, ranging from states with established sports organizations that are controlled at the government level, like the People's Republic of China, to states like the United States, which has a decentralized sports program which is largely independent of the government. Chalip, Johnson, and Stachura (1996) note what the status of sports policy is in each country and how it has affected each state's status in the Olympic movement. In several cases, this work will provide a basis for the sports policies affecting host states and the interaction of Nationalism with their Olympic efforts.

III. METHODOLOGY—THE HUNT FOR OLYMPIC NATIONALISM.

As this study is deeply embedded in the choices of the host, with only a small degree of IOC structuralist constraints, this analysis of nationalism in the Olympics is conducted almost entirely through the study of the choices of the organizers, in terms of how they intended their displays to appear. Therefore, the specific goals and choices of the actor will establish the relationship of nationalism and the Olympics.

Organization of the Olympics requires the involvement of representatives of the national government, region/state government officials if appropriate, city officials, IOC officials, the organizing committee, international sports federations, and other individuals with a vested interest in the games. Because this study is rooted entirely in the performance of identity through the Olympics as an international event, an "actor" will be defined as being either the OCOG, the "artist(s)" in charge of the performance of identity, or both. Moving forward with our concept of "actor," we then consider in what location(s) the cultural performance will occur.

Actor choice can be found in several locations, only some of which will be pertinent to this study. The focus here will be the two events of the Olympic games, both winter and summer, which carry a large audience at the domestic and international levels and which have within them a structured opportunity for the display of identity—the opening and closing ceremonies of several Olympiads. In addition to assessing the contents of the performances themselves, the final report of the organizing committee will supplement this analysis. Each host must prepare a final report analyzing the Olympic games from the perspective of the host. In most cases, this involves a descriptive analysis and assessment of both the opening and closing ceremonies.

By analyzing the opening and closing ceremonies through the actual footage of those events and through the text of the final report, I make several assumptions which help to effectively streamline this analysis. First and foremost, I assume that the opening and closing ceremonies are faithful renditions of the actor's goals. Furthermore, whether a specific identity embodies a specific trait is not relevant. Recall that Hobsbawn (1983) and Geary (2002) established that identities are constructs of myth, not fact. By deconstructing the elements of cultural performance, this study seeks to establish the existence of the relationship between nationalism and the Olympics without respect to the degree of success or failure of any particular host.

Since this study hypothesizes that nationalism and the Olympics have an inherent relationship, and since this study is framed in terms of actor choices, it will be more enlightening to study this in terms of "manifestations" rather than in terms of cases constructed by Olympiad. First, by not studying specific Olympiads in isolation, this study avoids arguments that the display is a result of structuralist situations within a specific state, OCOG, or games. Second, by analyzing in terms of manifestation and not host, we avoid any risk of biases in the study in terms of the effectiveness of a specific cultural performance, or its entertainment value, and instead construct meaningful observations on the role of nationalism and the Olympics that will remain pertinent regardless of what city/state acts as host.

By avoiding Olympiad-based case studies, we are able to more easily work within the understanding that nationalism in the Olympics does not simply manifest itself in one clear-cut way. Its manifestation is dependent on the goals the actor sets as well as on the specific attributes of the identity that the actor is seeking to establish. The benefit of this is that identity demonstration can be completely divested of cultural determinism and strictly be analyzed in terms of goals and selected attributes. Furthermore, by requiring each strategy to be established and justified with several examples from several different Olympiads, we are able to establish that these processes are symptoms of the relationship between nationalism and the Olympics and not a result of the having a specific state as host.

The manifestations of nationalism analyzed in this work are not presented with the intention of making sure that each Olympiad fits perfectly into any singular category. Recalling the Berlin games, nationalism was manifest in several forms; hence, a single Olympiad may fit into multiple categories and further diminishes the value of a case study format. Lastly, as we are focusing on the process, limitations on the basis of the commonality or rarity of a specific trait or routine has no bearing on their establishment. It is best to consider the breadth of tools instead of only currently popular ones.

While considering only goals and selected attributes apparent since 1980, the following manifestations or aspects of nationalism will be analyzed in this study:

I.   Historical Revision and Creation
II.   Indoctrination of Ideology
III.   Custodians of Culture
IV.   Core vs. Periphery and National vs. Regional Identity
V.   Race, Ethnicity, and the Native vs. Immigrant Issue
VI.   Religion and Mythology

Whether the goal is handling a diverse nationalistic identity(s) or whether it is reworking, in some way, a preexisting one, nationalism in the Olympics falls largely into one of the seven categories listed above. The next section will briefly consider, with reference to the ideas of other nationalism authors, each manifestation to establish precisely what each means before formal analysis of the opening and closing ceremonies of several Olympiads is presented.

IV. THE CONCEPT OF STRATEGY

Frank Zagare (1984: 11) defined strategies as: "the options available to [actors] to bring about particular outcomes." He further noted "strategies are linked to outcomes by a mathematical function that specifies the consequences of the various combinations of strategy choices..." (*Ibid.*). Thus, by establishing goals for the display, actors implement the strategy they expect will result in the attainment of their goals. The strategies that they can implement are thus seen as formulas for effective nationalism displays because they deconstruct displays of specific types of identities and establish the processes necessary for conducting these displays with specific goals in mind.

Paramount to this discussion are the concepts of *us* vs. *them*, as delineated by Thomas Eriksen and Frederik Barth. Eriksen (1993) noted that the purpose of a nationalist identity is to demonstrate that the people ascribing to an identity are noticeably different from everyone else. Traits chosen for objectification are therefore the collection of traits that describes an identity as unique. Recall the French Canadian example and the use of the French language in identity formation. To demonstrate a Quebecois identity as different from the rest of Canada, provincial policies have been passed making French the official language, changing road signs from English to French, and even requiring French literacy to qualify for certain jobs. Quebecois nationalism was a response to the preexisting socio-political and economic order in North America that privileged the English language and hence English speakers over those who spoke other languages (Barreto 1998). Eriksen's work is critical to understanding the concepts this study will examine. They become even more germane when one recalls that the processes of nationalism in the Olympics are performed in front of an international audience at an event with international participation. The objectifiers do not normally need to worry about the interference of the international community in their process. The display must pass domestic as well as international scrutiny as well; however, at the same time the Olympics, a phenomenon that has its own embodiment of legitimacy, can allow for a more radical redefinition as guests of the games are more likely to accept and less likely to question the images

Similarly, Barth's (1969) concept of boundaries must be considered. He noted that an individual's concept of "us" may persist regardless of the loss or acquisition of particular boundary markers (e.g., language, religion, folk customs, etc.) Still, Barth's study emphasizes that the discerning feature of a national identity may be a particular trait, or set of traits.

Weber's (1976), Lefebvre's (1979), and Popkin's (1990) studies of the French Revolution can be interpreted as concluded that at different stages of the revolution, different concepts of *us* and of *them* triggered the bulk of the violence. The symbols of the revolution, as well as the concepts of the ideology that pushed it forward, were continuously in flux, resulting in an excellent demonstration of the conceptualization and cyclical reconceptualizations of French identity. Regardless of which traits are used to delineate in- and out-group members, the actor promoting a new national identity must be cognizant of the consequences of the *us* vs. *them* dynamic.

In addition to Eriksen and Barth, every manifestation will use, in some manner, Richard Handler's (1984) tenets of objectification. According to Handler (1984), simply stating that a nationalist/ethnic identity is made up of a certain set of traits is not sufficient. Those traits need to be objectified. The process of objectification lends popular legitimacy to the traits of the identity and further reinforces those identities. Objectification, therefore, is a process that involves sanctifying tangible traits as symbols epitomizing an identity . The process is most successful when the symbol attains a hegemonic status. Florencia Mallon (1995) wrote about the role of hegemonic symbols, stating that hegemony is the ascendancy of an icon to such a level that that particular icon is a *de facto* expression of the idea vested within it. While objectification and hegemonic symbols will play a role in every strategy, some strategies treat them in slightly different ways.

Additionally, there are also concepts that deal specifically with performance and display, rather than with notions of nationalism. These include the ideas of Timothy Luke (2002), David Guss (2000), and Don Handelman (1990). Luke and Guss showed in what manner, whether static or metamorphic, display can put forward a nationalist agenda. Luke referred to the relationship between nationalism and display as involving both qualities of socialization of knowledge and entertainment. First, Luke (2002: 3) notes, "exhibitions formalize norms of how to see without being seen inasmuch as the curators pose as unseen seers, and then fuse their vision with authority." Display, whether on stage or in a museum, establishes our understanding of both an ideology and the elements thereof. Furthermore, Luke notes "museums are effectively embedded in establishing certain rules to stabilize regimes of artistic, historic, or scientific interpretations" (*Ibid.*, 223). Finally, museums, as a form of artful display, attempt to merge both ideological understanding of identity and of tools of entertainment to broaden audience size and thus spread the message of the museum to as many recipients as possible (*Ibid.*, 228). Thus, the pageantry of the opening ceremonies is not just mere entertainment; rather it possesses a quality of a highly subjective historical and cultural information exchange.

David Guss (2000) offered Venezuelan festivals as highly pertinent venues for anthropological research into culture. He saw a clear and calculated demonstration and re-demonstration of Venezuelan identity through their festivals. His ideas lay the domestic groundwork for this study, as the very same study of Olympic Festivals parallels Guss' on an international scale. The most pertinent change, and one of great importance for the reader to understand, is the framework under which the organizers are working, is that of temporality. Guss's study showed that the festivals were a consistent opportunity for the reassertion of the concepts of their own identity as each iteration of the annual festivals were an opportunity for both demonstration and reinforcement of demonstration.

In terms of national performance, the Olympics represent, in large measure, a one-shot deal. Only the cities of Athens, Innsbruck, Lake Placid, London, Los Angeles, Paris, and Charmonix have hosted games twice. The time between their two opportunities to host has ranged from 12 to 108 years.[1] The national Olympic committees of Greece, the United Kingdom, Switzerland, Norway, Australia, and Austria have hosted twice; Germany, Italy, Japan, and Canada have hosted three times, France has hosted five times, and the United States has hosted eight times. Of the states listed, only the United States has more than one city up for discussion in this study. As this analysis unfolds, the reader may notice that U.S. hosts tend more towards regional displays of identity, which would suggest the United States is not an exception in this study.

It is, however, worth noting that protocol-governed events, such as the parade of nations, are opportunities for regular (every two or four years) reassertion of identity. For example, consider the outfits of the Mongolian athletes in the parade of nations. Their flag bearer is quadrennially adorned in native Mongol attire and serves as a constant reminder of that state's ancient past.[2]

Within the framework presented, we turn to Handelman for a keener understanding of the concept of model and the scope of models for public events. First, I agree with Handelman's (1990: 24) statement "models abstract reality in coherent ways, by selecting out, simplifying, and condensing various of its aspects and relationships." It is worth noting that models are not mere simplifications of phenomena but is reductionist demonstrations of the real-world manifestations (*Ibid.*). In his analysis, public events were broken into three categories: those that model, those that present, and those that represent. Roel Puijk (1999: 100) explained that presentations are those events that "show the existing order directly," and that representation are those events that show the existing order indirectly. He also explained that events that model "affect the order and at least lay a germ for change" (*Ibid.*). Putting aside some of the problems of his analysis, his point rests in Handelman's explanation that most public events involve some combination of all three models.

V. DISCOURSES ON THE MANIFESTATIONS

This section introduces the core assumptions of each strategy. At first glance, some manifestations may seem to overlap in ways that would suggest they should be combined or some should just be eliminated in their entirety. The first category groups the first three tactics: historical revision and creation, indoctrination of ideology, and custodians of culture. These three manifestations share the common trait of being driven by matters of story and symbol. Each of these strategies represents an effect on the myth of the society as it is told and believed.

The three manifestations presented herein should be considered tools for the formation of a display. A goal-seeking construction of a performance must be established through tools that are crafted to assist the actor in attain his specified goals. In that sense, the performance of identity is handled through tactics, which are designed to meet the needs of the objectifier. The manifestations of historical revision and creation, indoctrination of ideology, and custodians of culture each are story driven because the represent elements of story as opposed to the story itself.

The first, historical revision and creation is an attempt to subtly, perhaps subversively, change what are perceived to be the historical truths of the past as a means of rewriting a national identity. The second, indoctrination of ideology is a process of taking a current myth and confirming, reestablishing, and/or strengthening the concepts and beliefs of that myth. The third, custodians of culture, demonstrates how the myth attempts to incorporate symbols into its mythology and then turn them into hegemonic notions. This is the concerted attempt to take historically "real" and significant artifacts and ascribe them to one's own cultural heritage, regardless of the historical validity of such claims.

The first two can be seen as the past, present, and future of a mythology. The first seeks to rewrite the past or to abandon the past—in part or in whole—in favor of a whole new nationalism with a newly described and accepted past and present. The second seeks to accept the present notions on itself and the past and to strengthen the people's understanding of those notions. The third affects the other two in that it is the deliberate attempt to insert claims on artifacts of history. In other words, regardless of the first two, this "cultural assimilation" can and often does take place. Historical revision and creation and indoctrination of ideology deal with a myth as a whole or deal with a specific part of it. The third, on the other hand, simply deals with the specific, usually single, elements of the myth as it stands or as it is being affected by either the first, second, or fourth manifestation as well. This would suggest that the third typically appears with another strategy; however such a statement should never be considered as an absolute.

VI. FINAL CONSIDERATIONS

The seven manifestations, as discussed, represent facets of the relationship between displays of national identity and the Olympics. To continue the metaphor, the final chapter of this discourse takes each of these facets and constructs the diamond. While each is grounded entirely in the specific goals of the organizer of the games and therefore represents processes, these processes are rarely in isolation. While some are more topically related to each other, the reader must remain mindful of the fact that each is merely a means of realizing the hypothetical statements of this study.

While each shares a similar "goal"—a process to represent nationalism through the Olympics—they also share similar conceptual grounding. However, each manifestation has its own specific form and therefore they each serve different goals that actors may seek. Therefore, while maintaining focus on nationalism displays at the Olympics as performances intended on deliberately attain specific goals, this study seeks to appreciate the many ways in which Nationalism has been manifested in the Olympics. From this point forward, this text justifies each of these strategies by primarily defining them in greater detail and then providing copious examples of their implementation.

NOTES

1. Such a brief iteration—twelve years—is quite rare and only occurs in times of emergency. In this case, Denver, Colorado resigned as host of the 1976 winter Olympics leaving less than the standard amount of time to construct all the venues. Thus Innsbruck, which hosted in 1964, was a logical option.

2. Examples of this can be found in either the flag bearer or the whole Mongolian team, during the Parade of Nations of many of the Olympiads discussed in this study. Specific Examples are present in: SLOC 2002d, and COOB'92 1992b.

CHAPTER 4
HISTORICAL REVISION AND CREATION: OLD HISTORIES AND NEW INTERPRETATIONS

> Nineteenth-century scholars, politicians, and poets did not simply make up the past; they drew on pre-existing traditions, written sources, legends, and beliefs, even if they used them in new ways to forge political unity or autonomy. Second, even if these communities are in a sense imagined, they are very real and very powerful. (Geary 2002: 17)

Some nationalist identities are based upon a myth or series of myths that are constructed out of the process of rewriting history. The revision of history could simply be an embellishment of some facts—commonly by leaving out one or more elements. These elements are either abandoned in an effort to gloss over a past the host may be ashamed of or are expanded with new elements in an effort to accentuate an altered cultural heritage. An example is the intentional elimination of the Korean massacre from Japanese textbooks. This policy was a single step in the process of rewriting Japanese history so as to divest Japanese culture of a racist past that has plagued opinions of this culture for more than half a century.

The process could also involve a much larger alteration, in which a nation's entire past is changed to fit current political or cultural goals of the political or other elite. Regardless of the degree of revision, historical revision involves any attempt on the part of an actor to change the facts of a nation's history so as to make those facts more compatible with their goals for a newer national identity.

Hugh Trevor-Roper (1983) is noted for his work on Highland Scottish identity, in which he accepted the concept of invented tradition to indicate set practices, typically governed by a set of rules, written or tacit, that seek to incorporate specific values into a national identity. First, Trevor-Roper pointed out that a very limited portion of Scotland, the Highlands, was the base for the overall concept of Scotland. Second, icons that today are intimately associated with Scottish heritage, notably the short kilt, is a garment designed by an Englishman.[1] These traditions are invented in that they tie a current national identity to a past, which was borrowed from other communities. The term "invented" is attached to the concept since it is intended to imply that the actual connections to the past can be real, exaggerated, or completely fraudulent. The most critical aspect of this concept for this study is the ritualization of invented traditions.

Hobsbawm indicates that the whole process of inventing traditions "is essentially a process of formalization and ritualization, characterized by reference to the past, if only by imposing repetition." (Trevor-Roper 1983: 21-24) When this is conducted through the Olympics, we are implying the direct ritualization and imposition through demonstration, most notably through icons incorporated into cultural displays. By suggesting repetition, Hobsbawm implies that the process occurs over time. Still, this does not have to imply a protracted process (*Ibid.*).

Regardless of the venue, if the invention is a simple one, or one that is built off of a preexisting tradition, it could be done discretely in a shorter period of time. The more complex the concept of the tradition or the more removed from people's current perception of their identity, then the more time that will be required for the process to be successful. This should not, however, distract from the more important issue of challenges to this process. The time involved, and even the possibility of success of revision through the Olympics, is dependent upon how entrenched the pre-revision identity is within its society and whether there are challengers to the revision. It must underscored that the process of historical revision cannot be successful if it seeks to push to far away from currently accepted notions about history. Sumiko Higashi (1995) indicated that members of a community will not accept a postmodernist historical representation if they feel it is contrary to traditions about their history that are still invested in their current belief structure. Higashi also indicates that revisions fail when they do not convince historians or the public. As this study is looking at success of a performance of national identity, we will be more concerned with how a revision is presented to an audience than to the historical community.

John Mraz (1995), in *Memories of Underdevelopment*, asserted that a revision of identity, similar to those suggested by Higashi and Hobsbawm, are more effective if the society is on the verge of a paradigm shift in history. I argue that this is true if the society is on the verge of a cultural paradigm shift only if the revision is conducted by incorporating already established definitions into the process of transformation. Mraz would suggest that the revision of a nationalist identity is best done by "selling" the new ideas by showing them as coming out of, connected to, or a logical synonym of the currently accepted myth. Mraz becomes even more pertinent to this study when one considers that he was discussing processes conducted through film. Historical revision through the Olympics is very similar to documentaries and docudramas in that they both can be used to demonstrate new concepts through combining new and old images into one overall demonstration of identity. New ideas or myths are more easily accepted when they are tied to previously accepted myths. Robert Rosenstone (1995: 202) stated that a dramatic presentation is successful when it "1) performs a variety of traditional historical tasks; 2) goes beyond these tasks to create new ways of visualizing our relationship to the past; and 3) provides a "truth" that can stand beside written versions." (Hobsbawm 1983: 4)

Thus far, most of our discussion on historic revision involves selling things to the public and, in some cases—particularly Higashi—selling it to the historians as well. The hardest sell, one would assume, would be to the historians, especially when they play a role in the interpretation process. For this study, we could easily substitute Higashi's "historians" with "elites," Gramsci's "Intellectuals," or similar ideas. Essentially, Higashi and Marshall Hodgson (1996) focus on the difficulty of altering the view of a myth when others have prior knowledge and the influence to challenge the new definition. Hodgson (1996) indicates that the process of rethinking history is one that is common among historians. This usually requires reassessing assumptions and reinterpreting facts that, when done, settle on a completely new understanding of the past.

As Hobsbawm and others indicate, creating a new national myth requires connecting people to a new set of assumptions about the past. The continuation of historical analysis, by its very definition, requires historians to do the same. Thus, when historians become a part of the invention or reinvention of tradition myths can become indoctrinated into the public's understanding of its own past and in the official historical analyses of that past. The result is that whatever the legitimizer displays may well be accepted in the scholarly circles as quickly as among the general public. As Roosens succinctly states:

> In the ethnic arsenal you can partially forget what you know if others do not notice or do not mind. You can add things if exact knowledge is not available. You can choose a suitable variant if different theories exist. You can combine and transplant. You can inject vigor and authenticity, ... Almost anything and everything are possible, as long as no falsehoods are

told that are too obviously refuted by common knowledge and as long as the adversary is not too strong. (Roosens 1989: 161)

In terms of the Olympics, we find that displays of a national identity can result in the rewriting of historically accepted traditions or facts. This process, in the Olympics, usually involves two elements. First, and by far the most prevalent, are the cultural displays of the newly constructed identity, usually sold through carefully designed presentations that incorporate both new and old elements of a national identity. The second involves documented histories, whether through documentaries, short news stories on historical points of interest, or through state-sponsored enterprises designed to educate insiders and outsiders about their society. This latter process is less common in that it tends to lack the showmanship that is tied to most Olympic events.

The concept of revision can occur in several degrees. A simple revision can involve the alteration of a single fact or trait. From there, the process can grow in degrees of complexity by altering more and more traits. Eventually, this can culminate in a total revision. In this scenario the root concept of the identity is deconstructed and rebuilt. The term revision than becomes less precise and we instead use the term creation. Thus, instead of seeking to alter the past, the actor is in fact seeking to recreate it in its entirety.

An effort to create, according the previously established problems with revision, should be doomed to failure because it is pulling the audience too far from their currently established myths. This is true unless the audience is ready for and expecting to be taken from the established myth. The willingness on the part of the audience to change is a necessity for a creation myth to be successful. It is helpful for the audience to be willing to accept a revisionist demonstration, but if revision is subtle enough, it can be done without the vast majority of the audience even noticing. The processes of revision and creation therefore are very similar but have a few key distinctions.

There is a difference, albeit subtle, when one considers the actor's intent. The first is an attempt to recreate by rewriting the past subversively. It is not a legitimate process and results in a lie. The second, on the other hand, is a reemergence. In other words, having accepting the past, the community now seeks to emerge as something different. This is the burgeoning of a new identity. Where the former is often done out of shame or disgust, the latter is done out to attain transformation.

The creation of a new mythology is an intended act in which the objectifier and everyone planning the demonstration are aware that the goal is to breathe life into a society by redefining its entire concept. The process of reinvention could involve new symbols, incorporation of regional, racial or ethnic, or religious qualities that previously were not a part of any national identity. After World Wars I and II, several new states were formed, needing mythologies that would attempt to unify them into one solid unit. When this was successful, a peaceful and harmonious state resulted. When this was not successful, civil disorder, violence and even civil war occurred. In much the same way as there was a necessity for this process in the formation of the state, the process could also be necessary for revitalizing an existing state.

Taken together, we find as our first strategy for national identity performance at the Olympics to contain two key elements. The first element is that of historical revision; the second is creationism. Both of these terms have deep connotations and their proponents and detractors. However, for this purpose we should accept them both for the processes they are and divest them of current baggage which would unnecessarily clutter the issues of this chapter.

Historical revision is a contentious issue. Some see it as a subversive pack of lies intended to misrepresent the "true" facts of history. Others find it a necessary, if not wonderful, process of rewriting and reinterpreting archaic understandings of history into new, more socially and politically acceptable interpretations. While in historical circles the term "historical revision" can spark heated debates, here the terminology is intended to illustrate a different concept of nationalism. By historical revision, in reference to one's national identity, I intend to indicate a process in which a currently existing national identity is altered to reflect modern trends in a society.

While historical rewrites are certainly a possibility in this scenario, it is not the only possibility. Simple emphasis, addition, or omission of a few facts is a sufficient enough change to warrant the label of historical revision. In fact, slight embellishment or re-emphasis on the past is the most common example in this manifestation. As part of an identity, there is a concerted effort at re-describing elements of the heritage of a particular group of people by actors with the goal of restructuring nationalism to suit their objectives. While minor changes are the most common, more catastrophic changes are not outside of the scope of this manifestation. The process, either way, requires carefully steering an identity in a specific direction without losing site of its origins.

Taking this to the opposite extreme, creationism is leaving behind a nationalist identity's original definition in favor of a completely new one. This is most common when a national identity ceases to be functional to the elite sponsoring it. If a national identity has fragmented to the point of having no utility, then a revision can become an effort at creation—a situation in which the present identity is scrapped in favor of a brand new one. History, in this sense, is not revised but completely rewritten. A completely rewriting one's history does not mean that every element of the old history need be altered. Instead, it means there is a calculated plan of starting with a new definition of nationalism and then using icons and histories of the previous identity only if the actor chooses to. These elements can be used as is, reinterpreted slightly, or completely redefined for use by the objectifiers. Therefore, while there are similarities in revision and creation, the difference between the two concepts is very important.

Both revision and creation involve rewrites of history. The difference is in how one goes about it. The former is accomplished by taking the currently existing myth and building on top of it as if it were a foundation. The latter, to continue the imagery, would take the foundation apart brick by brick and start a new foundation, using new and old stones. The nationalist elite's stones are the cultural traits used to differentiate *us* from *them*. While considering this, it should be noted that neither concept implies any degree of authenticity. The alarming trend of revisionist historians is frighteningly encouraged in this form of identity reformation. Here, identity is rewritten and sold with only nominal regard to the truth. But, Higashi (1995) was also right when he insisted that the audience would not accept a new definition of identity unless it incorporated enough older traditions that it felt real.

Consider Loring Danforth's study of the Macedonian question. Upon Macedonia's independence, the international community was joined by a new state, which emerged out of the rubble of the pan-ethnic Yugoslavia. The new state of Macedonia a formal and internationally recognized prior history as a self-governing entity. It lacked a cohesive sense of state identity as well, thus this new state had to employ a full-scale creationist process to identify itself. Macedonia, an exceedingly new state, built its own identity out of the legacies of Philip of Macedon and Alexander the Great (Danforth 1997). National symbols, ideas, and heritage were all built around the great leaders of antiquity and incorporated into official state iconography. For example, the use of the Star of Vergina on the Macedonian national flag is a blatant attempt by the state to link itself with Ancient Macedonia. The flag was later modified, but not completely revised. But, as is evident from this example, creation often involves co-opting symbols and historical legacies already in existence.

Marshall Hodgson (1996) explained that correct historical revision is more of a reinterpretation than a revision. To rethink the past requires taking old understandings and old truths and reinterpreting them in the light of a new, perhaps better, perspective on what counts as historic truths or newly discovered facts. While his study looks at taking history from the local and writes it on the global, the concept is nevertheless true for revisions of identity. Success, therefore, is only clear when the process of revision suitably supplants older definitions of identity so that it incorporates contemporary popular assumptions of their own identity while they are creating new suppositions.

If revision requires the incorporation of old traditions, with similar assumptions, then how is creation structured? In what is alarmingly simple, creation requires the mutual understanding that it is afoot. I argue that revision can be accomplished regardless of whether the audience is aware. As John Mraz (1995) pointed out, transformation is easiest when society is undergoing a paradigm shift. Should a society already be in an overt process of changing—whether by revision or creation—then it is aware of its redefinition. Under these circumstances, revision or creation at the Olympics is a part of an already established process, and therefore the audience is more likely aware of the process.

Audience awareness is critical. If the audience is aware of the revision and favors it, the process will be much easier because the objectifier is working with a receptive audience. If the audience is unaware, then the process must either make them aware or tread carefully enough to hide the process. The danger is when the audience is both aware and unreceptive, at which point the process is not likely to succeed. This is especially true when the process is a creation, not a revision.

Creation requires a mutual abandonment of the old identity in favor of a new one. During a creationist display, traditions may persist, and members of the community undergoing identity recreation understand that they are part of a new concept and not the continuation of the old. In this sense, there is no option to "trick" the audience or else the symbols that are being deconstructed would have to remain unchallenged. In short, a creation without audience awareness, and consent, must be limited in scope. Should the objectifier have both, then the creation can be as extensive as the actor wishes, including the construction and/or deconstruction of hegemonic symbols.

As Gramsci (1971) and Mallon (1995) pointed out, a symbol is hegemonic only if the members of the community universally accept it as vested with a specific symbolic meaning. If all members of society agree on its interpretation, then to change it requires the consent of the society and not just the objectifiers. Therefore, creation, while being far more like a paradigm shift in its degree of change than any other process of identity alteration, cannot be arrived at subversively or unintentionally. While revision and creation both require selling new concepts to an audience, the former may employ subtlety and subversion while the latter is only easily successful with the consent of the audience.

In both scenarios, demonstration becomes a key issue. Audiences must be shown the elements of the altered or new identity in a manner that accomplishes several tasks. First, and foremost, it must do so in a believable manner. Whether the attempt is subtle or subversive, the audience has to accept it. If the attempt is creationist in its design, then the audience must be able to accept it as a representation of a specific identity. We must also realize that identity revision or creation, when performed through the Olympics, is carried out on a stage in front of the affected group members and also in front of those who are uninvolved because they are not a part of the community. In all likelihood this latter group constitutes audience members who are simply present for the entertainment, enlightenment, or mere spectacle of the show.

Because cultural performance must inherently serve both audiences, objectifiers need to merge elements of identity formation and elements of entertainment in a manner that pleases both. The opening and closing ceremonies of the Olympics involve a highly choreographed and carefully engineered pageant. Luke (2002) explained that museum exhibitions help to formalize our understandings of historical events. Pageantry can perform the same tasks.

By visually demonstrating historical events, icons, and artifacts of culture, the pageant streamlines our definition of these elements of nationalism in light of a specific identity. Luke (2002) also confirmed that entertainment is not merely looked upon as such but is seen as embodying much more. That entertainment can inform, enlighten, and socialize is something of which entertainers are clearly aware. Bentein Baardson, the auteur[2] of the Lillehammer games, was well aware of this when he went about planning the opening ceremonies of the Lillehammer winter games (Klausen 1999: 105-106). Baardson was looking for a way to depict Norwegian culture through the entertainment portion of the opening ceremonies, therefore demonstrating that entertainers or, more accurately, the entertainment designers, are keenly aware of the dual role of their performances. Identity revision and creation in the Olympics are both processes of socialization conducted through entertainment that serves as indoctrination for those whose culture is being demonstrated and simultaneously as explanation for everyone else. Furthermore, when discussing cultural performance through festivals like the Olympics, there is a third structural constraint, which can be described as protocol.

A festival that has been institutionalized as a tradition, as Hobsbawm would use the term, has a set of rules and procedures that govern how the festival is celebrated. For the opening and closing ceremonies, there is a list of Olympic protocols, which include flag raisings, anthems, cauldron lighting, oaths, speeches, and others. The focus in this project is predominantly on the pageantry and not the protocol. There are times, however, when centering on the protocol will be somewhat useful when there are limited opportunities for expressions of nationalism. We therefore must identify specific elements of the pageant that have identity-altering qualities and interpret them in light of these and other strategies.

In this chapter we will build a case from several Olympic opening and closing ceremonies to demonstrate the clear presence of revisionist or creationist elements in the pageant. Multiple examples will be employed in order to substantiate the claim that the strategies defined in this, and other chapters, are not a unique result of a specific host, but are in fact general strategies utilized by many hosts. Much of this evidence is provided in the footage itself, in the explanation of the elements of the footage, and by looking at reports of the Organizing Committees of the Games OCOGs and broadcast commentary.

I. REVISION: HISTORICAL FICTIONS AND FICTIONAL HISTORIES

A good portion of revisionist identity demonstration involves wiping away past failings or atrocities. For example, the aforementioned example of Japanese textbooks excluding the Korean genocide. In cultural terms, this 'dark spot' is something that Japanese society would be more than happy to erase. Along similar lines, failure of a group, whether in war or other forms of conflict, can generate a need for a revision to justify, diminish, or erase a moment of history. In this age of historical and cultural awareness, this form of repositioning in light of historical events is more likely than the Japanese example, which is open to accusations of misrepresenting the past, similar to holocaust denial.

Most efforts at decisive historical revision start with the depiction of an identity in a metaphoric or symbolic way. For example, the 1996 Atlanta Summer Olympics presented a full sequence in the pageant section metaphorically depicting the history of the south from European colonization to the post-civil rights period. This segment, entitled "Summertime," creates a mythology for Southern identity and displays elements of that collective character in a highly symbolic manner. The beginning of the *Summertime* segment is a creation story that begins with a depiction of the environmental beauty of the region.

Two elaborately adorned characters representing the Sun and the Moon enter from opposite ends of the stadium. The two meet in the center of the stadium and form the Southern Spirit. The Southern Spirit, formed by a union of the Sun and the Moon, generated a symbol of grace. The costume is majestic, delicate, and flows smoothly with the movements of the performer. The use of white, traditionally a symbol of purity[3] and innocence in western cultures, and the elegant and simplistic design of the costumes suggest the traits the Atlanta organizers wanted embody in Southern identity. The Sun and the Moon then depart leaving the Southern Spirit to preside over the region's creation. The Southern Spirit moves toward the main performance entrance of the stadium, where it then leads the parade of symbols into the stadium. Symbolically, the Southern Spirit welcomes each part of the Southern identity as it enters. In a very interesting, and arguably quasi-religious, manner, we have here a creation story of a new identity.[4]

The order of entrances appears somewhat chronological. The most obvious flaws in the chronology were misplaced period dresses and the use of certain songs, none of which are significant to Southern history; these require further explanation. A hierarchy is not being presented to the audience. Instead this pageant is intended to be a concise "cultural" history of the South. What is most interesting here is that history is presented as the progression of culture. Music, dress, dance, and "past-time"—in manner that recalls Hobsbawn's (1983) general framework and Trevor-Roper's (1983) Scottish Bagpipes example, in particular—all merge to create a glowing chronology of Southern history that does not actually depict factual events. There is one exception, which is highly pertinent in this analysis. The Civil War is specifically referenced as a moment of history—one that was particularly destructive to Southern culture.

The Civil War period is depicted by the "Thunderbird" sequence. The Thunderbird segment begins with rolls of thunder and lightning flashes. It is followed almost immediately by a large metallic bird-like creature entering the stadium. The commentators are quick to point out that the thunderbird is a depiction of all the troubles the South has endured, but they also concede that the single event this segment is intended to depict is the Civil War (ACOG 1996b). Interestingly enough, the Southern Spirit positions itself in front of the thunderbird in a manner that suggests defiance and resistance.

This act occurs for two symbolic reasons. First, it shows the perseverance of the South and how it resisted changes imposed by the Union—the government of the North. Second, it symbolically situates Southern and Northern Identity face-to-face on the stadium floor. While this may be more pertinent for the core/periphery and regional strategy, it serves in this segment as an artistic depiction of the Civil War or the *War of Northern Aggression*, as it is sometimes still called. The thunderbird is a metaphor for tribulations that the South suffered but in this instance it can be seen as a depiction of one of two conflicting nationalist identities.

It would not be unreasonable to suggest that this is ascribing a nationalist aspect to the Confederate independence in the 1860s and further solidifying an independent Southern identity, both then and now. The Thunderbird segment is not just a metaphor for Northern and Southern relations it is also a depiction of the resilience of a self-determined South.

Following the thunderbird is a large piece of waving cloth that symbolizes the cloud of smoke left after the Civil War. Most would assume that this represents Sherman's burning of Atlanta during the Civil War. However, the commentators explain that the symbol and the soon-to-follow rebirth of the south is intended to depict the entire region's rising out of the ashes of the Civil War (ACOG 1996b) reinforcing interpretations that the thunderbird is indeed the burning of Atlanta.[5]

In this segment the Atlanta organizers easily could have been presenting a brief history of Atlanta during the Civil War. Instead, they chose to use this segment as a representation of the unification of all the southern states. Having a shared history is a very important element of the formation of a nationalist identity. Seymour Lipset (1990) argued that the lack of a shared history made it difficult to form and legitimize a nationalist identity. The South, seeking a nationalistic identity that was justifiably different from the national American identity, could benefit from a shared history that was unique from its Northern counterpart.

The thunderbird's exit reintroduces the audience to the themes and music of the Summertime segment. Here we have the South's rebirth. Although, a strictly historical interpretation of this segment would suggest that it represents the reconstruction period. This reprise of the themes of Summertime is not a direct copy of the pre-thunderbird version of the segment. Instead, it is artistically augmented to suggest a stronger more vibrant post-civil war society. Most notably, is the inclusion of fifty Southern Spirits, which is simultaneously an acclamation of the vibrance of the South and a symbolic reminder of its prominent place among the fifty United States. They are dressed in the same style as the Southern Spirit but more colorful. Their emergence comes immediately after the following William Faulkner quote is read to the audience: "To create out of the materials of the human spirit, something which did not exist before" (ACOG 1996b). Conveniently, what we have here is the pageant claiming that post-Civil War Southern identity is a revision of Pre-Civil War Southern identity.

The entire Summertime segment invoked criticism for the opening ceremonies, but this reprise is likely what some viewers displayed there displeasure with the ceremonies when they referred to the opening ceremonies as self-righteous. The Toronto Star quoted a Russian athlete who stated: "everything in Atlanta was aimed at Atlanta . . . at expressing and glorifying itself" ("World Heaps Scorn" 1996). The Summertime segment finally brings itself to a close with an upbeat Jazzy rendition of the Hallelujah chorus including all elements of the Summertime segment with the sole exception of the Mississippi River's depiction. The closing themes of Summertime added a very triumphal flavor to Southern identity.

Three interesting qualities, in terms of historical revision, can be identified from the Summertime and the Thunderbird sequence. First, Southern History is presented, or rather objectified, in terms of culture and not a political or social historical past. The elegance of southern dress and music is not underscored with any depiction of the Southern past, which would draw attention to its plantation heritage. Second, the Civil War is depicted as a temporary cessation of the vibrancy of the Southern Spirit. It is not presented as the destruction or alteration of that symbol. Conducting this demonstration as a reprise of a Pre-Civil War cultural lends credibility to my previous claim that the Summertime segment, complete with the creation of the Southern Spirit, should be viewed as revisionist and not creationist. Third, the period of reconstruction is not depicted as an event that had any lasting negative impact on the South.

The return of the Southern Spirit, the festival nature of its depiction, and the full embodiment of the South are now shown in an even larger tone. Reconstruction, historically, is usually depicted as a period of destruction against the South as punishment for the War. In this depiction, Reconstruction and the Civil Rights era are completely glossed over as the Summertime sequence returns. If interpreted for its historical and cultural merits, the reprise of the Summertime sequence could show that Southern identity was more vibrant in the post civil war period and therefore suggests that the "rebirth" that occurs after the Thunderbird sequence could in fact have been a re-creation moment for a regional Southern identity as opposed to just a Southern flavor of American identity. Clearly, the flow of Summertime to Thunderbird to Summertime Reprised is simultaneously a revision of the history of the South and a reminder of the reemergence of a vital Southern identity.

Furthermore, we should note a few benefits from this strategy. By conducting its history in cultural terms, the pageant avoids any need to depict political and economic aspects of Southern history. Slavery, oppression, and corruption are glossed over as incidental. In fact, Atlanta even claims for itself the antithesis of this history. After the Parade of Nations, the ceremonies pause to pay homage to Martin Luther King, Jr. A segment of the now famous "I Have a Dream" speech was played and images of the civil rights leader were put on the stadium's screens. The choir sang an arrangement of "I Have a Dream" in the background. Instead of a post-Civil War through mid 20th century depiction of Atlanta and Georgia as one of the battle grounds of civil rights, its shown as a leader in this cause. This is later reinforced by the performance of "Georgia on my mind," the Georgia state anthem. This discussion of the civil rights period does not suggest that Atlanta should not have depicted its pride-filled moments in the era. What this discussion points out, however, is that it is a revision of history to project only the tolerant side of Georgian history by dismissing the backdrop to the elements of the story they do in fact tell. Gladys Knight, a famous rhythm and blues singer from Atlanta, sang Georgia's official state anthem, which was proclaimed as an effort at smoothing race relations in light of segregation of performance halls that led performer, Ray Charles, to refuse to play in the state of Georgia (Cox 2005). By maintaining a strict cultural element to the pageant, and then supplementing this with glorifications of Atlanta's civil rights friendly moments and leaders, the Atlanta organizers effectively streamlined their display into a complete expression of the beauty and glory of their identity. This is particularly effective, as Higashi (1995) would explain, since the ceremonies focused on actual civil rights luminaries from Atlanta, thus diminishing Atlanta's history in the civil rights movement is more believable because of the demonstration's believability and authenticity—in other words, its proximity to the "truth."

This example of eloquent retelling of one's past is common in the Olympics. In the case of Atlanta, it was a more pleasant depiction of the revitalization of the South in the Reconstruction and civil rights period. Some states have used this opportunity, instead of rewriting a history, as a moment of atonement for that history. At the Nagano opening ceremonies, anti-landmine activist Chris Moon entered the stadium with the torch, surrounded by children singing "When Children Rule the World" (NAOC 1998c: 125). He was disabled, losing half a leg and an arm, while removing landmines with a non-governmental organization. The organizers choice of Moon symbolically represents the sadness of the Japanese heart for the atrocities Imperial Japan committed against Koreans in World War II (NAOC 1998b). Japanese demining efforts in Southeast Asia would also lend credibility to this interpretation and further explain the reason for Moon's placement in the ceremonies.

In this example, the opening ceremonies offered the Japanese an opportunity to express state solemnity over a past horror. This was also very conveniently timed for the Japanese government. One year prior, the Japanese Society for History Textbook Reform, was set up to begin the process of rewriting history textbooks. The organization was the first step in what Korean and Chinese officials claimed to be a conscious effort at removing Japanese war atrocities from their official state history ("Disputed History Text" 2001: 15). It is very interesting to see the dichotomy of a Japanese policy in a very international and public setting, in this case the Winter Olympics Opening Ceremonies, compared to a Japanese policy in a much more discrete and domestic setting such as classroom textbooks.

Lastly, in this discussion of revision, the Barcelona Games should be considered for their dichotomy of Catalonia versus Spain. Here we focus on two parts of the Barcelona Opening Ceremonies: the Creation Myth and the symbolism of the European Union. As with the games in Atlanta, the most important segment of the Barcelona Opening Ceremonies was depicted as a creation myth. There was, however, a key difference that separated the creation styles in these two games. Atlanta's creation myth told the story of how the "Southern Spirit"—an incorporeal, mythic, symbol of the region—was created by the joining of the Sun and the Moon. The Barcelona Olympics, on the other hand, showed how the ancient city of Barcelona, the region of Catalonia, and the people of that host city were constructed out of an ancient "Greek" myth. Again, like Atlanta, this is not an example of creationism. The Barcelona ceremonies did not attempt to create a new concept of Catalan identity. Instead, it took old symbols and elements and created a revised history for these symbols to be considered the legacy thereof. Instead of showing Barcelona and Catalonia as having a history that was a part of and growing out of the central Iberia, Catalan was shown as being a part of the Mediterranean.

By emphasizing the role of the Mediterranean Sea in its revised creation story, the Catalan organizers were effectively accentuating the disconnection of themselves from a Spanish history that had never effectively absorbed Catalonia into itself. These, and other, efforts at reinventing a creation myth are effective because they do not easily bereft people from their own sense of historical authenticity (Higashi 1995; Mraz 1995). Creation myths are loosely based interpretations of an ancient past, which tend to contain more symbolism than fact. As a result, audiences are more likely to accept massive revision to these elements unless the creation myth is so deeply invested into their cultural identity that its revision pulls the audience too far away from their own sense of identity (Higashi 1995). Therefore, it is a way of establishing a unique identity, along a Barthian *us versus. them* framework, by creating a clear understanding that "we" have a distinct historical origin from "them."

As ancient Barcelona's discovery and founding was being defined as distinct from the rest of Spain, the audience was more willing to be drawn into a very artistic and carefully conceptualized view of the creation of Barcelona and Catalonia. According to the Opening Ceremonies, the Sun sets the stage for Hercules to dash across the stage and symbolically split a column to allow the Atlantic Ocean to flow into the stadium, forming the Mediterranean Sea (COOB'92 1992b). The column had two symbolic meanings. First, it symbolized "the will of man" and second it symbolized the end of the world, which when split represented "the boundaries between Heaven and Earth, good and evil, life and death" (Cuyas 1993b: 56).

The water, depicted with the aid of hundreds of performers, rushed across the stadium floor, encompassing a giant Silver ingot. The ingot would slowly unfold to reveal a Roman ship, based off of the story of Hercules' travel from Africa. The final report claims that the ship and its passengers represent the warriors, thinkers, and artists of the various Mediterranean cultures (Cuyas 1993b: 59). The ship is a key element in tying Barcelona's identity construction directly to a Mediterranean and Roman heritage and therefore separates from an identity that links it with the rest of the Iberian Peninsula. The following sequence was particularly gritty and violent. It depicted a series of "challenges" for the ship to overcome in its journey across the sea. These challenges included a bull, a hydra, disease, which embodied the challenges any group would face in embarking on discovering and expansion.

The creation sequence ends with the founding of a new city: Barcelona. The survivors of the voyage symbolically and ritually pay homage to the efforts of Hercules and themselves in facing their maritime challenges. This ending served a dual purpose. On one hand, the entire sequence can be interpreted, as NBC's broadcast commentary described the entire sequence, "as representing Catalans' historic effort to defend their identity" (de Moragas Spà, et al. 1995: 16). On the other hand, this study can be reinterpreted as symbolically showing the Olympics being brought from Greece to Barcelona. First, Hercules traversed the stadium, followed by the ship. The effort here, regardless of which interpretation you choose to accept, is to draw Barcelona into a Mediterranean community (Rivenburgh 1996: 337). The obvious result of this depiction would be to symbolically and historically present a Barcelona and Catalonia that could easily be separated from Spain.

This latter manifestation in the Opening Ceremonies is further strengthened by further revisionist refocusing of Barcelona and Catalan identity as European. During the arrival of the torch and the lighting of the cauldron, audience members held up dark blue and gold lights. The stands were covered in a dark blue field with twelve gold stars: the symbol of the European Community. The European presentation was actually a highly contested issue, involving the European Community, the IOC, and the officials from Barcelona and Spain. Its overt political messages, which were conducted at the objection of several IOC members (Pound 2005), was the likely result of pressure from Madrid and the European Community.

Europe would have two more places of distinction the night of the Opening Ceremonies. First, twelve human pyramids, a Catalan tradition called *castells* (Cuyas 1993b: 71), were constructed; each one symbolized a member of the European Community. This uniquely Catalan tradition was tied together with the European Community in a gesture that clearly indicated the games were Catalan and European, as opposed to Catalan and Spanish.[6] Finally, the ending of the Opening Ceremonies involved a single boy, dressed in the flag of the European Union, singing Beethoven's *Ode to Joy*, the European anthem. Opera singers and then the chorus joined him. During these European elements, the crowd waved blue and gold flashlights that enveloped the audience in the blue field and 12 golden stars of the European Union.

In a very decisive manner, the Barcelona organizers revised their history to show that Catalonia's past was in a separate creation story from the rest of the Iberian peninsula and that its present and future lay within the European Community. While Spain played a key role in the opening ceremonies, on the basis of compromise and protocol (See Hargreaves 2000; de Moragas Spà et. al., 1995; and Rivenburgh 1996), Catalonia took center stage and Europe was afforded a very clear and but supporting role. It should be noted that the European context of the opening ceremonies were, "arbitrary symbolic referent" (de Moragas Spà et. al., 1995: 27). Europe was hinted at through Catalan devises, like the twelve *castells* towers. However, its presence was undeniable and a clear indication of future tendencies within Catalan and European revisionist identity formation.

II. CREATIONISM: THE PATH TO A NEW BELIEF

In the Nagano, Barcelona, and Atlanta examples, historical revision was employed as a manner of altering the domestic and international impressions as a means of *touching up* one's past. In the case of Lillehammer, Norway we see a very different goal, but with very similar if not identical processes, to those found in Atlanta. The Lillehammer Olympics presented Norway with a golden opportunity to give this small country a world stage to convey Norway's uniqueness.

The opening ceremonies were, if nothing else, a concerted effort at selling the idea of Norway to the public. In much the same way that Hobsbawm and Ranger's *Invention of Tradition* dictates, Norwegian organizers and ceremonies designers worked diligently to create a uniquely Norwegian event. Almost all Norwegian cultural expressions at the Lillehammer Olympics were vested into either Norway's ancient or folkloric past. Therefore, Bentein Baardson's script for the Opening Ceremonies provides a beneficial case study for studies of nationalism.

First and foremost, the Lillehammer opening ceremonies employed what has to be one of the most classic examples of tradition invention by depicting the country's folklore as Norway's cultural traditions. Even the 15th century "authentic" cultural dress, as the broadcast makes the audience believe, was patterned off folklore (Klausen 1999: 106). The script suggests that what is termed "low-mythology" actually exists and forms the base of modern Norwegian folklore. In a very similar fashion to Trevor-Roper's (1983) identification of the formation of Scottish identity, the Norse Pantheon[7] was replaced by the Christian mythos and a previously non-existing term, *Vetter,* was introduced to refer to the creatures in a modern version of Norwegian folklore (Klausen 1999: 106).

It is interesting to note that the Lillehammer organizers and the Norwegian government were trying to weave together a new folk-history for their country while maintaining a clear depiction of the diverse make-up of Norway. A possible explanation for this obsession with a creation is likely vested in the youth of the Norwegian State, having gained independence only 101 years before the Lillehammer Olympics. The Parade of Nations was designed to have Norwegian couples serve as the placard bearers.[8] Each couple was dressed in appropriate traditional costumes representing each of the country's regions. While the organizers were creating a costume and folklore history for Norway, the government office responsible for approving all traditional costumes refused the costumes of the Sunnmøre region. These costumes were rejected on the grounds that they had been newly created and therefore were not authentic depictions of Norwegian identities (Klausen 1999: 113).

The organizers and the Norwegian government were willing to accept the creation of a homogenous Norwegian cultural and folklore history, while at the same time, a regional identity was denied expression in the Olympics because it lacked authenticity. Therefore, the Norwegian Opening Ceremonies offer an interesting opportunity to study competing levels of historical accuracy in the invention of tradition. While the Lillehammer ceremonies tried to portray a general concept of Norwegian culture, it was drawing on elements of both deep-rooted and recently contrived to do so.

This is not to say that those elements of the culture that were presented, particularly those of the traditions of the Sami (Lapps) people, were not authentic or were not displayed as an historical icon of Norwegian society. This is meant to indicate the absence of overt and numerous Viking elements, which the Norwegian people claim as their forbearers. In fact, the Norwegians placed a very strong emphasis on their Viking heritage, not in the opening ceremonies, but in their architecture. The speed skating arena, which was called the *Viking Ship*, is an architectural visualization meant to conjure the image of the inverted hull of a Viking vessel.

While not a part of the opening ceremonies, this less-than subtle incorporation of Viking culture into Norwegian heritage is not surprising. Roel Puijk (1999) offers the best explanation for this when he explains that the "opening ceremonies may be viewed as a selection process by which certain elements from the national culture are chosen" (*Ibid.*, 128). He continues by explaining that choices on what to include in the ceremonies draws on "readily noticeable elements—material culture (costumes, musical instruments, artefacts [sic]) music, historical events, famous persons, etc." (*Ibid.*). Another possible explanation is that a Norse or Viking definition of Norwegian identity would not have effectively separated itself from other Scandinavian identities, particularly that of the Swedes.

Therefore, by considering Puijk's insight and the lack of Norse, Viking, or other heritages that could have been claimed as Norwegian, we can conclude that the organizers had a different goal in mind for Norway's nationalistic demonstration. Instead of a cultural demonstration as the main thrust of the presentation, Norway was seeking instead to trumpet itself as the custodian of winter sport elements and thus indoctrinate an ideology of it is the source of the Winter Olympics.

Norwegian Olympic organizers and the Norwegian Olympic Committee have long held claims of historical importance upon the heritage of Winter Olympism. Greece maintains a near monopoly on Ancient Olympism and its traditions. That Olympic symbolism and heritage is linked intimately to Ancient—and, as the Greek government claims, modern—Greek heritage has been a rarely questioned concept within the modern Olympics since the inception of the modern games in the years prior to the 1896 Athens summer games. Norway has repeatedly attempted to defeat this hegemonic concept in reference to the Winter Olympics both times they have hosted the Winter Olympics.

Starting with the 1952 Oslo Winter Games, the Norwegians began attempting to replace Greece's exclusive role. In 1920, Baron Pierre de Coubertin introduced a series of new symbols for the Olympic Movement. This effort was simultaneously an attempt to give the Olympics a stronger status by having symbols for people to demonstrate their pride as well as an attempt to reassert Olympic ideals in the wake of World War I. One of these symbols is of great importance here.

At the Antwerp Olympics, a white flag with five interlocking Rings, representing the five continents, was introduced. This flag, now referred to as the Antwerp Flag, has become a part of official ceremony. It is symbolically handed from the mayor of the previous host city to the successor mayor either during the opening ceremonies, the closing ceremonies, or both. This occurred during almost all winter and summer Olympics. At the 1952 Oslo Winter Olympics, the Norwegians replaced the Antwerp Flag with an Oslo Flag, claiming that the heritage of the Winter Olympics is vested in Norway. This Oslo Flag—the official banner of the Winter Olympic used for the first time in Oslo, Norway—has been used during several Winter Olympics for the traditional hand-over of Olympic colors between the mayors of the current and succeeding games.

Co-opting the Antwerp flag was a clear step towards Norway's ascent as a country whose Olympic heritage is as symbolically important as that of Greece. This challenge to Greece's hegemonic status as the sole epicenter of the Olympics saw its most obvious and clearly most vehemently rebuked moment at the Lillehammer Winter Olympics. The situation evolved from Norway's attempt to honor its heritage as the birthplace of skiing, an overarching element of the Winter Olympics.[9] The city of Mørgedal, Norway is considered by many to be the origination of skiing. In 1952, the Oslo organizers wanted to run the torch from Mørgedal to the stadium. This plan was denied the status an official torch. The IOC, in its official report on the Oslo Games "specifically stressed that this was no Olympic flame being carried from Mørgedal to Oslo, but a torch greeting... a natural form of greeting... as torches have been used for centuries in Norway for skiing in the dark" (in Klausen 1999b: 76).

Again, in Lillehammer, an attempt was made to run a torch from Mørgedal to the Opening Ceremonies. The multiple attempts to do so, as well as an attempt to unite the Greek and Mørgedal flames into one flame, were both met with caustic disapproval from the Greeks and the IOC. Eventually, the Mørgedal flame was recognized as a lost cause and it was only the flame lit in Greece that would burn in the cauldron over Lillehammer, Norway. The Norwegians failed in their attempt to co-opt Greece's exclusive status in the firmament of Olympic ideology.

While the Mørgedal flame failed, the Norwegians were not without their successes in challenging a Greek monopoly over Olympic symbol and tradition. The opening ceremonies, which were held in the ski jumping arena, were deeply laden with the symbols and suggestions of a complete marriage between Norway and skiing. The opening sequence, the introduction of many *vetter*, and several other aspects of the cultural displays of the opening ceremonies involved performers on skis. Several performers entered from the hill beneath the ski jump. The most stunning element of this display was the arrival of the Olympic torch. It may not have been run from Mørgedal, but it flew into the stadium in the hands of an Olympic ski jumper who carried the Torch into the stadium by taking the large ski jump. It was an awe-inspiring moment designed to insert a staunchly Norwegian feeling into the cauldron lighting ceremony.

Finally, the Nagano Winter Olympics are useful to highlight what is perhaps one of the most revealing examples Norway's primacy, second only to Greece, in Winter Olympic traditions. The Greek team has always led every Parade of Nations with the exception of the 2004 games.[10] During the Nagano Opening Ceremonies, the Parade of Nations was split into two segments. The first half of the parade was led by Greece. The second half was led by Norway. Norway, as leader of the second Parade of Nations, was not entering alphabetically; hence its placement was intentional on the part of the Nagano organizers. While Greece holds the heritage and birthplace of all the Olympics, the Japanese have accepted that Norway comes in second place as the custodian of the heritage of winter sports, and therefore the Winter Olympics.

In the Atlanta and Nagano examples, game organizers sought to rewrite darker passages of American Southern and Japanese history, respectively. In the Lillehammer example, the opposite form of revision took place. Norway tried embellishing its identity with a richer and more symbolic role in the realm of international sports. In both the American Southern and Norwegian examples, there are clear signs of creationism. Insightful examples of creationism also exist in the ceremonies for Seoul and Sydney. Seoul's place in this analysis is partly connected to the interesting conundrum that South Korea posed for the International Olympic Committee. First, this country was officially at war, although without actual combat, when it bid and hosted the 1988 Summer Olympics. Second, it was an industrializing country with an emerging global economy. The IOC awarded the games to a then-termed "third-world country" on only one previous occasion, the 1968 Mexico City games. The games were held a critical moment in the history of South Korea.

During the 1980s, most countries supported and recognized either Korean state; few interacted with the two states. Before the 1988 Olympics, South Korea had no formal relations with the Soviet Union and most its allies. Hosting the Olympics provided an opportunity to establish relations for the first time with these and other countries. These games gave South Korea a new avenue for political, economic, and trade opportunities with the Eastern Bloc and strengthened its ties to other countries around the world. Richard Pound (1994: 4) noted this turn of events and compared this Olympic opportunity to the 1964 Tokyo Summer Olympics, which marked Japan's "reentry into the world as a full participant in the international community."

Pound's study noted many economic and political benefits of the games, but neglected a very interesting and important metamorphosis within Korea at the time of the Olympics. South Korea was in the process of its global emergence. While this was predominantly an issue of money and politics, it obliged Korea to present a new facade. The opening ceremonies of the summer Olympics provided just such a moment in which Korea recreated itself on a global stage. The opening ceremonies were full of highly symbolic elements, emphasizing the "newness" of a modern South Korea. The theme of the Seoul Olympics was "Harmony and Progress." This theme was meant to encompass two important facts: peace is a state South Korean seeks and that all of Korea is moving towards its destiny as a fully integrated and productive member of the international community. The Korean Olympics were simultaneously a visual depiction of how Korea has helped bring together the East and the West.

The Seoul ceremonies started with the arrival of the Dragon Drum, symbolizing the convergence of ancient and modern Korea. The drum arrived at the Olympic Stadium via the Han River. The dragon drum was a "summoning of the world" to the games. After a third symbolic striking of the drum, the world tree floated into the sky, revealing the Olympic Cauldron. The drum, and its three strikes, is a poignant merging of ancient Korean, the City of Seoul, symbolized by the Drum's journey down the Han River, and the modern Korea as part of the global community.

Another interesting element in the early part of these ceremonies was what was termed the World Tree. This twenty-nine meter high pedestal, which would soon be revealed as the Cauldron, symbolized the universe. The large red sphere atop the world tree, as well as the formations of the drummers and dancers into discs, were all meant to signify the Sun. These solar demonstrations depicted Korea's new dawn. The spirit and symbolism of these ceremonies are best demonstrated by the words of Park Sei-jik, the President of the Seoul Olympic Organizing Committee. Early in his speech, he stated that his country "leapt over ideological and political barriers to share in a celebration of harmony and progress, which we earnestly hope will endure long after these games" (Seoul Final Report 1988: 388). In a more poignant moment in his speech, Mr. Park stated: "...these Olympics are a milestone for Koreans who have accomplished great things... these games will serve as a sign of the wonders we can accomplish together as we build a better future for all nations" (SOOC 1988: 390).

In addition to these examples, several other performance segments stressed symbols and youth in a continuing effort to promote harmony and progress. For example, the cauldron was lit by three Koreans: a school teacher, a high school student, and a grad student. They denoted the importance of education in progress. Other segments of the performance, including the Taekwondoists breaking boards, "demonstrated power and techniques through competitions and dismantling of the barriers" (SOOC 1988: 394).

Throughout many portions of the Seoul Opening Ceremonies, the use of symbols of peace, growth, and renewal were omnipresent. This was coupled with the involvement of many children in the opening ceremonies, which typically represents the future of a society. One highly relevant moment was a short segment of children happily playing as if on a schoolyard. The segment began with a seven-year-old boy at play. He was chosen because he was born on September 30, 1981—the date on which the IOC voted to give the 1988 Olympics to Seoul (SOOC 1988b). The Korean organizers chose to name the final segment of the Opening program the "Light of Genesis," which for the western and neareast world, is a callback to the first chapter of the Jewish and Christian Bibles, where God begins creation, on the first day, with light.

Next, we find similar processes in the Sydney Opening Ceremonies—specifically how the Sydney organizers attempted to depict a new form of

Aussie identity. The Sydney Olympics came at a very opportune time in the cultural, ethnic, and nationalistic history of Australia. The Australian government was in a process of deconstructing what had been a racist past that separated Australian society into a core western society and a peripheral aboriginal counterpart. A telling sign of how deeply this change was embedding into Australian society appeared in 2002, when the film *Rabbit Proof Fence* was named Best Picture by the Australian Film Institute. The is a dramatized narration of what aboriginal children were forced to endure during the period of recent Australian history. These children were forced into "schools" designed to dissolve their customary aboriginal practices and replace them with western traits

The Sydney Opening Ceremonies present two separate cultures: White/Western Aussie and Aboriginal. These two elements were exhibited separately as a prequel to their consequent merger. The ceremonies center on two individuals. A little girl named Nikki represented modern and white Australian society; meanwhile, an Aboriginal dancer represented ancient Australia. Each one is given the opportunity to command the stadium floor, but the most interesting moment comes during their convergence.

In the segment titled "Eternity" both Nikki and the Aboriginal dancer stand atop the center of a stage, which slowly rises above the performers on the floor. The two stand together, hand in hand, witnessing the creation of an eternal Australian Spirit that coalesces their two distinct societies. This symbolism is paralleled by the Arrival Sequence. In this sequence, the colorful tapestry of Australian identity—including Aboriginal elements, traditional British Aussie elements, and immigrants to Australia wearing their national dress, is presented. The sequence ends with all of them standing together in the shape of the continent of Australia, signifying that all peoples on the stage are the embodiment of Aussie.

Regardless of the clear distinction being made between core and peripheral elements of Aussie nationalism, the opening ceremonies represented a concerted effort at tying them together into a unified depiction of national identity. The unified demonstration represents a creationist moment as Aussie identity was redefined into a culture of inclusion and multiculturalism instead of its more restricted and racist past. This creationist moment, to continue the analogy from the beginning of this chapter, deconstructed two foundations, and took the stones from both to create a new base for a modern Australia. According to the Final Report of the Sydney Olympics, the Awakening Segment was "symbolizing the diversity yet unity of aboriginal peoples, was intended to project the confronting issue of Reconciliation between those who represent Australia's past, and its present" (SOCOG 2001c: 55).

Reconciliation was the overtone of several parts of the opening ceremonies. Another key moment for this occurred in the opening ceremonies during the Eternity Segment. As part of this segment, a crew of workers constructed a thirty-meter-high bridge entitled the Bridge of Life—a symbolic walkway towards connection and reconciliation (SOCOG 2001c: 57). Another key symbol was fire. Aborigines burned small areas of land in a process that encouraged new plants to take root and grow. "Fire purified the bush, began a new life cycle" (SOCOG 2001c: 55). From this, the pageant transitioned into the "Nature" segment that depicted the growth and beauty of Australia. A process of constant rebirth and growth took place on the stadium signifying renewal as with other elements of the Sydney Opening Ceremonies.

Finally, there are elements of historical revision that are a part of the opening ceremonies but are not a part of the pageantry of the ceremonies. These moments fall within the segments of the ceremonies that are outside the host-controlled elements but are not outright controlled by Olympic protocol. Earlier, Llinés (1996) was cited for her discussion of the nationalistic display during the torch lighting ceremony at the 1976 Montreal Games. The torch relay and cauldron lighting ceremonies are governed by Olympic protocols, which leaves only limited opportunity for nationalistic demonstration. The aforementioned role of Chris Moon in the Nagano cauldron lighting ceremony is further evidence of this kind of manifestation.

Two additional examples are worth note. One occurred during the 1984 Sarajevo Winter Olympics. It is necessary to make a few comments about Yugoslavia's history. Yugoslavia was a country formed in the wake of the two world wars. Several ethnic groups were tied into a single state. Although adhering to different faiths, an overwhelming majority of the new state's population spoke the same language—Serbo-Croatian. Yugoslavia, which translates as "Land of the South Slavs" combined several ethnic groups. The internalization of a pan-Yugoslav identity was largely limited to urbanites and intellectuals. The myth of a cohesive Yugoslavia was so weak, that shortly after the fall of the Soviet Union, the country went through several years of violent break-ups culminating in six internationally recognized independent states and one partially recognized state.

The torch relay during the Sarajevo games was a calculated effort to present a unified Yugoslavia. The flame started in the city of Dubrovnik, where it was split into two separate relays across the country. The western run traveled through the major cities and capitals of Croatia, Slovenia, Vojvodina, and portions of the ethnic communities of Bosnia and Herzegovina. The eastern run traversed the major cities and capitals of Macedonia, Serbia, Montenegro, Kosovo, and Serb portions of Bosnia and Herzegovina. The relay represented a carefully planned attempt to touch upon every republic, autonomous region, and ethnic group in this moment of "displayed unity." Both torches were carried to Sarajevo, where they were united and then brought into the Kosovo Stadium to light the cauldron.

The second example occurred during the Sydney Summer Olympics in 2000. At these games, a moment of transformation occurred for both North and South Korea. Australia, which had been instrumental in working towards peaceful relations between the two states, worked with the IOC and orchestrated a unified Korean team. During the Parade of Nations, North and South Korea entered the Olympic stadium as one nation. Two Koreans, one from the north and another from the south, co-carried a new Korean flag: a white field with a light blue silhouette of the Korean Peninsula. This was a great creation moment as both North and South Korea shed the icons and colors of their own states and adopted a new one for the Olympics. In addition to the new unified flag, all Korean athletes wore the same costumes, which used only the blue and white colors on the flag; they arrived in the stadium walking hand-in-hand.

At this point, two observations should be apparent. First, the use of the Olympics to revise a national identity is an effective means of deploying an invented tradition. Second, as is apparent in numerous examples including attempts at both regional and national identities, the processes of historical revision in the Olympics is not constrained to a specific identity, ideology, or ceremony. This study has not as of yet questioned whether any of these attempts, regardless of method or goal, have been successful. With the Lillehammer/Mørgedal example, there was indication of a degree of success evident in the Nagano games due to the placement of Norway as lead delegation for the second half of the parade.[11] In looking at Atlanta, accusations of foul play and over-doing 'southern equals spectacle' indicates that, while many people were upset about it, the organizers did convey their message of Southernness and elicit responses. In short, there is suitable evidence to claim a degree of success in historical revision as a strategy of nationalism in these international Olympic festivals.

NOTES

1. Rosenstone uses the term dramatic films in his analysis, but for our discussion, it is best to use "presentation," as it is not necessarily conducted exclusively through film. Film constitutes only one of many forms that history is presented through the Olympics.

2. Auteur is a term used in several art disciplines, including cinema, which describes an artist (in this case director) whose filmmaking is stylistically consistent and recognizable in most or all films they make. These individuals create for themselves their own sense of artistry that becomes synonymous with their work.

3. White, in the eastern tradition, is a symbol of spirituality and death; therefore, the significance of this color in the life-death cycle of creation speaks to eastern cultures as well as western.

4. Note that this is a revisionist demonstration and not a creationist one. While it is a depiction of a creation story, it is building off of pre-existing cultural artifacts and traits that had been accepted as Southern well before the performance.

5. During the bidding process, Billy Payne, the head of Atlanta's bid team, regularly said that Atlanta was the only city in the U.S. to have been burned to the ground and then re-built itself. He stopped telling the story when he told the story in the presence of the Mayor of Belgrade (another candidate city). The Belgrade mayor's response was that he could sympathize, since it had happened to his city seventy times. (Pound 2005)

6. Due to the possibility of Madrid's role in garnering the EC presentation, it is possible that the goal was instead to present a European identity in lieu of something Catalan. Or, even more likely, to present a common theme that unites both Catalonia and the rest of Spain.

7. The Norse Pantheon was the basis for Viking religious belief; the Vikings were the traditional founders of Norway.

8. The placard bearer was the individual that accompanied each flag bearer into the stadium in the Parade of Nations. They carried a sign inscribed with the name of the country in the official languages of the games. Their involvement in the Parade of Nations is the only part of this element of Olympic protocol the organizers can manipulate.

9. At the Lillehammer games, there were twelve separate categories of sporting competitions. Of those categories, six were forms of competitive skiing. Out of the sixty-three events in these sports, thirty-seven (in other words 58.7%) were skiing events (LOOC 1994c: 62).

10. In 2004, Athens hosted the Olympics. By tradition, Greece leads the Parade of Nations and the host country is the last team to enter. For the Athens games, Greece opted to be the final state into the stadium and asked France, with the permission of the IOC, to lead the Parade of Nations. France was chosen because it was the birthplace of the founder of the Modern Olympics, Baron Pierre de Coubertin, and the 2nd host country of the modern era.

11. It is arguable that the only reason Norway lead the second part of the parade was because they hosted four years earlier. There is no mention of either possible

justification in the final report. However, considering the symbolic importance of the placement of the Norwegian team, especially after the observations on the Lille-hammer Games, it seems to be more likely that the interpretation here is the correct one.

CHAPTER 5
INDOCTRINATION OF IDEOLOGY

Whereas the previous chapter dealt with the process of changing an identity, whether by revision or creation, this chapter is centered on presenting and reinforcing preexisting concepts. The organizers seek to indoctrinate the audience into the accepted national myth through the demonstration of that belief in multiple ways. While this can imply repetition, as both Hobsbawm (1983) and Handler (1984) discussed, it does not necessarily mean that the opening ceremonies will display the same types of imagery over and over again. Indoctrinate, according to the *Imperial Dictionary*, literally means "to instruct in any doctrine or science; to imbue with learning; to teach; to instruct" (Ogilvie 1884: 597). Noah Webster's (1869: 684) definition is slightly more in-depth, by adding that *indoctrination* is meant "to instruct in the rudiments or principles of learning," and "to furnish with the principles of doctrines." Both definitions are necessary for a complete understanding of the scope of this ideological goal.

Actors intentionally use of the opening or closing ceremonies in order to: 1) teach, instruct, or otherwise imbue the audience with the necessary knowledge, understanding, and beliefs to tangibly experience the national identity on display; 2) supply the audience, both domestic and international, with the necessary information to understand the elements of an ideology as well as the entire ideology; and 3) impart on the audience the guiding principles of the ideology. Recognizing that each definition of a national identity, as well as its individual parts, has an internal and external meaning, the purpose here is to instill in the audience a particular subjective understanding of the ideology in question.

The installation of these concepts goes beyond what was accomplished by the previous strategy. Historical revision and creation adds entirely new facets to an identity, often replacing older aspects in totality. The strategy of indoctrinating an ideology attempts to solidify an established national identity. Elements that had tacitly become a part of an identity are now being reinforced. This is clearly different than revision and creation because this nationalist manifestation does not need to convince an audience of the authenticity of new traits.

This is the purest example of Handelman's (1990) performance mirror. Under this definition, the currently accepted statement of a society's identity is simply reflected back to that society and all others watching, without alteration, interpretation, or qualification. Therefore, since the majority of the members of the community already accept the elements of the national identity, the majority should accept the display without doubt. It only needs to be confirmed, and in so doing, defined in a more specific manner.

We must return to Benedict Anderson's (1983) concept of *imagined community*. Anderson's main point was that all identities are imagined because they are based on assumptions of shared ancestry. Anderson asserts that no one can know every member of a community. Community members are bound by the assumption that the community actually exists on the basis of characteristics that supposedly unite it. The indoctrination of ideology is a process that would call for a reinterpretation of Anderson's statement that all communities are imagined. Obviously, it is unlikely that every member of a community is watching the Olympics, but a large enough number of them are to make this an effective enterprise. Therefore, this strategy allows the organizers to demonstrate, for one of the largest gatherings feasible,[1] the currently accepted statement of the identity of their community. In other words, they are attempting to confirm the imagined identity is real.

This is also compatible with Barreto's (2001a) concept of elite-driven identity construction. Once the identity has been constructed, meaning the specific elements that will make it up are agreed upon by an elite, the new identity must be "sold." Elite choice, as Barreto (2001b) demonstrates in the case of Puerto Rican ethnogenesis in the early 20th century, does not mean creating a complete myth out of thin air. In Puerto Rico, the main question was whether to use language (Spanish vs. English) or religion (Roman Catholicism vs. Protestantism) as the core facet of Puerto Rican identity. Both traits already existed among the vast majority of Puerto Ricans and did, to varying degrees, differentiate islanders (*us*) from Americans (*them*). The local intelligentsia's decision to promote language as identity rather than religion was strategically advantageous safeguarding the role of secular intellectuals as culture's guardians rather than clerics—themselves members of a rival elite. The power of ideological indoctrination is very much derived from Barreto's (2001b) language vs. religion study of Puerto Rico. With two already understood competing possibilities for dominance in the new Puerto Rican identity, this elite had to indoctrinate their preference as the bulwark of *Puerto Ricanness*.

The strength of this strategy can be illustrated by taking a lesson from the French Revolution—specifically, by looking at revolutionary news, as described by Jeremy Popkin (1990). During the French Revolution, there were competing presses—each with their own goals for describing the political, social, and nationalistic directions of the revolutionary movement. The lack of a unified attempt at depicting French nationalism, through journalism, led away from consolidation. Popkin (1990: 181) explained that ". . . the press sabotaged the revolutionary dream of national unity." Rather than mutually indoctrinating the new French ideology by both agreement and repetition, they were fermenting disunity within French society. Had the opposite been true, the revolutionary press, as a whole, would have been effectively unifying France through the calculated indoctrination of ideology into one French people.

In addition to the aforementioned scholars, we must revisit Mallon. Her explanation on hegemonic symbols was already stated as having pertinence, but it requires special attention. Indoctrination is especially compatible to the processes of objectification that result in the raising of an icon to the status of hegemonic symbol. The elevation of an item to *de facto* representation of the identity is a dangerous game. Once the item has taken on hegemonic status, even the actors that created it cannot question its status. The concept requires special attention here because the Olympics offer interesting options for dealing with potentially hegemonic symbols.

First, it is common for elites to take their ideas and attempt to institutionalize them. Once they attain such a status, the symbols become longstanding presentations of their concepts. Elites aspire to establish their identity in hegemonic terms. The risk, however, is that hegemonic symbols, if too powerful, take on a life of their own and can be turned against the elites that created them if cognitive linkages between the symbol and the elite fractures.

The indoctrination process does not have to result in the creation of an uncontestable hegemonic symbol. It can be avoided with careful planning on the part of the actors. Most demonstrations of nationalism through the Olympics are done in the form of cultural displays that are necessarily complex. They involve multiple traditions and cultural traits that are all concurrently or consecutively displayed. By doing this, the would-be symbol can be completely buried among other icons diminishing its long-term impact.

Regardless of the process within indoctrination or the identity under scrutiny, the utmost goal of the project remains constant. The objective of indoctrination is not just to establish the traits of an identity, but rather to define that identity in broad terms as well as to impart to the audience the opportunity to experience what it means to be a part of that ideology. These three "elements" should be analyzed as phases of one coherent goal, and not as individual goals. Therefore, unlike other manifestations where multiple goals can be handled individually, simultaneously, or consecutively, these phases require separate consideration.

The three phases of indoctrination all have to do with degrees of understanding and the imparting of knowledge. The first phase involves establishing the specific meaning of an identity, symbol, or characteristic. The second phase emphasizes the individual components of identity and explores the construction of the overall identity. Lastly, the third phase is the reincorporation of each constituent part of identity into its total meaning and then institutionalizes it as the official definition of a national identity. In total, the process is a clear facet of identity construction and as such its individual phases fit comfortably into established understandings of identity, especially those of Anderson and Barreto.

Anderson (1983) explained that identity is based on the assumptions of shared characteristics. These assumptions extend not just to the characteristic, but to a shared understanding of that characteristic's meaning. If the meaning is self-evident, or universally known to both local and international audiences, the establishment of the meaning (phase one) is unnecessary. Otherwise, phase one must establish the breadth of identity by presenting its context and characteristics to individuals within and outside the community.

The second indoctrination phase harkens back to Barreto's (2001a) concept of constructed identities. The indoctrination of ideology deals with the post-construction period of identity formation, but it must still recognize the constructivist element of nationalism, especially as this manifestation is only effective if it establishes the constructed elements with their own meaning. This is different from the first phase. Phase one lays the groundwork to allow the audience to receive the elements being indoctrinated within the necessary context to gain a full understanding of their meaning. Phase two begins with the identity, in its deconstructed form, and supply both the individual meaning(s) and the meaning of the sum of its parts.

This latter part, demonstrating identity as a whole, leads directly into the third phase, which establishes the governing ideology(s) of a national identity. Ideological institutionalization is the culmination of this process; it implies that the audience has fully experienced a national identity and can now comprehend its existence, contents, and meaning. In this latter sense, we revisit Mallon (1995). An icon only attains hegemonic status when the object, as an embodiment of some idea, is no longer questioned as embodying that specific meaning.

The indoctrination of ideology can aim to accomplish one of two tasks. First, it can attempt to demonstrate a unitary and complete identity, meaning that the full understanding of what it means to be ascribed to a specific concept of "us" can be established on stage. Second, a concept of "us" can be broken into more manageable units and these units could be established on stage. In this latter task, there is reasonable question as to how much of an identity must be displayed for the manifestation to have value.

In general, the case with this form of identity formation and demonstration is that there are elements, which are central to a national identity and elements that are peripheral. According to Barth (1969) and Eriksen (1993) briefly, there are limits to how far away from "us" one can get before one becomes part of "them." The degree of effectiveness of indoctrination of ideology is directly related to the degree of importance of the element of the identity being indoctrinated. This is necessarily due to two important structural elements of the phases of this manifestation. First, the establishment of both the ideology of symbolic meaning, in the third phase, as well as their specific understanding of the traits, allows the audience to tangibly experience them are effective only if the audience does not have incompatible preconceived notions of their meaning. Should the facets of the identity on display be more peripheral, possibly a part of more than one identity, then the performance becomes less effective.

As much as the degree of consolidation of the presented identity affects the effectiveness of this manifestation, the degree of cartelization of a society likewise weakens this manifestation. Furthermore, regardless of the degree of consolidation or cartelization of formal identity, success or failure of this manifestation is dependent upon the decisions of the actor and how they implement those objectives. The more convoluted a demonstration becomes, the less likely the audience will get the point. Even if an identity is both unified and hegemonic, if too many elements are displayed at once then the audience may become confused and therefore the demonstration will fail.

Taken together, ideological indoctrination is not concerned with any single trait or any collection of traits. This manifestation focuses on a preexisting idea or concept. As King (1997a) suggested, these are the attributes possessed by people who ascribe to a specific ethnic or cultural identity. Furthermore, there is a direct correlation between the degree of repetition of the same concept through different symbols or presentations and the higher likelihood that the indoctrination will be successful.

I. LOS ANGELES: THE MUSIC OF AMERICA

An excellent example of indoctrinating a specific ideology, specifically through the presentation and then reinforcement thereof, is found in the 1984

Los Angeles summer Olympics. The Los Angeles opening and closing ceremonies indoctrinated two concepts. First was the spectacle and bombast of Los Angeles as an entertainment city. Second was to show the spirit of America, predominantly through its unique and vibrant musical heritage. In several sections of the opening ceremonies, both are demonstrated simultaneously. For ease of analysis, they will be discussed separately.

At this point, it is necessary to recall that there was a subtle but well-known competition between Los Angeles and Moscow over who had the best Olympics, including the best opening and closing ceremonies. Moscow, whose games will later be described for their attention to precision and formality, were lauded by the Los Angeles organizers as being impossible to improve upon (Perelman 1985a: 202). Even during the actual ceremonies, American broadcasters commented, with a certain degree of pride, about the precision of the Moscow ceremonies and how the American dance sequences were similarly precise in movement (LAOOC 1985a). Several key attributes of the Los Angeles plan for the opening ceremonies were based on the need to offer distinction between the Moscow and Los Angeles ceremonies, while still paying appropriate respect to Los Angeles and the United States as hosts of the games.

Part of the goal of the Los Angeles ceremonies organizers was to add an element of vibrancy, enthusiasm, and spectacle to the opening ceremonies, a trait that seemed somewhat lacking from the austere and dignified Moscow opening ceremonies. David Wolper was chosen to lead the efforts of these games because he was keenly aware of the need for spectacle (Perelman 1985a: 200). Furthermore, the Los Angeles Olympic Organizing Committee LAOOC staff members were particularly interested in having the ceremonies present an "emotional, majestic, and inspirational" tenor (*Ibid.*).

The planning stages of the opening ceremonies, as discussed in the *Official Report of the Games of the XXIIIrd Olympiad Los Angeles* (Perelman 1985a: Ch. 8), emphasized that the organizers were consumed with paying homage to Hollywood. The official report noted that David Wolper, an internationally renowned filmmaker himself, was aware that the reputation of Hollywood and the United States was at risk if the ceremonies were not an appropriate depiction of Hollywood's spectacle of entertainment (Perelman 1985a: 200). As a result, the ceremonies paid special attention to successfully lauding Los Angeles as the entertainment capital of the world and commending the host country for its spirit of creativity and art.

Musically, song and dance numbers were either taken directly out of American musical heritage and Hollywood productions or were new pieces written specifically for the games, by Hollywood's acclaimed composers. For example, the opening song of "Welcome," Los Angeles's formal greeting to the world, was written by Oscar and Golden Globe winning composer Marvin Hamlisch.[2] John Williams,[3] another Oscar and Golden Globe winning composer, wrote the "Olympic Fanfare and Theme," the official theme of the Los Angeles Olympics. Walt Disney Productions, the original company hired to organize the games and thus bequeath them with a Hollywood "feel," originally hired Williams for the job (Perelman 1985a: 200). The only non-Hollywood luminary, at least prior to the 1984 games, was Philip Glass. He was previously known mainly for his operatic and theatrical scores. Glass was selected to write music for the opening ceremonies, specifically the theme song for the torch lighting.

The process of sustained deference to Hollywood's entertainment history is apparent within each segment of the opening ceremonies' pageantry. The Los Angeles games, for the purposes of this study, can be broken into four segments: Welcome, Music of America, Olympic Protocol, and Reach Out and Touch. The Music of America segment can be further broken down into five component parts: Americana Suite, The Pioneer Spirit, Dixieland Jamboree, Urban Rhapsody, and The World is a Stage. This analysis will focus predominantly on the Music of America segment and the Reach Out and Touch segment. The Welcome segment was nothing more than a formal greeting to the Olympic audience and competitors. The Olympic Protocol segment involved the standard IOC-mandated elements, which were not laced with elements of the target ideology.

The Music of America segment will be the main source of material for a discussion of the Los Angeles ideology indoctrination process mainly, because its emphasis is clearly Hollywood, entertainment and America's musicology. The sequence started with an 800-member Olympic marching band. The audience is informed this is a vestige of Revolutionary war drum and fife corps (LAOOC 1984b; Perelman 1985a: 208). The marching band segment emphasized Americana by first performing pieces by noted American composers, for example Aaron Copeland's *Fanfare for a Common Man*, and a medley of Union and Confederate civil war songs. Second, the marching band's performances ended with the players standing in a large outline of the continental United States and performing Jacob and Raye's "This Is My Country" (LAOOC 1984b).

The map of the continental United States formed the basis for section two: the Pioneer Spirit. With the map in place, the public announcer heralded the music of the pioneer era. Featuring Aaron Copeland's *Rodeo* as the backdrop for the race across the United States to tame the west, the pioneer segment offered a brief history of Los Angeles and the American West as covered wagons with horses and pioneers arrived and then built a mock-up of a frontier town out of Hollywood sets (LAOOC 1984b : 200). At the start of the segment, the announcer explained the pioneer spirit of America and paid tribute to the music inspired by the new world (*Ibid.*). The segment ended with an old-fashioned western hoedown.

From a depiction of the celebratory western expansion, the Music of America Segment modulates into its tribute to Dixieland and Jazz. The marching band reforms itself into a steamship, to emphasize southern rivers and bayous and allows the band to reposition itself for the process of building a New Orleans congregational church (*Ibid.*). Using colored tapestries for stained glass windows, performers in white to shape the walls of the church, and pews to represent a congregation to form the community of the church, a southern revival took shape to laud gospel traditions and African American spiritual music. This segment departs from the Hollywood spectacle and instead replaces it with a more refrained yet vibrant tribute to America's sacred music literature.

Thus far, the audience has been introduced to the history of American music. Although not specifically in the historical occurrences that led to the formation of pioneer and Southern Spiritual and Jazz music, the ceremony does establish the importance of each historically bounded period of musical history and then gives the audience a well-known, if not universally known, set of examples. So far we have seen both phases one and two of indoctrination at work within the ceremonies. By establishing the musical segments with announcements and dramatized historicity, the organizers have supplied the audience with an understanding of both the importance of and the pertinence of these three musical forms. Tying to each of these elements a clearly Hollywood-entertainment feel to each segment, especially through the use of Hollywood film composers and sets, the audience is also reminded of the performance history of Los Angeles in addition to that of the United States.

Returning to analysis of the ceremonies, the Southern sequence next moved into what was titled the "Urban Rhapsody." This segment followed Jazz's incorporation into classical styles of American Music, which included the music of American legends such as George Gershwin. The Urban Rhapsody segment offers one of the best examples of indoctrination through repetition that has occurred at recent Olympic ceremonies. In this segment, two important depictions occur. First, Gershwin, as representative of classical jazz, is performed with the use of eight-four grand pianos. Commentators explain that each performer represents composer George Gershwin and the dancers depict the elegance of this American musical form (LAOOC 1984b).

As the Gershwin performance unfolds, grand pianos are pushed forward from the main performance end of the stadium to reinforce the entire depiction of the grandeur of the American Music Tradition. This sentiment introduced echoes the performance within the Urban Rhapsody and introduces the next segment, "The World is a Stage." These two segments together signify the return of the process of indoctrination (phases one and two) of both Americana and Hollywood. One of the quintessential moments is the performance of "Stepping Out With My Baby" and "Dancing Cheek to Cheek."

While being played, two dancers, representing Ginger Rogers and Fred Astaire, pay tribute to two legendary Hollywood Musical performers.

The performance first establishes the sense of the American Hollywood Musical, emphasizing its music and dance numbers. The concept is then reinforced by having more dancers take the stage, each of which represent the same Hollywood couple, and having them dance to more than just the initial song that started the sequence. The World as a Stage segment continues forward, beginning with the music of the Big Band era and continuing chronologically through the various musical traditions from the 1940s to 1984 (Perelman 1985a: 208; LAOOC 1984b). During this final segment, the demonstration switched from phases one and two of indoctrination to phase three and the main premise of the entire demonstration took shape.

A few comments should be made about the entire segment, the Music of America. From beginning to end, musical selections included only well-known and classic examples of each genre. Each piece of music, while possibly unknown for its historical and genre roots, was most likely recognizable to the average audience member. Second, the concept of each musical performance as uniquely American was further established through announcements and reinforcement of American symbols (including the outline of the continental United States). As the audience became more accustomed to the presentation, as it was intended to understand, the pace of presentation increased. No longer needing to worry about phase one and two of indoctrination, the musical form and selection of composer flowed almost effortlessly from one performance to another. This included music by Duke Ellington, Glenn Miller, and Lenny Goodman, as well as pieces from American musicals, such as *Chorus Line* and *Fame*.

The whole process ended with a quintessential example of phase three of indoctrination. With the history of American Music defined and demonstrated, the audience was given the necessary tools to understand the concept of American music. The concept was then formally placed within American identity once the audience had experienced the uniqueness and vibrancy of America's musical heritage. The final segment of the Music of America, entitled "Finale," featured one simple and direct demonstration of everything that came prior in the "Music of America" sequence. All singers, dancers, and other performers of the different music segments came together onto the field. The marching band reformed the country's cartographical outline, which was first established as representative of the United States through the song "This is Our Country," while all other performers stood inside the outline and sang "America, the Beautiful" (LAOOC 1984b).

It is important to note what elements or factors of American identity were established for the audience. It was not defined in terms of ethnicity, race, or a political or social history. By focusing on the cultural elements, namely music and dance, the opening ceremonies avoided defining American national identity in terms of a multi-cultural legacy of immigration. This was emphasized in every segment of the "Music of America" sequence by not illustrating ethnic or culturally historical costumes. The main dance sequence of "welcome" had all performers dressed in white with Olympic or LAOOC logos. The Dixieland Jamboree sequence featured performance-appropriate choir robes, and the Urban Rhapsody sequence featured tuxedoes, evening gowns, and the return of the dressed-in-white performers from the opening "Welcome" number. The only exception to this was the mid 18th century style "western" work attire that adorned the dancers of the "Pioneer Spirit" segment. There was no attempt within that segment to present cultural distinction between settlers or between settlers and Native Americans.

The entire opening ceremonies described thus far, including all facets of Olympic protocols, were devoid of cultural or ideological traits that were not entertainment-centric. Therefore, implicitly, American identity was presented as the America that Hollywood personifies: a show whose ethnic, racial, and historical connotations are present as elements of the performance, but not independent of the entertainment. This trend in the opening ceremonies ended in the final sequence of the ceremonies, during which America's cultural diversity was shown, but was not emphasized.

The final segment, "Reach Out and Touch," featured three key elements: musical performers, multi-cultural ethnic displays of Los Angeles as well as the attending national Olympic committees, and international participants on the jumbo screens. The sequence began immediately after the entrance of the torch and the oaths by the judges and athletes. At that time, 2,000 people dressed in their native costumes entered the stadium and positioned themselves in a large circle around the track (LAOOC 1984b). The circle completely encompassed the athletes. An international children's choir started performing Ludwig Van Beethoven's *Ode to Joy*. This was immediately followed by the performance of "Reach out and Touch." While the choir and many performers on the stadium floor sang the song, the multi-culturally dressed people held hands, followed by an impromptu joining of hand by both the athletes and the audience. A total of 180,000 people took part in what was dubbed a celebration of international brotherhood (Perelman 1985a: 215).

In addition to everything occurring within the stadium, the final sequence also featured a display, projected on jumbo screens, of people holding hands all over the world. This final segment is important for a few key reasons. First, it is outside of the process of indoctrination that occurred throughout the ceremonies. Furthermore, it was both international and local. Evidence of the first exists in the use of an acclaimed German song, performed by an international choir, which was used to encourage international peace among all people. Evidence of the latter can be found in the demonstration of America's "national" identity as embodying a sense of equality of all peoples within one state. Therefore, this multi-cultural presentation of goodwill can be seen as having intrinsically international and domestic relevance.

We could argue that the Olympics are a festival of peace, on an ideological level, and that this final segment featured a reinforcement of that facet of Olympic ideology. However, whether the audience accepts this as a display of an Olympic principle, or sees it as something else, is not the important fact of this display. Rather, the emphasis here is that the only concrete display of ethnic and cultural American identity was conducted within the context of the show of internationalism and not just an intrinsically American sequence. American, therefore, is still being defined as multicultural and diversity-tolerant, as the ideology being defined is not one that exemplifies one set of traits within the fabric of American identity. Instead, it emphasizes an entertainment-culture that cuts across all elements of society.

The extent to which the organizers continually reinforced this sequence as "multi-national" and not strictly American lends credibility to previous statements that the traits of the American identity, presented in the Los Angeles Olympics, were vested within the context of American entertainment instead of a presentation defined in terms of ethnic or multi-cultural heritages. This is even further emphasized by the fact that the United States was represented in the multi-cultural framework only by its Native American people, and not by a depiction of a melding of both its native and immigrant communities (LAOOC 1984b).

As Handler (1984) noted, and Hobsbawm (1983) reinforced, objectification is a process of indoctrinating the masses into the new myth, typically through repetition. Several components of repetition were indicated within moments of the opening ceremonies as well as between elements. One more illustration of repetition, which should be discussed to further establish that the Los Angeles ceremonies are an effort at indoctrination of ideology, occurred within the pageantry sequence of the closing ceremonies.

The ceremonies that ended the games started with the final of the marathon and the necessary ceremonies for awarding the medals for the final competitions. The extinguishing of the flame was next. During this time, the only cultural manifestations within the display were those cultural accoutrements that accompanied athletes, including their national flags, in the parade of nations, with one exception. This exception is irrelevant to the topic of Los Angeles but will be mentioned solely for the edification of the reader. At every summer and winter Olympics studied in this monograph, except the 1980 Moscow Olympics, the host city of the following Olympiad is allowed a brief period of time during which it may conduct any presentation they wish in order to allow the world to preview their own Olympics. This sequence was therefore embedded with the cultural icons of traditional Korea, as a preview of the Seoul summer Olympics in four years.

Returning to the main theme of this study of Los Angeles, after all the necessary elements of the closing ceremonies were concluded, the audience was then treated to one final piece of entertainment. The sequence featured two helicopters and a spaceship. Lights from the infield stage and the spaceship symbolized communication. The ship landed and an alien emerged next to the cauldron to show his satisfaction with the Olympic games. The sequence was followed by a fireworks display and musical tribute to each host of the previous summer Olympics. The display was then followed by a tribute to Los Angeles and concluded with Lionel Ritchie and 300 break dancers performing the song "All Night Long."

The 1984 Los Angeles summer Olympics ended the same way it started; with a Hollywood flair. Where the opening ceremonies focused on the musical paradigm, the closing ceremonies were appropriately a look to the past and the future with a science fiction overtone. Further reinforcing the ideology of American identity as being the collection of its cultural and artistic entertainment, the last segment of the Los Angeles Olympics was a finale to the opening ceremonies' musical sequence, now featuring 80s rock and dance style. Therefore, by being both a reminder and a continuance of the indoctrination of ideology in the opening ceremonies, the closing ceremonies provided a compelling final piece of evidence to establish the Los Angeles ceremonies as an example of this manifestation.

II. SEOUL: HARMONY & PROGRESS

While Los Angeles relied on strategizing the ceremonies into a chronological demonstration of the concepts being reinforced, Seoul sought to indoctrinate an idea by its placement within multiple areas of the opening ceremonies. This included chronologically specific settings as well as general pageantry and general concepts of Korean culture. The overwhelming theme of the Seoul opening and closing ceremonies was progress and harmony. The notion that was embedded within this theme was that of reconciliation, predominantly between the two Koreas. Therefore, the ideology that was performed was that Korean nationalism was a peaceful and progressive identity that, in the hands of the South Koreans, was moving towards reconciliation with the North.

According to the final report of the Seoul summer Olympics, the concepts of harmony and progress needed to be vested in a concrete object—they chose barriers—that would be able to symbolize these concepts (SLOOC 1989a: 392). In a very apropos manner, the Seoul organizers seemed to be aware of the concepts in this study as they attempted to struc-

ture and then present an idea within their national identity as an almost perfect example of this concept. Without question, the organizers applied Handler's (1984) notions of objectification and how intangibles are objectified
through physically real ideas. The organizers formally called the theme of
the opening ceremonies "Beyond All Barriers" (SLOOC 1989a: 392).

The goal of the organizers, as illustrated by the ceremonies and discussed within the final report, was to establish Korea and the Korean people
as a progressive, harmonious people, who are simultaneously looking to establish a state of peace on their peninsula and in the global community. As
this was the stated goal of the Seoul organizers (SLOOC 1989a), the Seoul
opening and closing ceremonies provide a wealth of evidence for how indoctrination of ideology functions within a performance framework.

The concepts of peace, harmony, progress, unification, and the break-
down of borders are all ideas that do not need to be defined for the audience
to understand their meaning within the presentation of Korean identity. From
the very beginning of the opening ceremonies, the symbolism of these broad
ideas was being objectified. As noted in the previous chapter, the Dragon
Drum has a symbol of three intertwined colors, within one circle, which
symbolizes the unity of heaven, earth, and man (SLOOC 1988b). The procession of the Dragon Drum, much like many other elements of the opening
ceremonies, was dualistic. In this case, Koreans were dressed in yellow costumes to the right of the drum and in red costumes to the left, reminiscent of
the existence of two Korean states.

The dualities in these games extended beyond the North-South Korean
divide as it also encompassed the east-west political and social divide.
Shortly after the Dragon Drum and World Tree Sequence, 44 Korean
nymphs and 44 Greek maidens (SLOOC 1989a: 404) performed "Heaven,
Earth, and Man," symbolizing both the unity of the east and west in terms of
the Olympics and in terms of the world. From this point onward, most elements of the opening ceremonies were laced with the meaning and sym-
bology of that ideology. In some cases, this was very subtle. For example, at
the start of the parade of nations, the more than 70,000 audience members
used fifes to play the notes "do," "mi," "sol," and "do," which forms a tonic
chord, or put another way, perfect harmony (*Ibid.*).

The Seoul organizers were effective in weaving their message into the
protocol segments. In SLOOC President Park Sei-jik's speech, he noted, "we
have leapt over ideological and political barriers to share in a celebration of
harmony and progress" (SLOOC 1988b). At the end of the formal declaration of the opening of the games, the audience members held up large cards,
creating a placard display that spelled out harmony and progress (SLOOC
1989a: 406). There is another example in the torch lighting ceremony. Sohn
Kee-chung, a Korean gold medalist from the 1936 Berlin Olympics, carried
the torch into the Olympic stadium (SLOOC 1988b). It is an interesting

symbol of both harmony and unification, as the torchbearer symbolically represents a unified and independent Korea. By choosing an Olympian from the pre World War II era, the torchbearer represented a time before the east-west conflict that led to the division of Korea into two states. Furthermore, it was also a reminder of the independence of Korea because Kee-chung was a participant on the Japanese team[4] but labeled himself as a Korean athlete for his competitions (*Ibid.*).

At the end of the protocols of the opening ceremonies, the pageantry returned in the form of a seven-part epilogue. The segments of the display were: "A Great Day," "Chaos," "Beyond All Barriers," "Silence," "New Sprouts," "Harmony," and "One World" (SLOOC 1989a: 406). Several of these sequences are particularly useful for this analysis. The first segment, "A Great Day" was a depiction of the dawn of the world of mankind. It recalled an age of peace and innocence among all human beings. The presentation featured 74 parachutists descending into the stadium carrying flags of several of the participating nations. They were greeted by high school dancers "expressing the yearning for peace created by harmony of the heaven and earth" (SLOOC 1989a: 406) through a Korean cultural flower dance.

The segment that depicted peace was interrupted by "Chaos," a dramatic presentation of Korean folk masks, dancers, and fountains of fire, which symbolized the end of peace and the advent of bedlam. Afterwards the "Beyond All Barriers" segment replaced chaos with the precision and discipline of martial artistry. 1,008 children ceremoniously brought down the barriers to peace, harmony, and progress with a demonstration of board breaking (SLOOC 1989a: 410). According to the final report, this segment specifically "display[ed] the power of mankind who had come to the place of reconciliation beyond the barriers" (*Ibid.*).

The "Silence" and "New Sprouts" segments quickly followed the departure of the child Taekwondoists. The "Silence" portion of the ceremonies featured a boy, born on the day Seoul was awarded the games eight years prior, playing with a hoop. The circular hoop had three meanings: first, the circulation of the cosmos, depicting the heavens; second, the harmony of the world depicting the earth; and third, the five Olympic rings representing mankind. In a simultaneously symbolic and reminiscent manner, this segment recalled the depiction of the Dragon Drum and the performance that featured both Greek and Korean artists. The idea of the "Silence" section was the reinforced by the "New Sprouts" segment, which featured more than 1,000 children that ran out onto the arena floor and played with hoops and other toys.

The next segment to be featured, "Harmony," is one of the most pertinent parts of the opening ceremonies in terms of the study of ideological indoctrination. The piece featured a Konori battle game. The game features two teams, Hong and Chong, Red and Blue, respectively, which recall the duality, of east and west and north and south, in the pre-protocol pageantry segments. The game is symbolic of the struggle for unity and harmony. It begins with both teams carrying ropes weighing over 3,600 kilograms (SLOOC 1988b) that are positioned opposite of each other and then charged towards each other. On the first charge, the two teams missed each other completely. On the second charge, they clashed but result only a stalemate. On the third, and final charge—again, symbolically reminding the audience of the Trinity of Heaven, Earth, and Mankind—the two ropes clashed and the result was to thrust the two teams into the air. Atop the ropes representatives of each team stood and exchanged flags connoting harmony's arrival. As the demonstration also depicted failed attempts at this unity of the two teams, we can also interpret this demonstration as a reminder of the trials of unification of North and South Korea.

The "One World" segment then follows in which performers from many countries around the world, and all previous performers, join together in a hand-clasping symbol of international brotherhood and peace. Representatives of countries, flowers, animals (through former mascots), and other symbols all weave together to create one mammoth presentation of all of creatures on earth together in harmony, signaling the end of the Seoul opening ceremonies.

The Seoul closing ceremonies continued the indoctrination in the closing ceremonies, starting with a friendship dance that celebrated the strides towards peace between competing nations. After the entrance of the athletes, the theme of togetherness and harmony continued with the construction of Ojakkyo, or the "Magpie Bridge," which symbolizes love (SLOOC 1989a: 414). The S-shaped bridge became the stage for a special dance that depicted the meeting and parting. The concept of the duality of Korean existence and the hope for reunification was obviously a key theme of this segment of the closing ceremonies.

As occurred in the opening ceremonies, SLOOC President Park Sei-jik incorporated the theme of harmony and progress into his speech. Recalling the east-west demonstration of Greece and Korea, the closing ceremonies featured a dance of Korean and Spanish (Barcelona, Spain would host the summer Olympics after Korea) performers. At the end of the symbolic elements of the pageant, two balloons representing the mascots of the Seoul and Barcelona games rose up and out of the stadium into a fireworks display as one final reminder of the goal of unification of the Seoul games and the continuity of the Olympic movement.

A final note on the symbolism of the Seoul Olympics in terms of this duality of a divided country seeking peace was in the design of the stadium. The stadium was constructed so that its two entrances faced each other and were positioned at opposite ends of the stadium: north and south . Having its participants enter from opposite entrances only to join together on the arena floor augmented the symbolism of the Spanish and Korean dance, which signified the unification of Korea.

III. FINAL THOUGHTS

When considering the two examples presented within this chapter, a few commonalities emerge. First, the display of the concept(s) of the indoctrination occurred multiple times. Recalling Handler (1984) and Hobsbawm (1983), repetition can play a key role in the success of an objectification. Second, the process, which was defined as involving three phases, only requires the last step if the audience is already aware of the meaning of the icons and of the context within which the must be placed.

Third, it is necessary to note that indoctrination can be either the focus of the pageantry (as in Los Angeles), or an underlying current within the whole ceremony (as in Seoul). In the case of the latter, the concept(s) indoctrinated can recur in other elements of the opening ceremonies, but the whole process is contained in each segment, such that if it were shown without the rest of the ceremonies its integrity would be maintained. Last, the complexity of concept has no bearing on this manifestation.

The Los Angeles and Seoul presentations were diffused throughout the ceremonies. The Los Angeles ceremonies involved multiple periods of American musical history and therefore involved a complicated set of traits and symbols for the process of indoctrination of one main principle. The ideology being indoctrinated is incomprehensible should only one segment of the display be shown. Similarly, the depth of the concepts of reunification, harmony, and progress, would have been lost if the Seoul Games limited the ideology to one segment as well. The effectiveness of the Seoul indoctrination is due to the faithful depiction of the concepts being reinforced in every segment. As a result, the different sections of the Opening Ceremonies have, as the main continuity element, the concepts being indoctrinated.

The Seoul ceremonies required presentations and symbols that were vested with the same meaning as part of a concept that Korean identity was said to possess. While the definition and pertinence of these ideas were simple, a main focus of the Korean expression was in how important these notions are in Korean identity. Unification as the source of harmony and progress for all of Korea was not just indoctrinated but it was being treated as a hegemonic concept. The repetition of this idea throughout the ceremonies is therefore a necessary and powerful technique for convincing the audience.

The depths of meaning, the complexity of the idea and its context, and the purpose or goal of the presentation all influence the display on a structural level. Furthermore, as degrees of complexity, context, and goals influence the implementation of this process, it is reasonable to conclude that while the outcome may be different, the process can be utilized regardless of the content or the context of the display. The only necessity of this manifestation is an ideological conception of one's own identity that is vested into traits or icons that may be both defined and displayed. It is, therefore, necessary to point out that this manifestation deals with ideas, which may be objectified into symbols, but not with symbols directly. The symbol is nothing more than the language of the dialogue between presenter and audience.

The point of departure for this manifestation, from the next, is when the goal is to take a symbol, which already has a vested meaning, and assimilate it into the total concept of one's national identity. Whereas this chapter dealt with taking a concept, which may be represented by one or more symbols, the next chapter deals with the meaning and incorporation of a single symbol into a state's national identity. Where the previous manifestation focuses on a core concept of identity, or a soon-to-be-core concept of identity, the next focuses on a single trait and defines it vis-à-vis the current national myth. Therefore, the next chapter will be more circumspect in its scope and specific in its treatment than indoctrination of ideology.

NOTES

1. The gathering is not limited to those in the stadium, but to every community member, including those watching on television.

2. Oscars: Best Original Score: *The Way We Were* (1973); Best Adapted/Song Score: *The Sting* (1973); Best Original Song: *The Way We Were* (1973). Golden Globes: Best Song: *Kotch* (1971), *The way We Were* (1973),

3. (Only awards won prior to the 1984 Games listed) Oscars: Best Original Score: *Jaws* (1975), *Star Wars* (1977), *E.T. the Extra-Terrestrial* (1982); Best Adapted Score: *Fiddler on the Roof* (1971). Golden Globes: Best Original Score: Same as Oscars;

4. During the 1936 Berlin Summer Olympics, Korea was under Japanese occupation and therefore Olympians from Japanese-controlled territories competed under the Japanese flag.

CHAPTER 6
CUSTODIANS OF CULTURE

I. THE CONCEPT OF CUSTODIANSHIP

The custodians of culture is a strategy that incorporates the use of hegemonic symbols in nationalism. A hegemonic symbol has a meaning that is very powerfully vested within a people's shared understanding. Actors seeks to incorporate a symbol and its meaning into their overall statement of national identity. There can be multiple purposes behind this. First, and foremost, if the symbol already has a hegemonic status it can be used to lend credibility to the overall display of nationalism. For example, several countries have switched their flag from its previous design to a display of red, white, and blue in a symbolic acceptance of new democratic ideology and institutions. These colors are usually associated with three regimes—France, the United States, and the United Kingdom. The adoption of a new symbol can also be an attempt to control history.

Consider the Macedonian question, as put forth by Loring Danforth (1997). Danforth highlights the conflicting yet overlapping identities between two states: Macedonia and Greece. Both, in an attempt to objectify their national heritage, have claimed the heritage of Ancient Macedonia. Particularly for Greece, the state claims an exclusive and "legitimate" claim to the ancient Hellenic past. These states have attempted to do this through a series of rather claims as the custodians of the legacy of Philip of Macedon and Alexander the Great. These two figures, which conjure images of glory and power, attest to the greatness in which "someone's" national history revels. But who is the custodian? Both the Greek and the Macedonian governments have incorporated the Star of Vergina, the symbol of Philip of Macedon, and by extension the leader himself. Whether they put this symbol on flags, buildings, or statues, both are fighting for the right to be the heir of this portion of ancient Greek or ancient Macedonian history.

Danforth (1997), through his analysis of Greek-Macedonian relations and of the interplay of Greek and Macedonian communities in Australia, established the strength of the custodianship of culture manifestation. Control over the symbols of Ancient Macedonia is important enough for both Greece and Macedonia to vehemently argue over, because these symbols are vested with meaning that both states see as critical to their survival. We must keep in mind that this debate over antiquity is fueled by two modern states— one created in the early 19th century and another constructed at the end of the 20th century.

Greece and Macedonia played a dangerous game because both sides have attempted to establish themselves as the sole representatives of "Macedonianness." This fiction is even more pronounced when we are reminded that Lewis and Wigen (1997) underscored the great myth that is geographical borders. Lewis and Wigen (1997: 191) were right when they observed that geographical definitions of the world were tenuous and that "nationalist revivals have exposed the vulnerability of existing state borders." A major part of the Macedonian question is rooted in Greece's fear that Macedonia may use its national identity, rooted in its claimed historical legitimacy, to annex the Greek provinces of Macedonia.[1]

The custodians of culture strategy can consolidate or fragment a state, depending on what type of identity is being established. This is more prevalent in states with vibrant regional or peripheral identities, but the concept is no less valid in supposedly "homogenous" states. In many of the demonstrations discussed in this study, the attempt is to bolster the concept of the nation-state as a means of consolidating its power and establishing its stability. Lewis and Wigen (1997: 8) put it best when they said: "In this process, states [seek to] become reified as natural and fundamental building blocs of global geography, rather than being recognized as the constructed, contingent, and often imposed political geographical units that they are." While they use the term "state," predominantly because they are dealing with the concept of boundaries, we can substitute it with the term "nation" because this study intends this to imply both sovereign and would-be sovereign states.

Combining elements of Lewis and Wigen's analysis, together with Danforth, we find that this strategy is a concerted effort to establish both ownership of specific socio-cultural and historic legacies, as well as an attempt to legitimize those claims. In these examples, tangible elements are incorporated into the display and therefore the definition of the identity being depicted. However, this strategy is not limited to this for its possibilities.

Arne Martin Klausen (1999) shows us that this process is not necessarily limited to a physical icon. It can, instead, be linked to an idea, a history, or even an event. Klausen showed us how Norwegians tried to rewrite sports history in an attempt to take ownership of the heritage of all winter sports. By harkening to a past in which skiing, the mainstay of Olympic Winter Sports, was created in the city of Mørgedal, Norway. It is a reasonable statement to claim that skiing is a vital part of Norwegian Society. However, claiming itself as the source of skiing and all other Winter Olympic sports does seem to go a bit too far.

In short, this strategy does not necessarily deal with just the incorporation of a physically apparent icon that has its own meaning above and beyond the item itself. This strategy, in fact, deals with the incorporation, based on some degree of fact or facts, of a historical moment, icon, idea, or artifact into the currently existing mythology of any given nationalism, without attempting to alter the current understanding of that identity.

Whether we are using ideas put forth by Lewis and Wigen, Danforth, or Klausen, we are dealing with the concept of possession. Most nationalist identities survive thanks to the belief that they possess certain attributes that differentiate them from others. In this sense, we recall Antonio Gramsci's *Intellectuals* (1971), in which he demonstrates that the concept of intellectual is a characteristic unique to a specific segment of the population. In a sense, this strategy would argue that intellectuals took custodianship of the concept of their own ability for leadership.

Finally, we must realize that this strategy almost always appears in tandem with other nationalist manifestations. Where the previous two strategies are a story arc in which the mythology is presented with a sense of a beginning and an end, this strategy represents the physical or ideological manifestation of one element within that story. It is separated, and expanded upon, herein as its own strategy because of how it plays out in the Olympics.

Often the Olympics can represent a single step in a process of an overarching alteration to a mythology. In the Olympics, the segment of the process could involve simply the custodianship of a specific icon or series of icons. The rest of the process could be a protracted one that starts before and finishes after the opportunity to host the Olympics. Therefore, since the Olympics can contain an entire myth-affecting process, or could contain just this one part, it must be considered herein as a separate strategy.

We can make one final note on the concept of display in terms of process. Luke (2002) and Handelman (1990) are both directly pertinent to this manifestation. Mixing concepts of modeling, presentation and representation together with the concept of display as established through museums, we must realize, "hegemony is constantly under construction, and relentlessly subjected to deconstruction" (Luke 2002: 217). By way of Olympic demonstration, the objectifier can redirect nationalist tendencies within a state and prepare the audience for the indoctrination of a new identity conception.

The single most important difference between custodians of culture and the previous manifestation is breadth. Here we focus on individual elements, not the broader idea of a specified nationalism. This process focuses on aspects of an identity instead of establishing the total identity or a major trend within that identity. It does, however, seek to augment that understanding through the incorporation of old or new symbols within a dialogue on national identity.

In this manifestation, we see the objectifier reaching out for a specific symbol and taking custody of it as though it were their rightful property. The symbol, as well as its meaning and history, are then assimilated into the objectifier's statement on the definition of national identity. The icon over which the objectifier claims custodianship may already be a part of the existing national identity. In that case, the agent reasserts ownership or restructures the symbol to make it more or less important.

The first mechanism, simply restating ownership of a symbol, will be discussed later. The subsequent reevaluation process has superficial similarities to historical revision. Revision involves the reinterpretation of cultural icons within a national identity. In this system, the actor has as a goal of either revising historical aspects of his identity through reassessing the icons that have been used to symbolize it or by emphasizing some symbols while deemphasizing others as a path to a new definition of the self.

For example, emphasizing the Spanish language while deemphasizing the Catholic faith, as Barreto (2001b) explained, was a strategic choice by Puerto Rican secular intellectuals who were attempting to define their identity in a manner that promoted their elite status. Barreto's example shows how elites can restructure their own identity by taking specific cultural icons within their identity and re-ordering them in a calculated plan to maintain their elite authority. The choice of the Barcelona elite to emphasize the mythology of the *barca nona*, the Roman mythological ship from which the name Barcelona is derived (Cuyas 1993b: 61), provides another example of reassessment of an icon to meet the goals of the organizers. In this example, the *barca nona* was used to emphasize Barcelona as a Mediterranean rather than a Spanish city. In this sense, the reassessment lies in the degree of importance of a symbol and not the interpretation of the symbol. This is an important distinction, because the goals and processes are slightly different.

If the revision occurs as an interpretation of the icon under review, then it could be one step within an indoctrination of ideology. As indoctrination of ideology was previously established as a process through which symbols, ideas, and histories are woven together to establish an identity, then custodianship of an already-present cultural icon can be one step in that process. Examples of this can be found through consideration of specific elements within the Los Angeles musical and entertainment indoctrination. In addition to a reassessment, the addition of a totally new symbol ultimately may be conducted through indoctrination and custodianship.

Taking custody of a new symbol requires a process that utilizes the construction of a symbol followed by an acquisition of guardianship. Therefore, it involves a process similar to indoctrination of ideology, as it must define the new symbol for the audience. The symbol's space, meaning, and purpose are all constructed for a specific goal that tends to be ideological in its purpose. Take, for example, the myth of the Mørgedal flame. In this example from the 1952 Olympic Winter Games, the Norwegian government started constructing an entirely new symbol to legitimize its claim to a winter sports heritage.

Outside of performance, we find another example of this kind of custodianship in the Macedonian question. By claiming the star of Vergina as part Greek history, the Greek government attempts to appropriate the star, the legacy of Philip of Macedon and Alexander the Great, and the history of Macedonia into an exclusive definition of Greek and Hellenic identity. The heritage of ancient Macedonia becomes a descriptor of modern Greece rather than the modern Macedonian state—a process benefiting Greek elites and the Greek state rather than their Macedonian counterparts.

Custodianship of culture generally involves a symbol that already has been vested with a specific meaning. The issue of competing control over a symbol, as in the Macedonian question, usually concerns the meaning vested into the symbol rather than the physical object itself. It is common for that meaning to be universally valid, or at least valid between the groups of elites involved in the competition. As a result, a main feature of this process is the assertion of the symbol, possibly through repetition as noted by Handler (1984) and Hobsbawm (1983).

According to Handler (1984), actors have a certain degree of control over the process of incorporating traits, including their meaning, in the process of objectification. Therefore, custodianship of new and old symbols, whether foreign or familiar to identity, involves a degree of definition. In this context, performance is similar to displays of identity found within festivals or museums (Guss 2000; Luke 2002). According to Luke (2002: 12): "art exhibitions are performances of power, creating states out of the narratives, images, practices endorsed as authoritative in the power plays of the artwork put out on show." In the first manifestation, the narrative was either created or revised to reflect a change in the overall concept or minor details of the identity. Here we are less concerned with the outcome of the narrative than with a specific element that has been, or will, be vested with meaning.

By assimilating a trait, custodianship can welcome peripheralized identities, seek to conquer communities outside of the current definition of the objectifier's identity, or create a new concept within the identity. It is simultaneously a process of claiming ownership of an icon, its meaning, and its historical legacy, as well as exercising the privilege of redefining those traits. So far, this explanation has identified the assimilation and reinterpretation of external or peripheral identities. In addition to these options, custodianship can reinterpret or exhibit older icons as part of a process of internal recitation.

Taking custodianship of a cultural symbol is not only conducted on external elements. This process can also affect symbols already indoctrinated into the identity because, as several authors have illustrated, identity is a construct of the choices of actors and is therefore malleable (see Barreto 2001a, 2001b; Handler 1984; Mallon 1995). Unless we are discussing the revocation of an icon from the concept of identity, then custodianship involves strengthening, weakening or restructuring the current interpretation of one's identity. This is best accomplished by seeking to alter the status of a symbol within the firmament of objectified traits of the identity. As Guss (2000: 9) noted, cultural performances are both contentious and ambiguous and as a result can change their structure and direction.

The Puerto Rican and Catalan examples presented earlier both dealt with the alteration of identity through reassessment. Recitation is also a key form of this manifestation of nationalism through performance. Recitation will play a key role in this chapter as it focuses on taking a single icon and presenting it multiple times. This takes Hobsbawm's (1983) assertion that creating identity involves a process of formalizing and ritualizing identity through reference to the past and imposing it through repetition. Of the various manifestations discussed in this study, this is the most faithful and specific implementation of Hobsbawm's ideas. This is also tied to concepts of hegemonic symbols and their ascendancy, which is a critical facet of the presentation of any icon.

Someone's belief in the symbolic meaning vested into an icon grows in strength until such time as the icon becomes an *ipso facto* representation of that meaning or idea. Thus, taking custodianship of a symbol becomes a process by which actors take ideas and imbue them into symbols that are then incorporated into the total definition of the actor's identity. In other words, the actor has taken custodianship of the icon and defined it in terms that meet his goals for national identity formation.

The custodian of culture manifestation is intended to demonstrate how symbols and icons are depicted, defined, and then assimilated into an identity. Thus far, it has been assumed that these symbols are tangible. A large part of Handler's (1984) argument concerning the process of objectification explained how the "intangible" was given physical reality by embodying the traits of an identity into concrete symbols. Therefore it is a logical conclusion that, when discussing the process of custodianship of a symbol, we are discussing a physically manifested item. That, while true, is also misleading, because custodianship can seize ideas and ideologies that do not have a physical embodiment. By recalling Klausen's (1999) study of Norwegian culture, we are reminded that identity formation can often incorporate ideas, histories, or specific events in addition to material symbols.

The assimilation of a non-corporeal trait has its costs and benefits. First, the demonstration presents special difficulties due to the lack of a physical object to present to the audience. Part of the main point of objectification is to present the members of the imagined community with pieces of their identity through symbols they can see and touch. The main issues put forth in this study are, in fact, the different strategies through which an identity, which is in itself insubstantial, is demonstrated on stage. The idea of demonstrating an incorporeal symbol or icon is a microcosm of this entire study. Therefore, it is necessarily difficult since even an insignificant element requiring demonstration must itself be artistically rendered for it to be successful.

While this poses a hurdle for the organizers, the efforts are well worth it as the necessary complexity of the concept and its demonstration shields it from a simplistic refutation on the part of those opposed to the definition or its incorporation into the national identity on display. As the trait being demonstrated is displayed through artistic rendition, its interpretation is necessarily impressionistic and automatically accepted as being more symbolic than explicit in its definitive meaning. Taken together, custodian of culture represents an entire range of possibilities of actor's goals for the assimilation of an icon, physical or metaphysical, into the community's mainstream understanding of its nationalism.

II. ATHENS: KEEPER OF MACEDONIA AND THE SOURCE OF MODERN ART?

The opening ceremonies of the Athens 2004 summer Olympics provide an excellent series of examples of the utility of custodianship. The Macedonian question had its moment of presentation at the Athens opening ceremonies. The issue was over the legacy of Alexander the Great and the star of Vergina. The history of Macedonia, as embodied in the Macedonian general and his symbol, is a poignant example of an icon being fought over by two sets of elites: the governments of the Hellenic Republic and the former Yugoslav Republic of Macedonia (hereafter Greece and Macedonia). Any attempt by Greece to claim Alexander the Great or the star of Vergina as an exclusively Greek icon represents an example of Greek elites attempting to take custody of an icon that is claimed by at least one other elite.

Before continuing, a few notes on Macedonian history will assist the reader in better understanding the main point of this subchapter. First of all, the concept of Macedonia, as it existed a few thousand years ago, is not *ipso facto* the same concept as the modern sovereign state of Macedonia. The borders of Macedonia and Greece have both fluctuated over time and any connection between the modern political boundaries of the states of Macedonia and Greece and their ancient counterparts is pure invention on the part of modern Macedonian and Greek elites.[2]

Claiming control of an icon that is as visibly in dispute as the star of Vergina requires careful work by the organizer. If the display is too obvious, the result could be international condemnation and accusation of imperialistic aims; however, if the display is too subtle, then the audience could overlook the appropriation. Moreover, if the symbol is deeply embedded among other icons, even well-educated members of the audience specifically acquainted with the imagery could fail to differentiate it from the other elements. The challenge for the actor is to be clear in the demonstration of the target of assimilation but at the same time subtle enough to not seem ostentatious. In the case of the Athens example, once the crafter of the opening ceremonies has handled this delicate balancing act, there remains one final challenge: establishing the icon as overwhelmingly Greek.

It is insufficient to just present an icon. The symbol must be placed within a context of Greek identity that establishes it as Greek, as opposed to Macedonian. The Athens organizers managed to handle the issue of Alexander the Great and the star of Vergina expertly, providing us with an impressive example of skillful presentation of an internationally delicate icon. During the Athens opening ceremonies, a segment titled Clepsydra presented a history of Greece. A Clepsydra is an ancient Greek invention, better know as a water clock, which keeps track of time. This segment featured a parade of floats, upon which were depicted moments in a chronological history of Greece.

Each float established a different stage of the development of ancient Greece. The demonstration began with a depiction of Minoan culture with the subjugation of a bull marking an ancient rite of passage for a child to become an adult. There is already a degree of symbolism within the structure as the birth of Greek culture is almost immediately followed by a rite of passage indicating how Greek culture went from childhood to adulthood. The segment ended with a depiction of the 1896 Olympics, modern Greece, and an artistic presentation of the future potential of mankind. From the beginning to the end of the Clepsydra session, Greek history was presented as a series of historical and cultural icons.

By presenting a complete field of Greek history in a series of fifteen elements, each single element is bolstered by the presence of the other fourteen. Using, for example, the standard depictions of Greek theatre, sports, Orthodox Christianity, and other established icons of Greek identity, less well-established icons are given an added sense of credibility. Notable among these non-traditional elements was a single float dedicated to Alexander the Great. The Macedonian float featured Alexander the Great on horseback. In front of the horse were several spears leaning in the same direction Alexander was facing. The side of the float was lined with eight simple shields affixed with the star of Vergina. This formed the only overt demonstration of Greece's claim to ancient Macedonia in the Olympics.

The Greek assimilation was successful for a few reasons. First, the Macedonian float is unmistakable in its representation. While a broader international audience may be less aware of the history of Alexander the Great or of the imagery of the star of Vergina, the symbols are readily apparent to the Greek and southeastern European regional audience. In addition to being straightforward in its meaning, the presentation was carefully embedded in a manner designed so as to reduce its audacity and diminish the opportunity for internal or external attacks on the display. First, the Macedonian float was one element within fifteen. Each float was adorned with multiple elements, many of which were ornate and vested with symbolic meaning. Audience awareness of each element would have been diffused enough to limit emotional response to any specific element. Furthermore, as the presentation was filled with so many elements, the degree of perceived authenticity of each element helped to influence audience perspective of icons perceived to be less authentic or fraudulent.

Second, the placement of the Macedonian float was placed with great intention within the Clepsydra sequence. Prior to the Macedonian float was a depiction of the ancient Olympics. The ancient Olympics are historically accepted icons of ancient Greece, and due to the modern Olympics, universally accepted as contained within the identity of modern Greece. Histories of ancient Greece, particularly Herodotus (1998), record Alexander the Great as having competed in the ancient Olympics. Therefore, a presentation of Alexander the Great following a presentation of the ancient Olympics helped to make the Macedonian issue more innocuous than had it been displayed without such a precursor. The irony is, of course, that Greece is trying to assimilate Macedonian symbols and history, which includes the Macedonian Conquest of Greece by Philip of Macedon.

The Alexander the Great float was then followed with a highly symbolic and artistic rendering of Heaven and Hell. The depiction of the Greek notion of Heaven and Hell, which incorporated elements of Greek Orthodox Christianity and Hellenistic mythology, included the transformation of Greek religious practices from the Greek pantheon to Orthodoxy as the primary religion of the Greek people. By following the assimilation of Macedonian icons with an involved set of mythological presentations of religion, the audience's attention and cognitive understanding became occupied by, and therefore distracted from, a longer and more analytical consideration of the validity of the display that came immediately prior.

Evidence of the success of this display can be seen in the commentary from NBC's broadcast. During their discussion of the Macedonian float, the NBC commentators accepted without mention that Alexander the Great was a Greek icon (Athens 2004 Organizing Committee for the Games 2004b). They did comment on the relative lack of success of Alexander as an Olympian, which suggests that the misdirection of placing the ancient Olympics float prior to the Macedonian display was successful (*Ibid.*). The facts of the conflict were not unknown to the NBC commentators, as they referenced the conflict between Greece and Macedonia during the latter's entrance in the parade of nations. Therefore, the placement of the Alexander demonstration was not only cunning in that it misdirected viewers into accepting Greece's claim, but it was embedded well enough that educated audience members (i.e., the journalists), who were aware of the Macedonian question, did not perceive it as worthy of comment.

The custodianship of culture concept along the recitation form is demonstrated within both the Clepsydra segment and the opening ceremonies as a whole. While there are arguably several possible examples of recitation in the opening ceremonies, I will focus specifically on Greek art and sculpture to establish this process. The Greek organizers sought to take custody of the long history of modern art, specifically the depiction of the form of the human body, as a history that is totally Greek. To make such a claim, the Athens opening ceremonies had to both establish and then reinforce that statement.

Incorporating the steps of this process, the organizers first needed to physically take custody of the progress of artistic depictions of the human form. This required more than simply presenting a beginning and an end of the development of art. It required presenting the audience the earliest Greek examples of display of the human form through sculpture and then illustrating the progress towards increasing degrees of detail and accuracy in its portrayal. Once this was established, the second step of the custodianship via recitation involved restating this idea through its display as an icon within the framework of other Greek elements of the games.

Once established, this demonstration merely requires presentation. It does not require being center stage, re-explained, or even overtly interpreted. Once the depiction of Greek status was established, the depiction was reinforced by then simply involving it in other artistic or protocol moments of the festival. The Greek organizers were actually very effective in both establishing the custodianship of this form of art and also embedding this cultural icon within many facets of the opening ceremonies.

The recitation of Greece's custodianship of art began with a woman dressed in black holding a bust. The following is heard as a voiceover:

I woke up with this marble head in my hands. It exhausts my elbows and I don't know where to put it down. It was falling into a dream as I was coming out of a dream. So our life became one and it will be very difficult for it to separate again. (Athens 2004 Organizing Committee for the Games 2004b)

At the end of the voiceover a large Cycladic Head, one of the earliest forms of sculpture found in the Greek archipelago, rises up out of the water (*Ibid.*). As it rises, a javelin of light was tossed at the statue by a centaur, most likely symbolizing the role Greek mythology played in ancient Greece's development of art.

Once aloft over the stadium floor, geometric patterns and grids are projected on the Cycladic head, depicting the elements of it that were refined during ancient Greek history as the phases towards more accurate depictions of the human form. The sculpture then breaks into eight pieces, which reveal a Kouros statue within the Cycladic head. The Kouros statue, which is a more accurate but still a rigid and not wholly realistic display of the human body, also breaks into several pieces. The breakup of the Kouros statue reveals the final stage in the evolution of Greek art: statues of the classical period. The last stage of this depiction of the evolution of the human form in art, presents statues as true to form of the actual subject.

Through the voiceover, Greek artistic forms, represented by the bust, and Greek society, represented by the woman, are merged together such that they become inextricably linked. Then, artistic form is established, from its earliest forms to the culmination of its evolution as faithful representation, as a quintessentially Greek element. The total concept is presented through the style and color of the Greek statue. The segment's title, *Artistic Tale: A Journey Through Ancient Greece Through Culture*, further establishes modern Greece's custodial claim over these ancient Greek icons.

At this point, it should be apparent that the first step of recitation of custodianship is more or less the same as the simplest form of custodianship—e.g., the appropriation of Alexander the Great and the star of Vergina. At this point, the two strategies for this process diverge. The Macedonian "moment" had its presentation in only one float. The ancient Greek sculpture presentation was established in the Artistic Tale segment and then recited eight times during the opening ceremonies and in one appearance in the closing ceremony. First, immediately after the break-up of the statues, a rotating cube upon which a man slowly walked depicted the Greek search for knowledge. Around him, the disassembled statues floated. The interesting element of this depiction is that the large fragments were used as video screens, upon which technological developments, images of people and images of Greece were projected. The symbolism being depicted was that ancient Greek statues were not just a part of Greek culture but a reflection of it as well. The next seven recitations occurred within the last cultural tribute in the opening ceremonies: the Clepsydra. All of the remaining reinforcements of ancient Greek art as property of modern Greek society were demonstrated through the placement of performers dressed and covered in makeup to appear like Greek statues.

The presentation of the polis, or city-state, period featured these types of performers. The theatre segment featured statues of a Greek woman and the renowned smiling/frowning drama masks. The gods of the Greek pantheon were each displayed as statues with some of their symbols. The presentation of the Parthenon was particularly interesting, as it included human reproductions of the statues that once decorated the external frieze, which now are mostly found in the British Museum,[3] were presented as the main theme of the Parthenon and Greek architecture. Arguably, we could claim this moment as another example of custodianship, in this case reasserting Greece's right to the statues that Britain still keeps in London. Another part of the depiction of architecture relevant here was the presentation of Caryatids (female statues which function as columns).

The last two elements of the Clepsydra segment that dealt with ancient Greece provide the final examples in this segment. First, the presentation of the ancient Olympics featured a series of performers, dressed as statues, pantomiming the competitions. Second, Alexander the Great was also depicted as a statue on the Macedonian float, which was noted in the previous example. The use of the statues in these two floats simultaneously reinforces modern Greece's claims of ownership of the ancient Olympics, ancient Greek sculpture and art, and Macedonia by intertwining these elements together. Individually, each has its own justifications for being considered property of modern Greece; however, when taken together, they share in each other's supposed validity and each helps to legitimize the others.

The final example present in the opening ceremonies appeared during the parade of nations. Once the artistic and parade elements of the pageant ended, the stadium was reset for the parade of nations. The fragments of the various periods of Greek sculpture were arranged to form a centerpiece for the athletes to encircle after marching around the stadium. Atop the center-piece was an olive tree, which would later be the main feature on the stage from which speeches were made during both the opening and closing cere-monies. The olive tree supplies the necessary link between the opening and closing ceremonies, reminding audiences of the continuity of the ceremonies and of Greek history.

Lastly, the entire concept established in the opening ceremonies was once again reinforced in the closing ceremonies. At the end of the pageantry segment, which began with a very elaborate presentation of a Dionysian fes-tival, the demonstration broadened to include more and more facets of Greek culture and identity. As part of this broadening, a return of the ancient ele-ments, depicted with two Greek statues, reinforced the legacy of ancient Greece as part of modern Greece. Such a subsidiary presentation seems al-most unworthy of mention, but even a trite, practically inconsequential, demonstration is sufficient to remind the audience of the idea. So long as the presentation is visible (in this example the statues were placed on a raised stage in the center of the stadium with adequate space around them to allow them to be seen from all over the stadium), it has the desired effect on the audience.

III. NORWAY: BIRTHPLACE OF THE WINTER GAMES OR JUST SKIING?

The Lillehammer Olympics offer a third example of custodians of culture, albeit far less structured than the two Athens models. The unstructured na-ture of Lillehammer's presentation is due in part to its ethereal nature. The "icon," in quotes as it is not physically manifested, is Lillehammer's claim over the legacy of winter sport. As previously discussed, Norway attempted to claim all winter sports, particularly skiing, as the legacy of Norwegian history, and thus establish the Mørgedal flame as an icon within the modern Olympics' firmament of symbols and ideas. It was an insubstantial presenta-tion due to two factors, the first of which was that the Mørgedal flame, the quintessential icon of their attempt at taking custodianship, was banned from Lillehammer's official Olympic presentations (Klausen 1999b), and the sec-ond required a degree of subtlety to avoid condemnation by Greece or the IOC.

The Mørgedal flame story is an effective example of creationism that, when pulled back from its hegemonic goal, is one of many carefully planned pieces of the indoctrination of a winter sports culture into Norway's identity. Arne Martin Klausen (1999b) established the Lillehammer organizer's goal of instituting the Mørgedal Flame and defining that new symbol as representing the birthplace of skiing and the home of Sondre Norheim, who is remembered for bringing skiing to the new world, for his skill at slalom and for his ski-journey from Telemark to Oslo, which is the basis for the famous Holmenkollen race (*Ibid.*, 80). In fact, had the symbol been allowed defini- tion and demonstration at the opening ceremonies, this example would dem- onstrate both custodianship of culture and indoctrination of ideology, since the steps of the latter would be necessary for it to be explained to the audi- ences.

The extent of the effort to get the Mørgedal Flame incorporated into the cauldron lighting, and the subsequent diplomatic mess with Greece which resulted in several unrealized threats of boycott by the Greek national Olym- pic committee, further supports my and Klausen's (1999b) assertions that gifting Norway with the legacy of skiing, and therefore much of winter Olympic sport, was one of the primary nationalistic goals of the Lilleham- mer organizers.

The second reason for the ethereal nature of this display was that pre- senting Norway as the home of winter sports, especially skiing, risked upset- ting the IOC and Greece had the imagery been to intractable. Therefore, coa- lescing this broad concept into one symbol prior to taking custody of it was impossible in the socio-political climate present before the Lillehammer Olympiad. Instead, organizers had to embed presentations of skiing and win- ter sports recreation into their display and allow it to impart onto the audi- ence the "sense" of their custody of winter sports without overt statement of the claim.

Establishing an ethereal demonstration required both subtlety and repeti- tion. Both were accomplished through careful reiteration of the necessary concepts as discrete parts of other portions of the pageant and protocol of the opening ceremonies. The process was made easier by the fact that it was a reasonable assumption that audience members at a winter Olympics had at least a minimal understanding of skiing as sport and skiing as transportation. Therefore, establishing Norwegian society's linkages to winter sports in general, and skiing specifically, did not require definition. Because of this, the Lillehammer organizers were able to permeate the entire opening cere- mony with the icons of skiing and winter sport.

The first major step in the process of indoctrination involved the estab- lishment and connection of sleighing and skiing as a part of Norwegian his- tory. Establishing skiing was an almost immediate step for the attending and television audience, primarily because the site of the opening ceremonies, Lygårdsbakken, was the ski-jumping arena. Therefore, the dominant con- trast, meaning the single element within the field of view that audience members see first, was the two ski-jumps. For the presentation of skiing to be successful, the concept had to be embedded into Norwegian culture and history. Therefore, simply celebrating the ceremonies in a skiing sports venue and having some performers on skis would not be sufficient. The custodianship would only be successful and non-antagonistic to the IOC, if skis appeared to be a natural part of the exhibitions during the opening ceremonies.

This process began with the presentation of an indigenous Nordic tribal people known as the Sami. They were represented at first by a single Sami musician, Nils Aslak Valkeapää, singing a Sami joik (LOOC 1994c: 154). The sequence is reminiscent of the aforementioned example of Sydney and how it incorporated Aboriginal culture. The lone performer entered the arena on a pair of skis and stood center stage. During his song, other Sami performers entered, this time riding sleighs pulled by reindeers. It was a brief, but colorful demonstration of an ancient culture of northern Norway. For this analysis of custodianship of culture, it is important to note that this demonstration established skiing as an ancient Norwegian artifact, even though the modern nation-state of Norway is roughly a century old. The concepts of skiing and sleighing are also interconnected in this demonstration. First, the combination of skiing and sleighing performers places the two snow sports into the same physical and historical space. Second, the sequence ended with the Sami singer taking hold of a rope on one of the sleighs and catching a ride out of the arena. The next phase of the ceremony featured performers from the Telemark region, who entered either by the skiing the slope below the ski jumps or on the backs of fifty sleighs drawn by Norwegian horses (LOOC 1994c: 154). The whole sequence, which was embedded with demonstrations of folk-dances and ethnic music (mostly fiddlers), was a tribute to the people and heritage of Telemark, the purported home of skiing and the county that contains Mørgedal.

Two pieces of evidence illustrate the importance of skiing to the organizers in this segment. First, the sequence began with a single skier descending the K90 hill and performing a somersault while playing the fiddle (LOOC 1994b). The other skiing performers followed him immediately. Second, the final report of the Lillehammer Olympic Organizing Committee (LOOC) described the entrance of the other performers by stating they "skied Telemark down the ski jumping hill" (LOOC 1994c: 154). In their own description of the event, Norwegian society and history are propelled by skies as a means of further emphasizing the linkage between the sport and the identity. The next segment, the entrance of the royal family of Norway, wove sleighing back into the performance by utilizing it in a moment of great distinction. The King and Queen entered on the same sleigh which brought King Håkon to the Holmenkollen Ski Festival (*Ibid.*), which was established by the aforementioned father of skiing, Sondre Norheim.

The most impressive moment of the opening ceremonies involved the cauldron lighting ceremony. The torch was brought to the stadium through the woods around Lillehammer and then brought up a flight of stairs to the top of the K120 ski jump. The Torch was then taken down the ski-jump and soared into the stadium. The torch was then skied around the arena and carried up to the cauldron by the Crown Prince of Norway. The symbolism herein is very important. One of the most prominent and symbolic icons of the modern and ancient Olympics, carried into the stadium by the indoctrinated national sport and then handed off to the Crown Prince. The symbolism suggests that skiing is both richly vested into the Olympic movement and that it is both an official icon of the state, by handing the torch to the Crown Prince, and an icon that will endure for the future of the state. The use of a legitimized and hegemonic Olympic symbol in tandem with the legitimate heir of the crown of the country can be seen as an attempt to establish the hegemonic stewardship of skiing within the Norwegian national myth.

In summary, from the opening moments of the ceremony to the end, skiing and sleighing maintained a highly visible role in the presentation. The Lillehammer Olympics offer an excellent example of how a subtle presentation of a large concept can be accomplished, and the custodianship of that concept can be legitimized in one sweeping display of nationalism. It is also apparent through the Lillehammer example that there was an effort at elevating skiing, separately from sleighing, to a hegemonic status or, if already established, further strengthening that status.

Similar to Athens, the Lillehammer closing ceremonies reasserted the lessons the audience learned from the opening ceremony by returning to the *vetter* and allowing them to "play" in a winter festival. The drama, which featured a story of good and evil, included Vetter on skis as occurred during the opening ceremonies. To accentuate the message, all the good Vetter assembled at the foot of the ski jumps for their moment of victory over the evil Vetter (LOOC 1994b). The final report, in its section on the closing ceremonies, indicates that the hope of the organizers was for "Norwegians [to] have a very special feeling for winter activities, and that winter can be a time for festivities and fun" (LOOC 1994c: 164). It also emphasizes the important relation between these activities and nature.

In each of the examples presented in this chapter, a single idea or concept was appropriated by the organizers as an integral part of the organizer's definition of its own identity. In the case of the first example, the Greek organizers asserted their claim over the legacy of Macedonia in a calculated attempt to incorporate Macedonia deeper into the concept of Greek identity. The goals of the organizer included preventing Macedonia from establishing itself as the heirs of what, in the opinions of Greek elites, had always been a part of their heritage. The second example similarly built upon the organizer's pride in the ancient Greece through its legacy as the source of modern art, particularly sculpture. In the last example, the same processes used in both Greek examples were utilized to establish a less concrete idea. Its intangible nature was partly due to limitations on the use of a specific icon, the Mørgedal Flame, and was partly due to its nature as a concept too broad to be embodied in a single icon or symbol that could be established as Norwegian rather than Greek.

All three examples, however, took a concept vested within one or more symbols, and then placed them and therefore the concept under the umbrella of the self-conceptualization of the nationalistic identity of the host country. In so doing, audience members were instructed, as in indoctrination of ideology, to accept Greek identity as construing the evolution of art and containing Macedonian history, or to accept Norwegian identity as the source of skiing and winter sport, and as a society intricately and intimately linked to winter activity.

It should now be obvious that these examples represent a facet of identity, one that is within the total concept of definition of nationalism as seen by the organizers of a specific Olympiad. In the previous chapter, the focus of the manifestation was on the total impression of the identity, or alternatively the current trend or goal of that identity. The distinction between that concept and the single ideas presented in this chapter is apparent. The processes are similar in that they instruct the audience as to the meaning of the concepts and their pertinence to the actor's identity; but they are distinct in how each is structured due to the specific goals of each host.

NOTES

1. The three regions in Greece's northeast are all referred to as Macedonia. To exacerbate the problem, the region has been considered an ethnic extension of the state of Macedonia by Macedonian irredentists.

2. Note that much of the ancient Hellenic world was located on the Anatolian peninsula—modern day Turkey.

3. The statues, called the Elgin Marbles, were originally a part of the frieze of the Parthenon, but were removed by British officials in the early 19th century. Currently, they are a source of argument between the British and Greek governments, both of whom claim the right to house them in museums.

CHAPTER 7
SOCIETY DIVIDED: A CORE AND A PERIPHERY, A REGION AND AN ETHNICITY

The following two chapters will deal exclusively with the interplay between core and peripheral identities. They share significant commonalties in their implementation while nevertheless maintaining distinctive individuality, which will become apparent over the course of this chapter and chapters 8 and 9. The separation of this topic into three chapters should be seen as the result of structural concerns that affect the concept of identity within the host and not as a result of different goals.

Regardless of whether the objective is exalting a core, a periphery, or attempting a game of equilibrium, the goal remains the same: to present a nationalistic identity as the organizers (elites) see it and in such a manner that the demonstration accomplished the elite's desired outcome(s) for the ceremonies. Regardless of whether the objectification is in favor of the core or the periphery, it is still conducted under the same premise that elites are directing these processes in order to fulfill their specific goals. In using the term "elite," it is necessary to make two distinctions while discussing a host with internal cleavages. In a state in which we have two or more competing definitions of identity to describe the population, there are elites within the core and also within the periphery. By stating "elite," it should be assumed that the term references the elites in control of the organizing committee of the games (OCOG)

While the concept of an elite-driven presentation remains consistent in the following chapters, a distinction on their structure must be made. It will become apparent that these examples will possess traits found in other manifestations, particularly in their attempts to alter a mythology in a manner so as to adopt consideration for the elements of society under discussion in these strategies. However, the process of attaining these goals is different if the identity being demonstrated is solely a core identity, is a core and a peripheral identity together, or if it is solely a peripheral identity. Therefore, chapters 8 and 9 focus on the processes and objectives that are contingent upon the societal structure of the identity being demonstrated.

Chapters 8 and 9, therefore, are structured, not in terms of the process through which the manifestation is accomplished but instead into the type of identity being presented. Core, regional, and peripheral identities ultimately function as the same base concept but with different parameters—typically geographic—that help to establish the extent of the identity. Bear in mind that there is a distinct difference between a state cleaved along geographic lines and a state cleaved along racial or ethnic lines. The state formed with a geographic construction of identity separates its inhabitants into those pertaining to a core group and one or more peripheral groups. Unlike a racial and ethnic cleavage, the core and periphery or regional identity distinction supposes a coincidence between cultural and geographic boundaries.

The use of geographic differentiation does not preclude identity traits such as ethnicity. Often, a core and peripheral cleavage has racial or ethnic attributes. These traits are even more apparent in the difference between core and peripheral identities when a region possesses within it a community that claims their identity is different from the rest of the state. These differences often become the foundation for secessionist or irredentist movements.

State borders are rarely drawn to group together all people of one racial, ethnic, or cultural community. Native and immigrant cleavages also deal with a core/periphery argument, but in tandem with racial and ethnic issues, require separate consideration. While these two concepts are merged into one manifestation, readers should understand that some states, as part of their national myth, have included multiple diversities but have continually failed to include a native culture in its definition of an authentic national. It is also worth noting that native and immigrant displays can often include regional setups, racial distinctions or religious differences, all of which are represented in this group of strategies.

While the following sections will draw a few distinctions between identity cleavages that are based on a core-periphery divide and those that are a divide based on ethnic or racial differences or native and immigrant differences, their treatment in cultural performance will remain largely the same. They will be demonstrated through the same three processes. Divesting these concepts of their traits and complications, they all involve a balance between degrees of presentation of a core and a periphery, regardless of the traits that divide the periphery from the core. In that relationship, three options exist for the actor: exalt the core, exalt the periphery, or consider them equally. This leaves us with three different ways of demonstrating identities within an ethnically or geographically cleaved state all three of which are defined in terms of the goals of the designer and the challenges for these organizers.

Where, in previous chapters these options assumed a singular (or static) definition of identity and therefore constructed strategy on that premise, the following chapters consider actors that had not only strategy of presentation but a politicized strategy of competing identities as well. The next two chapters will maintain the methodology of this study through the emphasis of the actors' goals in handling the traits and cleavages pertinent to the aforementioned manifestation. However, the emphasis is now on structural concerns within the concept of the identity and not on the processes by which elites attain their nationalistic objectives through demonstration. Therefore, the specific elements of the national identity are not the focus of these chapters, but instead the framework around which these elements are established. Through the identification of these two types of presentations, this study provides an expanded opportunity for analysis and understanding of the unique roles peripheralization plays in the performance of nationalism in the Olympics.

Displays involving the contrast between a core and a periphery, regardless of the trait(s) involved, all seek to establish a power relationship between the two or more identities present in such a performance. This relationship manifests itself in one of three ways: a conscious attempt to supplant the core with the periphery, the periphery with the core, or an attempt at a compromise that depicts both with a degree of equality. Therefore, the demonstration of the two aforementioned manifestations can be designated as occurring in the following situations: one, where the demonstration of the core/national identity is crafted so as to replace the peripheral/regional and to bolster the "core" of the country over other identities; two, where the demonstration of a peripheral or regional identity is crafted so as to supplant the core/national identity; and three, where the demonstration of a peripheral/regional identity is crafted and demonstrated along side of a core/national identity.

The first two processes are significantly more common than the third, a fact that is predominantly a result of practical concerns. Because there is a limited amount of time, in either the opening or the closing ceremonies, for a demonstration of identity, performance of multiple identities with any degree of detail in the displays is rendered nearly impossible. Furthermore, it should be noted that type three does not include the redefinition of a core to encompass a regional or peripheral identity. Because we are dealing with a balance between two "distinct" groups, there exists the potential for a balance between them.

The third option indicates a situation in which the national and the regional identities are shown in parallel, but are not combined. The idea here is to demonstrate that the host-society is stratified and therefore possesses two or more concepts of the same identity, with the "periphery" usually separated from the core by a weak sense of regionalism that is geographically defined. As part of this dichotomy, the regional identity may have its own "cultural flare" to help define it as a specific entity within the core. The definition within the core is the key element in this concept. A demonstration that shows a redefinition of the core to encompass both the core and the regional is an assertion of the core. Therefore, it is conducted by the same rules of the core and will not have separate consideration in this study.

The structure of a core versus periphery cleavage in society offers a structural and procedural understanding of the identities discussed in the following chapters. Briefly, let us examine two methods in which this "division" can be defined. By understanding the nature of this structural division, one can more easily understand later discussions on cultural performance in the Atlanta, Barcelona, Calgary, and Sydney examples. The two most common division of this are accomplished with geographic or demographic definitions.

The geographical distinction is used mostly by states whose boundaries were drawn in such a manner so as to include culturally distinct regions. Non-core cultural groups may even spill into neighboring states. Indeed, as Lewis and Wigen's (1997) asserted, the geographic breakup of the globe is quite artificial. Based off of a practical need to carve the world into manageable pieces for the purpose of analysis, discussion and administration, elites have often employed nationalism to incorporate these political and administrative boundaries into their definitions. The regional strategy can either bolster existing notions or attempt to strike them down, replacing them with alternative geo-political definitions of the state. Whichever is the final result, articulations of national identity start with the state's current demarcation as the starting point.

Continuing with Lewis and Wigen (1997), the typical first step starts with a geographically bounded definition of the "identity." This physical construction constrains a national identity Anthony King (1997) also emphasized the problems of geography on nationalism. He explained that most cultural studies are flawed simply because of the use of the nation-state framework (King 1997: 9-10).

Stuart Hall (1997b) used Gramsci's notion of the war of positions to establish the basis of a process of countering assertions of a core identity. Identity through difference, as Hall (1997b: 57) puts it, "is the politics of recognizing that all of us are composed of multiple social identities, not of one." Demonstration of peripheral identity in the Olympics can take one of two forms. First, it can be a process of directly asserting a regional/peripheral identity as a subset within a particular national identity. This of course assumes compatibility of both identities. Second, it can be a war of position in the Gramscian sense (Gramsci 1971: 238-239).

The war of position is a long engagement in which the ideological battle is fought among the institutions of civil society. This is, therefore, a process of ideological indoctrination on the part of the periphery, against the core. Olympic performance, especially in the Barcelona and Atlanta examples, can be seen as depicting the process of supplanting one culture with another in a kind of war of position. This is all tied to Gramsci's understanding of hegemony which is, in Hall's (1997b: 58) words, "not the disappearance or destruction of difference. It is the construction of a collective will through difference."

We should consider the opposite manifestation, that of exalting the core over the periphery. The manifestations of historical revision and creation, indoctrination of ideology, and custodians of culture, are compatible with any type of identity, including core/national and regional/peripheral. Those manifestations were described with the assumption that we were talking about a national identity.

Note the difference between incorporating the periphery into an existing national identity and creating a new national identity. The difference between these two manifestations is that the incorporation of the periphery is not a homogenization of multiple identities into one new display; such a demonstration would be solely an effort at historical revision or creation. The demonstration of a national identity along side a peripheral identity would imply an effort at appeasement, on behalf of the core, as opposed to a process of redefinition.

The degree of presentation of elements of a national or regional identity is a complicated problem. Assuming that we are not seeking an equalization, then either the core or the periphery will be de-emphasized during the formal demonstration of an identity. This is much more of a problem for the periphery than it is for the core. Olympic protocol privileges states, which means that the national identity is already being given a degree of prominence. Thus, elites seeking to bolster the periphery at the Olympics have to carefully limit the degree of symbolic presentation of the core or national identity.

The demographic distinction has elements that are quite similar to the previous one just discussed. However, it requires separate attention in this study because of how this topic is treated in the Olympics. Certainly, racial, and ethnic cleavages and disparities between native and immigrant groups can be discussed in terms of peripheralized groups. However, in its treatment in nationalism and the Olympics there are two specific facts that necessitate separate treatment. Racial and ethnic cleavages can exist within the core or within the periphery, and the "national" definition of a society can be multi-racial or multi-ethnic. Anthony Marx's (1996: ch. 7, 10) discussion of Brazil offers an example of the process of integration of racial identities into the Brazilian national identity and David Guss' (2000: ch. 2) study of multi-ethnic celebrations of identity in the "Selling of San Juan" demonstrates the process of multi-ethnic indoctrination. The opposite is true, in which one ethnic or racial identity is established as "national" and others are peripheral-ized. Examples of this can be found in Danforth's (1997: 144) study of the Macedonian constitution and in White Anglo-Saxon Protestant definitions of America (e.g., Steinberg 1981: ch. 2).

The core, periphery and regional strategy, unless it is trying to indicate a unification of national identity, always demonstrates a power relation be-tween either competing elites or elites and the masses. In a racial or ethnic basis for cleavage, "the impetus for the construction of hegemony by moti-vating the dominant to incorporate ideologically the discourses, beliefs, or traditions of the subordinate" (Guerra 1998: 12) is the basis for partial or total assimilation of the subordinate identity into and beneath identity in power. Identity demonstrations based on a racial, ethnic, or native and im-migrant cleavage are always power relationships between elites and their subordinates.

Power relations between elites, or between elites and subordinates, exist whether or not there is a racial/ethnic or native/immigrant dynamic to the core versus periphery setup. They are treated slightly differently in this study because of a problem that racial/ethnic or native/immigrant demonstrations have when conducted on an international level. First, racial, ethnic, native or immigrant conceptions of identity are just as artificial as the geographic ones that were explained in the previous section. While this is true, the organizers have to remain cognizant of audience perceptions, however inaccurate they may be. Part of the difficulty of incorporating racial or ethnic identities within a demonstration is that these attributes are often times viewed as tran-scending state boundaries. Therefore, even though they are artificially con-structed, audience members maintain their own views about these identities in terms of their meaning and in their placement within the *us* vs. *them* dy-namic. Since this study is of an international event, that very fact requires the separation of this manifestation from the previous one. For there to be an immigrant culture within a state, there must have been an identity elsewhere in the world that was its source. Furthermore, there must not have been enough time for that transplanted culture to be indoctrinated into the national identity of their new home. In terms of demonstration of an immigrant cul-ture, a new challenge exists for the organizer conducting this demonstration on an international level.

Having delineated these two categories and defined the terms and elements of them, we are now at a point where we can discuss identification of these processes and differentiation from the strategies previously discussed. First of all, it should be stated that the three processes mentioned in chapters four, five, and six are all feasible manifestations in a core, periphery and regional presentation. In fact, the process of performing any of the three types listed above requires the use of the strategies of the aforementioned chapters. This is because the core/periphery and regional processes simply, but decisively, involves two levels of "us" vs. "them" objectification while the previous demonstrations only required one. The first three manifestations discussed in this study indicate how a single identity is established cognizant of the "us vs. them" dynamic. This process pays special attention to the intricacies necessary in handling two or more identities within a single national identity. As a result, performance of identity(s) in the forthcoming chapters requires a careful balancing of core/national vs. periphery/regional so as not to disrupt the wider perspective inherent in international display.

Objectifiers seeking to perform a peripheral or regional identity are as bounded by the theories of Barth and Eriksen as those performing a national identity. Thus there are two levels of "us" vs. "them" that the actor must consider. "Us" in this instance, is defined as the peripheral/regional identity, while "they" is defined first as the rest of the world, against which the nation is compared, and second as the national identity, from which the peripheral or regional identity seeks distinction. The opposite is also true. A core identity can be established against a global "them" and a peripheral "them."

Because there will always be at least two levels of "them" when issues of peripheralized groups are present, the objectifier is presented with an interesting, and highly pertinent, challenge. The protocol of the Olympic movement dictates specific duties and observations granted to the national government. Therefore, the peripheral/regional objectifier is tasked with adequately representing the national in its ceremonies while still bolstering the uniqueness and the primacy of the peripheral/regional identity. The national identity is often promoted within a country due to elite-controlled state policy. Thus, the various elements of a national identity are more likely to be recognized by the entire community. The peripheral or regional identity, however, may only be understood within the (small) community, which claims that identity. Therefore, indoctrination of ideology, custodianship of culture, and historical revisioning, which would focus on revising the regional identity to either appear as an alternative to of or as a facet within the national identity are all likely strategies of objectifiers using the core, periphery and regional processes.

Chapter 8 will look at the process of utilizing these tools to exalt the core. By focusing on examples from the Moscow, Sarajevo, and Sydney games, the chapter identifies three subsets to exalting the core and theorizes the subtle differences inherent in the goals of each of these cultural displays. By either diminishing or incorporating peripheral identities, hosts are able to create the illusion of a national identity that is unified and singular in appearance. Chapter 9, on the other hand, looks at cultural displays in which the aim was to diminish the core in favor of a peripheral or regional identity. In the Atlanta, Calgary, and Barcelona examples, sub-national identity is augmented to have equal status compared to its American and Spanish counterparts. The outcome of said demonstration is a full dismissal of notions of a unified national state identity in favor of a multi-regional identity—the Atlanta example—and a compelling argument for the distinctness of a Catalan identity within Europe, instead of within Spain—the Barcelona example. Calgary provides an example in which a regional identity can be tied to a representation of the region's cultural dichotomy encompassing both native and immigrant cultures.

CHAPTER 8
EXALTING THE CORE

I. THE CENTER EXALTED!

Exalting the center represents a deliberate attempt by state-level elites to perform their regime's concept of a national identity. The process results in either a redefinition or a reassertion of the organizing elite's authority, and in most cases also responds to peripheral identities within the society. As a result of this dichotomy, we can identity three possible paths of core exaltation: periphery dissection, core reassessment, and core isolation.

Periphery dissection represents an attempt to dismantle the periphery's identity and incorporate select traits of the periphery that seem useful to the actors conducting the dissection. The process indicates how an elite based on the center may attempt to subordinate a peripheral identity to one they sponsor—one focused on the core. Not all cultural traits associated with the periphery will be incorporated into the core's self-definition. Periphery dissection, if successful, would result in a fractured peripheral identity that lacked key elements and therefore would be less likely to successfully challenge the core. The process and outcomes of dissection can be compared to Hall's (1997a) theory concerning the suppression of local identities by a global identity. In this process, the periphery is torn apart to bolster a state-sponsored core identity. This is best illustrated by excerpting "token" elements from peripheral societies in a process of placation. Indoctrination then sells the "multi-cultural" core to these peripheralized subjects. Regardless of the presence of peripheral elements, this demonstration focuses on the core. Non-core elements are handled strictly by elites in charge of the display and are defined to meet their particular goals. Elites peripheral to the core identity of the host, if presented, are presented under terms determined by the elites in charge of the display. The Moscow, Sarajevo, and Sydney games are all examples of this structuring of decision processes.

Beyond incidental incorporations, core reassessment involves a concerted effort to redefine a centralized identity. In tandem with the historical revision and creation strategy, this should involve a genuine attempt to reconcile peripheries with the center, resulting in a new national (core-centered) definition. Obviously, this process is conducted by the existing core's elites. In effect, the center is publicly displaying its willingness to embrace its periphery, and hence, peripheral elites into their fold, albeit with a subservient status. While it involves a greater incorporation of the periphery than periphery dissection, it has the same underlying result: maintaining old-core elite authority in a new core identity. An example of this attempt to integrate a peripheral group is found in Anthony Marx's (1996) analysis of the incorporation of racial identities into a coherent Brazilian identity. He noted that Afro-Brazilian culture was "inescapably absorbed into the impressive project of Brazilian nation building" (*Ibid.,* 175) through state-sponsored social structures (Marx 1996: 159).

In subsidiary goals of periphery dissection and core reassessment, the national identity is always on display, and its presentation is under the control of the ruling elite. However, both of these objectives for the periphery are present only at the behest of the core elite, who interprets them with or without advisement from the periphery, at the core elite's discretion. As the first manifestation involves bolstering the core against the periphery, the presence of a periphery must be affirmed and its identity defined in juxtaposition to the core. The second goal, as a reassessment of the core, by its nature must present those elements of the periphery that are to be incorporated or reconciled.

The extent of the periphery's presence in the first two pathways depends entirely on the objectifier's need for peripheral traits. Implicit in these two pathways is the necessity not only for peripheral cultural traits, but also a need for an agreement with peripheral elites. Furthermore, as the former represents the periphery's relative decline and the latter its incorporation, the first goal will logically present fewer elements of the periphery than the second. It is also worth noting that core reassessment tends to present the periphery closer to the periphery's self-definition as the nature of this process is to conduct a faithful presentation of the periphery.

This leaves us with the third subsidiary method of core exaltation. In core isolation, the state feels a need to be unified along cultural lines. Under these circumstances, central elites feel no obligation, or have no desire to, contend with a peripheral identity. However, it is also possible that a peripheral or regional identity is simply ignored. In short, this process involves a deliberate portrayal of the state as a culturally homogeneous entity. Peripheral elements are not only diminished, they are completely absent from the display. Core isolation results from the elite's view of the irrelevance of the periphery, or from elite concerns that incorporation of any portion of the periphery could destabilize their authority.

The Moscow and Sarajevo games provide the best evidence of periphery dissection. Their ceremonies will be shown as mindful, even fearful, of the peripheral elements of their society. The Sydney games provide most of the evidence for core reassessment, as reconciliation between Australia's core and periphery was a main feature of the performance.

II. THE PERIPHERY DIMINISHED

The marginalization of the periphery is distinct from all other manifestations of nationalism in the Olympics as it deliberately depicts specific nationalistic traits as either minimized or subjugated. The Moscow Olympics offer a very clear and decisive demonstration of the primacy of the Socialist world over local and state nationalities. Therefore its opening and closing ceremonies provide excellent source material to demonstrate periphery dissection. The Moscow opening ceremonies were an impressive display of Soviet precision and athletic prowess. A sense of the goals of the opening ceremonies can be based on the type of specialists hired to coordinate the ceremonies by OCOG-80, the Organizing Committee of the Moscow Games. In addition to a Chief Artiste, they appointed a Director of the Sports Section, Conductor, Choirmaster, and Chief Ballet-Master (OCOG-80 1981: 280).

The opening ceremonies emphasized the Soviet Union's ability to run a "tight ship." Throughout the final report, the ceremonies are lauded for their precision, exactness, timeliness, and accuracy to Olympic protocol, repeatedly emphasizing a sense of Moscow's success and praiseworthy accomplishments (OCOG-80 1981: 307). Interestingly enough, Moscow, and therefore its controlling elite, was presented as the literal center of the Soviet Union and its various peoples and cultures. The only cultural displays in the entire ceremony involved performers in the various national costumes of the fifteen Soviet Socialist Republics. While politically Moscow can be seen as the "center" of the USSR, culturally, the elite could have presented Soviet identity as a pure center, as a facet of many identities, or instead focused on the concepts of identity within each republic, including Russian as an element of the local identity for Moscow.

The minimal "cultural" demonstration in the opening and closing ceremonies was symbolic in its depiction of the incorporation of these various cultural heritages as falling within the Soviet ideology. Gymnasts, athletes, and other physical-artistic performers first entered and formed a large solar disk. After this, youths in national costumes from each of the fifteen Soviet Socialist Republics ran towards the disk, forming sunrays. Athleticism, prowess, and structure formed the center of the Soviet Union and its multiple subsidiary cultures, represented the incorporation of the fifteen republics. This artistic display suggests the Soviet Union's selection of specific national identities within the republics to become, as Valery Tishkov (1992: 42) states, titular nationalities. Thus, the Soviet system, which is demonstrated neatly through the Moscow opening ceremony, is represented as the successful integration of the republics under guidance of the Soviet elites. Further, the Soviet system, exalting the definition of the core at all levels of the society, ties "official ideology and politics of ethno-nationalism ... with ethnic groups forming pseudo-federal administrative units or republics" (*Ibid.*).

The process of integration is repeated elsewhere in the opening and closing ceremonies. In particular, the construction of human vases on the field by athletic performers during the Moscow ceremonies can be interpreted as symbolizing Soviet structure and athleticism containing the diverse cultures of the soviet-controlled areas. This type of demonstration also typified the motto of the Moscow Games: "Sport, Peace, Progress."

A second significant moment in the opening ceremonies was the "Friendship of the Peoples Dance Suite." This segment involved performers in national dress alternating control of the field in a series of ethno-national dances. The "Friendship of Peoples Dance Suite" was a symbolic display of the peaceful interplay of nationalities within the Soviet Union (OCOG-80 1980). The necessary coordination and cooperation between the performers representing these national groups symbolized the "peace" among national identities that the Soviet Union claimed. Behind the performance, athletes in the eastern stands used shirts, flags, panels, and caps to create 174 colored mosaics (OCOG-80 1981: 297). The final report omits the symbolism of these designs, but the colors and patterns appear to reflect the costumes of the performers.

The cauldron lighting ceremony provides a third, and final, example of Periphery Dissection. Socialist state ideology supports a collective support of the socio-economic system. Individuality and individual efforts must be combined for the good of the whole and of the state. This idea is best typified by the cauldron-lighting ceremony. After the torch was brought into the stadium, some of the athletes on the eastern side of the arena lifted "planks" above their heads. These planks formed a pathway connecting the field to the base of the cauldron. In a very symbolic moment, the torchbearer approached the cauldron atop a metal platform that was supported by the soviet people.

Earlier, the work of Valery Tishkov (1992) helped explain Soviet consolidation of the fifteen republics through the selection of specific identities within each republic for official identities of that republic. The result of this process was a deliberate demonstration of official state-sponsored identities, both on their own and in cooperation with each other. As this system was centralized, control of it was in Moscow and not in the republics. The core was therefore presented as its own identity, containing specific elements (namely dress and folk dance) of the peripheries subjugated under Soviet control.

A very similar, but more limited, demonstration of periphery dissection occurred during the Sarajevo winter Olympics. The Sarajevo organizers were obviously influenced by the success and popularity of the Moscow precision demonstrations. The presence of these precision demonstrations is also indicative of a culture of conformity, which is a common attribute of socialist states. However, whereas the technical aspects of the Moscow opening ceremonies were repeated in Sarajevo, the Sarajevo organizers limited the multi-cultural displays. Moscow's multicultural display was ultimately brought under the Soviet Star, depicted through a starburst pattern on the field. Yugoslavia's display essentially sought the same outcome, but divested the pageantry of overt ethnic connotations.

The Yugoslav organizers were actively pursuing two goals through asserting their core: first, the establishment of the authority of Yugoslavia above the republics, autonomous regions, and other ethnic minorities; and second, a further diminishment of the sense of regionalism and ethnic cleavages. This was generally established through the futuristic costumes worn by performers, which reminded the audience that Yugoslavia's strengths lay in its future (Organizing Committee of the Fourteenth Olympic Winter Games, 1984b). Part of this is likely a symptom of Yugoslavia's legacy of a very frail sense of its own "Yugoslav" identity.

Although Susan Woodward (1995: 21-22) chastises many political scientists and historians for concluding that Yugoslavia's disintegration was the direct result of the presence of many autonomy-seeking or separatist nationalist groups, this may represent an oversimplification. She notes the efforts taken to establish economic, security, and trade equilibrium within Yugoslavia (*Ibid*, 21-26). But she also effectively underscores the very limited efforts that the Yugoslav government made towards establishment a single cohesive sense of national identity (*Ibid*, 30). Yugoslavia's history in the post-World War II period provides an example of poor pan-ethnic identity formation.[1] In fact, "the peoples of Yugoslavia had rights as founding nations of the member states of the federation (the republics) and also as individual members of those nations (ethnic peoples) to express their nationality and culture freely and without discrimination" (Danforth 1997: 53).

Woodward (1995: 31) asserts that "for Yugoslavs faced with national assertiveness in the late 1980s, the concept of sovereignty needed revision to reflect their reality of a layering of partial sovereignties and shared rights to self-governance." Thus, the Yugoslav system of socialist self-management never fully developed a discernable sense of Yugoslavian pan-national identity or a stable position of each ethnic within the post-Tito Yugoslav state (Flere 1992: 263-264). The 1984 winter Olympics occurred in an atmosphere of anti-nationalist rhetoric within this tumultuous period four years after Tito's death. Therefore, it makes sense that Sarajevo's exaltation of the core was as devoid of ethnic presentation as possible; including Sarajevo's republic of modern-day Bosnia and Herzegovina.

The delicate balance required by a demonstration of Yugoslavia's core forced the Sarajevo organizers to imitate Moscow's example of precision rather than its incorporation of multi-cultural ethnicities. Because of this, the main features of the pageantry segment of the opening ceremonies involved performers in brightly colored dress dancing in a series of geometric shapes. The colors were taken from the Olympic rings, with purple in place of black. Unlike the Moscow display, which featured ethnic patterns, the Sarajevo demonstration was almost completely devoid of cultural connotations. Commentators did note that a few of the geometric shapes were taken from designs often knitted into sweaters and other local dress, but further noted that these patterns were popular due to their aesthetic quality and not for any connection to an ethnic heritage (Organizing Committee of the XIV Olympic Winter Games 1984). In fact, commentators during the broadcast lauded the precision, unity and conformity of the opening ceremonies (*Ibid.*).

The Kollo dance was one of the few clearly ethnically driven elements in the Sarajevo opening ceremonies. This native dance, which originated in Serbia, is actually performed in several Slavic societies (Organizing Committee of the XIV Olympic Winter Games 1984). Significantly, however, the dance was modernized and performed with modern music—even music from cultures outside of Yugoslavia. Those commenting on the opening ceremonies noted that the use of this pan-Slavic dance, with modern steps and music, was an effort to suggest Yugoslavian unity (*Ibid.*). The Yugoslavian organizers' focus on the future was also noted as the purpose behind modernizing the Kollo and other elements of the pageant (*Ibid.*).

Beyond the actual pageantry, the trends of anti-nationalist and pro-modernist demonstrations were found throughout the ceremony. Notably, placard bearers in the parade of nations, guards in the stands, and some performers in the pageant were dressed in futuristic solid-white costumes that had no connection to any ethnic or national tradition in Balkans. However, the entrance of the Olympic flag was escorted by a procession of Yugoslavs dressed in the traditional costumes of the different ethnic groups in Yugoslavia. The flag bearers themselves, however, wore aforementioned white costumes, further diminishing the role of the state identity in the games.

Both the Olympic flag and the torch-lighting ceremonies were devoid of powerful displays of ethnicity and nationalism. In spite of the token presentation of traditional dress escorting the Olympic flag, the flag was still handled and raised by performers in white costumes. Yugoslavia's torch-bearer ascended the stairs to the cauldron while stripes of black, blue, green, red, and yellow followed him, covering the stairs upon which he had traversed. Even in the most important symbolic moments of the opening ceremonies, Yugoslav organizers focused exclusively on its efficiency, unity, and continuity.

These trends continued to the end of the games. As previously mentioned, the closing ceremonies contained only one moment of cultural distinction—the Kollo dance performed by young female ice-skaters. The girls from Sarajevo and Zagreb represented the limit of ethnic or nationalistic displays at the closing ceremonies (Organizing Committee of the XIV Olympic Winter Games 1984b). Further, the ceremonies were only very limitedly commented on in the final report; there was not a section devoted strictly to the ceremonies (Organizing Committee of the XIVth Winter Olympic Games 1984c).

Whereas Moscow sought to exalt its core by depicting "official" ethnic groups within the concept of the Soviet Union, Yugoslavia exalted its core in a more neutral, systematized way. The Soviet Union allowed multiple ethnic minorities to express their identity through dance in the opening and closing ceremonies, but only through a specific structure delineated by the Soviet organizers. Yugoslavia, on the other hand, maintained the demonstrations of socialist unity, precision, and accomplishment, but did not allow significant expression of the subservient nationalisms.

Depictions of regional identity, specifically the six republics and two autonomous regions, occurred through ethnic dress and cultural dances. However, unlike the Soviet demonstration, these displays occurred in only one segment in which all Yugoslav ethnic cleavages were shown in one large group. Second, the Yugoslav demonstration clearly modernized older identities by incorporating modern dress and dance/music styles into the performance.

In both the Moscow and Sarajevo examples, the regional and the peripheral identities were afforded minimal roles. Nevertheless, they were still shown as facets of the society, albeit lesser in importance than the Soviet national identity or Yugoslav socio-political unit. The former represents a concerted effort at showing the concept of Soviet, instead of the concept of Russian, Kazakh, Azeri, or any of the other ethnicity, while the latter demonstrates an effort at display of a unified state, whose regional identities were the historical antecedents and baggage of, but not the definition of, modern Yugoslav identity. The latter still represents an exaltation of the core as part of a Yugoslav policy of the 1970s and 1980s that abandoned the process of definition of a national Yugoslav identity in lieu of defining its internal stabilities. In short, since the creation of a national Yugoslav identity had failed to strengthen the state, a definition of stability, uniformity, and modernity became the path to maintenance of power by the elites.

III. THE PERIPHERY INCORPORATED

Core reassessment clearly differs from the de-emphasized expressions of the periphery depicted in Moscow and Sarajevo. This second path prefers faithful reproductions of the periphery as part of the core. The Sydney Olympics provides an effective example of this process of merging the periphery into the core. At these games, aboriginal society was assimilated into the broader concept of Australian identity

It should come as no surprise to the reader that the quintessential example of core reassessment is the Sydney Olympics. Reassessment of the core asserts two observations: first, the redefinition of the core through the incorporation of at least some elements of the periphery; and second, a reassertion of the remaining elements of the original core. Therefore, a creationist element naturally exists in this process. The Sydney opening ceremonies were shown as an almost perfect example of historical creationism. The ceremonies unfolded as a deliberate attempt to merge Aussie/Western culture, Aboriginal culture, and immigrant societies into one sweeping demonstration of the Australian spirit. This new identity was embodied in the presentation of these various groups standing together in the outline of the Australian continent. This chapter examines the fragments of the unified whole, how these three elements of Australia were displayed as separate from each other. The purpose of which was to attain the overall goal of a reinterpreted sense of Aussieness. According to the final report, the true success of the opening ceremonies lay in how it "offer[ed] a series of seemingly contradictory approaches to the texture of Australian and [made] them blend palatably" (SOCOG 2001c: 53). The very heart of core-periphery assimilation is a successful and equitable representation (reconciliation) of the "seemingly contradictory" elements of a society.

We begin our analysis with the dream sequence. The whole progression began with the arrival of Nikki, a nine-year old Caucasian girl running onto the field and fell asleep. The dream sequence involved a series of segments: *Deep Sea Dreaming, Awakening, Tin Symphony, Arrivals, and Eternity.* The *Deep Sea Dreaming* segment starts with the establishment of Australia within its physical space: the Pacific Ocean. Nikki dreams of swimming in the ocean and among the reef. She swims through the air as sea life surrounds her, a stunning reminder of Australia's love of the sea, love of swimming, and status as a continental island-state. The segment is completely devoid of cultural icons as well as historic representations; instead it simply establishes the country's environmental and geographic location.

From this point forward, however, each segment represents a specific Australian community: *Awakening* illustrates the Aborigines, the *Tin Symphony* corresponds to the advent of colonization and British settlers, and *Arrivals* signifies the non-British (i.e., non-English, Scottish, Irish, or Welch) immigrant communities. Finally, the *Eternity* segment represents the new Australia formed out of the legacy of the continuing period of reconciliation in Australia.

The aptly named first segment, *Awakenings*, possesses several symbolic meanings. First, the title of the Aboriginal sequence harkens back to the importance of the current movement towards reconciliation within the Australian community. Furthermore, the sequence was intended to represent "the diversity yet unity of the Aboriginal peoples" (SOCOG 2001c: 55). The opening ceremonies were therefore not just an awakening of all of Australia and the world to the diversity of the Aboriginal people, but also were a symbol of the revitalization of these older traditions. Finally, the *Awakenings* segment references the constant revitalization of Australia through the unique role of fire within the country's history and geography. Australia's hinterland often burns in brushfires caused by lightning and/or severe drought, a process of revitalization of the land. According to the final report, Aborigines conducted slash and burn agriculture to encourage new growth and attract wildlife (SOCOG 2001c: 55). The Fire sub-segment culminated in a display of the natural beauty and wonder of Australia. The first two segments, Deep Sea Dreaming and *Awakening*, together symbolized a renewed awareness of the environment of Australia tied to the rich heritage of the Aboriginal people.

The Wandjina cloth, a depiction of an Aboriginal creation spirit, further reinforces the concepts of *Awakening*. *Awakening* merges the practical and mystical functions of fire in Aboriginal society, a depiction of the cultural and societal reconciliation of Aboriginal culture into the broader definition of Aussie civilization. Throughout each sub-segment of the Aborigine display, native dances, music, and traditions—such as the burning of Eucalyptus leaves (SOCOG 2001b)—accentuated symbols of rebirth and reconciliation as a constant procession of Aboriginal culture. Therefore, the process simultaneously represented two ideas: Aboriginal identity and reconciliation or rebirth.

The *Tin Symphony*, which depicted Australian settlers through recalling the industrial technology of British colonialists, was titled to emphasize the metallic nature of the performance. As Aboriginal customary practices relied heavily on Australian natural resources, depicting the northern European settlers through the use of metal provides two important statements. First, it declares the settlers as culturally different from the Aborigines, and second, it demonstrates the legacy of the settlers and explorers to the history of Australia.

The *Tin Symphony* represented the energy, ingenuity, and spirit that drove the settlement period. Relying heavily on mechanization and corrugated iron, the segment depicted life in settlement Australia, including sheep sheering, timber cutting, and the birth of gold-rush towns. In addition to life within the settlements, the principle of exploration was established through bicycles, telescopes, and explorers sketching the "new" terrain and its features. The settlement and explorers sub-segment was embodied principally in the presentation of several bicycles that together represented Captain Cook's ship (SOCOG 2001b). Therefore, the *Tin Symphony* represents the spirit, vitality, irreverence (SOCOG 2001c: 56) and contributions of the colonial period to modern Australia. The *Tin Symphony* refused to take itself too seriously, an appealing quality referred to in the final report as *larrikinism*, "a distinctively Australian sense of irreverence, wit, and mistrust of authority" (SOCOG 2001c: 56). The segment ended with an odd ballet of lawnmowers, bringing the tin symphony from the early days of colonialism through to Australian independence and modern suburban life.

After the *Tin Symphony*, the pageantry of the Sydney opening ceremonies turned to its other immigrant communities. The *Arrivals* segment depicted the multi-cultural tapestry that is a valid part of present-day Australia. This segment was simpler, since it involved procession of multiple identities rather than an ostentatious celebration of a single identity group. Five groups of people dressed in the five Olympic colors, but adorned with the accoutrements of dozens of immigrant identities, paraded across the stadium.

The *Arrivals* segment was conducted as a series of immigrant representatives, entering in by continental grouping: Africa, Asia, the Americas, Europe, and Oceania. Present within the groups were costumes and icons representing many ethnic, national, and religious groups currently present in Australia. The culminating event of the entire pageant occurred after the entrance of all of the performers in the *Arrivals* segment. The representatives of the immigrant communities, the settlers, and the Aborigines assembled to form the outline of the Australian continent. Moreover, both adults and children created this tapestry of human identity. In a symbolic gesture that reminded the Aussies and the world that Australia's display was not just a present creation but also a hope for the future, all adults left the field leaving the stage to the children of the country.

The final segment, *Eternity*, paid tribute to the workers of Australia: specifically the people responsible for the internal growth of infrastructure and cities. The main feature of the *Eternity* segment was the erection of a 30-meter high bridge by teams of tap dancers (SOCOG 2001c: 57). According to the final report, this was the "Bridge of Life, a walkway towards connection and Reconciliation" (*Ibid.*). Not only is the bridge a symbol of a journey to a new state, but it is also a symbol of reconciliation.

Bridges played important roles in both the opening ceremonies and in the broader Reconciliation movement. The Final report mentions that four months prior to the Games "250,000 Australians, of all backgrounds walked across the Sydney Harbor Bridge to symbolize unity of purpose in achieving Reconciliation" (SOCOG 2001c: 55). This event did not specifically relate to the Olympics, but was mentioned in the final report due to its relevance to the goals of the opening ceremonies. This reinforces the importance of the Reconciliation movement in the broader context of Australian history.

First, it should be noted that the Sydney organizers did not attempt to exhibit the core as more important than the two peripheries. All three demonstrations were equally impressive and, arguably, equally entertaining. Furthermore, the organizers did not place the former core identity in any position of prominence. The four segments follow a chronological pattern, which relegates the old concepts of "Aussie" identity, that of the pioneers and the bushwhackers, to the second segment.

An important difference between Sydney's display and the opening ceremonies at Moscow and Sarajevo is the absence of the old core from segments, which depicted peripheral identity. Soviet and Yugoslav identity was present in all aspects of the performance, not just those areas that paid direct homage to them. In the Sydney ceremonies, the only "Western-Aussie" presence in the Aboriginal and in the Immigrant segments was Nikki, who was present merely to observe the unfolding cultural history of Australia. By allowing each segment, and therefore each historically established cultural identity, its own period of direct prominence, the Sydney organizers were able to give the appearance of independence to each segment. This is important because it further emphasized the separation between different groups in Australia. This divergence then gives stronger and more symbolic meaning to the *Eternity* segment, during which these groups became divested of individual identity to form a coherent concept of a new Australian identity.

From the *Eternity* sequence, we can perceive two important elements in terms of our strategies. First, this clearly demonstrates an effort at creation. Granted, this definition evolved throughout the entire Reconciliation period; however, the specific demonstration at the Sydney Olympics (SOCOG 2001c: 55). Second, the establishment of the creationist strategy was deeply rooted in the core and periphery strategy, in which each periphery was faithfully demonstrated along with the core in a process of redefinition. Regardless of the unique differences between the Moscow, Sarajevo, and Sydney games, all three used essentially the same process: restricting the demonstration of one identity in favor of another. The Sarajevo games directly restricted what was allowed in the ceremonies while the Sydney games only limited the time allotted to each identity. Moscow, on the other hand, represents a combination of those two controlling techniques.

Thus, these two processes represent a concerted effort to nullify the objectification of a peripheral identity—the intentional dismissal of specific traits or identities from the presentation of the core. In contrast, Sarajevo represents the extreme example of this process, dismissing any sense of the identities that could conflict with Yugoslavia's decentralized style. Therefore, Sarajevo represents a deliberate exaggeration of the Moscow policy.

The three processes of core exaltation can be seen along the same spectrum, ranging from no display of non-core nationalisms to a process of core reassessment, as in the Australian games. Finally, Moscow and Sarajevo exist in the center of this spectrum. These three sub-goals promoted by the center are essentially different degrees of the same demonstration, handled in an identically in terms of process. Each establishes the core and then displays the exact amount of peripheral traits chosen by the objectifier. Core versus periphery demonstration can exist anywhere along a spectrum of none to all, time permitting. As a result, one final comparison can be made in terms of our other manifestations.

The third option displayed no presence of the periphery, and therefore the demonstration was conducted akin to the processes described in chapters four through six. Continuing with our analysis of this category as a continuum, then the first three manifestations of nationalism can *ipso facto* be presented within any exaltation of the core. Examples from Moscow, Sarajevo, and Sydney can all offer examples of the other strategies. For example, see the discussion of Sydney's *Eternity* sequence within the historical revision and creation strategy.

In short, we have identified that core vs. periphery displays, whether involving exaltation of the core or the periphery, function within the same rules as all other displays. They are therefore different only in requiring multiple levels of identity demonstration, and hence multiple incarnations of the Barthian "us vs. them" concept. In terms of the actual planning of the display, these performances require a careful balance of in order to navigate a multi-leveled nationalistic pageant. These balances, while different from example to example, all share the deliberate attempt by the organizers to maintain their position as the elite objectifiers of their society's identity. Regardless of how much or how little peripheral elements are displayed, the definition of the core will not be altered to challenge the elite's authority.

NOTES

1. The topic of Yugoslavia's disintegration is well documented, but Glenny (1993), Sekulic (1994), and Woodward (1995) are good sources for the state of identity in Yugoslavia before, during, and after their period of hosting the Olympics.

CHAPTER 9
THE FRINGE WITHOUT THE FLAG

National identities do not always take center stage at the Olympics. In many instances, a peripheral or regional identity may take on that role. The terms *periphery* and *regional* can often describe different concepts. Periphery indicates only that the country in question has a clear difference between its center (core) and its hinterland. The center—typically the location of the country's major cities and capital—has an identity, culture, and socioeconomic structure that is seen as different from the rest of the country. Regional identities may share the same connotations, characteristics, and treatment (by the core) as periphery; however, there is a pertinent difference. Regional concepts almost always are defined in terms of geography. Noting that regionalism glorifies supposedly geographical differences is an oversimplification.

For example, consider Dixie as a regional identity and the primary focus of cultural elements of the Atlanta Olympics. For this study, the term Dixie refers roughly to the geographic area east of the Mississippi River, south of the Mason-Dixon Line, and excluding the states of Maryland and Florida. As a historically conceptualized geographic region, Dixie includes the states of Alabama, Arkansas, Georgia, Louisiana, Mississippi, North Carolina, South Carolina, Tennessee, and Virginia. In some definitions of Dixie, Florida Kentucky, and Texas are included.

As this study posits that Dixie is defined in historical, cultural, and geographic terms, it makes sense to omit Florida, Kentucky, and Texas from the list as they are not as deeply rooted in the traditions and legacy of the Antebellum South. Research by John Shelton Reed (1976), later extended by

Christopher Cooper and H. Gibbs Knotts (Cooper 2010) provide sociological analysis and backing to establish Dixie as encompassing these states. Their analysis, however, is rooted in cultural distinctions within the region of Dixie while dismissing a use of geography as ipso-facto establishing its range (*Ibid.*, 1083–1089). The kind of geographical differentiation typically assumed in the Dixie case is not necessary; the concept can be drawn culturally without geographic/terrain distinctions.

Lewis and Wigen's defined the geographical breakup of the globe as nothing more than the practical division of the world into manageable units. The distinction between periphery and regional, therefore, rests in the fact that region must have either an actual or invented sense of its own geographical space, whereas periphery simply refers to those areas not considered "core" regardless of their physical location within the state. The fact that geographical connotations of identity are constructed does not dismiss the fact that topographical structure of a region, due to nature, can be either augmented or diminished by the objectifier.

In this chapter, geography will necessarily play a crucial role. A region is defined as a physically bounded area of land or water or both within which is an identity that is clearly distinct from the rest of the country. Periphery does not require a geographical definition, but instead will be defined as an area of a country, which is distinct from the core of the state. It may be differentiated on the basis of economic, phenotypical, ideological, historical, or other traits.

The second element constructs cleavages in terms of historical origins of the communities involved. Native vs. immigrant or immigrant versus immigrant comparisons are both based in historical discontinuity between communities. The Native/Immigrant strategy requires that the host have a legacy of colonialism that settled Europeans to a land previously occupied with an indigenous community. Furthermore, the process of colonization must have left enough vestiges of the native culture to allow a distinction to be drawn. The same temporal restriction remains true in terms of immigrant groups. To have an immigrant versus immigrant comparison, there has to have been a "first" wave—e.g., the settlers in the Australian example, and a later wave of immigration from different ethnic/national communities arriving. Lastly, these cleavages must also appear as persisting to the current members of the community for them to be the source of ethnic/cultural division.

While the potential types of identity and conflicts within them can move in multiple directions, certain common trends exist in a demonstration that diminishes the core in favor of a periphery or regional nationalism. Three specific Olympiads—Atlanta, Barcelona, and Calgary—will be used to illustrate how the organizer utilizes the core, periphery, and regional strategy and the racial, ethnic, and native/immigrant strategy. They will also be used to illustrate the traits common to demonstrations of these two strategies in the context of extolling peripheralized nationalism.

While several of the other ceremonies under review in this study have displayed concerted efforts at peripheral or regional displays, the Atlanta, Barcelona, and Calgary games are perfect examples of the second category. Thanks to the involvement of regional governments and non-central elites, all three involved carefully planned demonstrations of regional identity in lieu of depicting the national identities of the United States, Spain, and Canada respectively.

I. THE REGION TAKES CENTER STAGE

In the case of Atlanta, the organizers developed a very calculated plan of showing the world what it meant to be Southern. The Atlanta Opening ceremonies began with a summoning of the youth of the world, which was then followed by "a traditional Olympic ceremony that honors the national government of the host country" (Watkins 1997b: 69). From the very beginning, the Atlanta organizers drew distinctions between global, national, and regional identities. The global "summoning" was as un-cultural and non-specific as possible. Olympic colors, each representing a specific continent, represented the tribes of the world. They were dressed in complicated costumes that were groups of circles and spheres layered together. Each of the performers wore a gold mask, hiding his/her ethnic and racial origins.

The global demonstration portion of the opening ceremonies attempted to strip people of their ethnic/national identities. The music was an especially composed drum arrangement that, similarly, did not evoke any specific cultural traits. Similarly, the United States was afforded only the minimum recognition dictated by Olympic Protocol. Even during the Parade of Nations, American identity was reduced as much as possible. At the Los Angeles Opening Ceremonies, the American team entered to the sounds of "Stars and Stripes forever;" however, at the Atlanta Games, the American team entered to "Summon the Heroes," which was the Official Anthem of the 1996 Centennial Olympics. It was played to start the Parade of Nations and introduced as the culminating moment of the colorful, tribal sequence (Watkins 1997b: 58).

The American Sequence, "a traditional Olympic ceremony that honors the national government" (Watkins 1997b: 58) was simply protocol intended to recognize the federal government. This entailed the entrance of the president, a color guard, the national anthem, and a fly-over by F-16C Falcon aircraft. It was short, discrete, dignified, and acultural. From that point, the ceremonies moved into the celebration of Atlanta. The "national" (or federal) tribute ended with the start of Atlanta's official welcome, which involved an energetic sequence of cheerleaders, precision dancers, steppers, cloggers, and a marching band. The performers spelled out "Atlanta" and then "How Y'all Doin'!" The entrance of thirty chrome trucks followed this with spotlights mounted on the back. The final report of the Atlanta Summer Games refers to these trucks as "represent[ing] an important contemporary icon of the American South" (Watkins 1997b: 71).

The end of the welcoming sequence culminated with Gladys Knight's performance of "Georgia on My Mind," the official state anthem of Georgia. The example of the Georgia state anthem is an appropriate to note that the Southern display used modern presentations of the South, as opposed to older confederate icons. The battle hymns and anthems of the Confederacy were not the focus of the Atlanta games. The stars and bars, the official state flag of the Confederacy, was not presented during any element of the ceremonies. The purpose of these omissions was intended to paint a modern Southern identity, instead of a modern rendition of a slave-holding Confederate identity.

The state anthem was followed by the most important sequence of the Atlanta Ceremonies for this study: Summertime. The Final Report elaborates further on the organizers' goals when it recorded that the artistic segments of the Opening Ceremonies were intended to "convey the essence of southern culture and history to the world" (Watkins 1997b: 71). In other words, the organizers understood the opportunity to host the Olympics as an occasion to objectify Southern identity for the global audience assembled for the Games.[1]

Although chronological, it is also interesting to note that the concept of the South starts with an incontestable quality of this region: geography. Anthony King (1997a) argued that geography was an unnecessary element of identity, but does not entirely preclude it from identity formation. In fact, geographical constraints of identity are particularly effective at streamlining "us versus them" arguments. For the Atlanta Organizers, the Mississippi River formed a natural boundary that is also important for its symbolic roles in landmark fiction like Mark Twain's "Huckleberry Finn."

The first segment of Summertime was discussed in Chapter Four. The second segment, titled "The River," offers a geographical definition of the South by binding it to the Mississippi River; which is more of a symbolic definition than a literal geographic one as some traditional parts of the south lay to its west. During this segment, the audience was presented with a musical history of the region, which included classic waltz, Christian religious music, something akin to a hoe-down, and jazz. Specific songs included the Southern classics *When the Saints Go Marching In* and *Skip to My Loo My Darling*. The reprise of the Summertime Sequence, a jazzy version of Handel's Hallelujah Chorus and a much bigger version of *When the Saints Go Marching In* were performed later in the Opening Ceremonies.

Even the Thunderbird Sequence, presented in Chapter Four as an example of Historical Revisioning, contains important elements of regionalism. First, the final report refers to this segment as depicting the events that have "tested the South and southerners during the region's history" (Watkins 1997b: 72). Furthermore, there is even more compelling evidence within the artistry of the Thunderbird Sequence. The other Southern elements were depicted as very elegant, natural, and flowing; a metaphor for the simplicity and charm of the southern ideal. The Thunderbird, on the other hand, a metaphorical representation of the North, was very mechanical, dirty, and rigid; a reminder of the north's industrialization. This dichotomy symbolically emulated the Civil War—industrialization is associated with the North, while the South is associated with agricultural traditions and rural grace.[2] The Thunderbird's "invasion" into this Southern celebration further reinforces a line between the South and its Northern counterpart. The Opening Ceremonies moved into the formal proceedings after the Summertime Reprise and never returned to a strong national or regional display.

Regional display continued briefly during the Closing Ceremonies. The celebration began with the presentation of a large quilt symbolic of the Olympic Games and of the gathering of peoples of different colors, origins, and creeds. The Final Report referred to the quilt as a "historically rich and meaningful cultural expression of the American South" (Watkins 1997a: 268). All expressions of identity cease at the Closing ceremonies in favor of a series of songs and ceremonies that paid homage to the Olympic Movement and its spirit. The evening concluded with a Southern, New Orleans-style, funereal celebration of music, dance, and partying. This musical jamboree was stylistically limited to American genres rooted in Southern traditions.

Both ceremonies contained a carefully designed demonstration of Southern identity. The Final Report, combined with the footage of the Opening and the Closing Ceremonies, effectively ties together a quintessential example of regional demonstration on the Olympic stage. During these two events, the obligatory deference paid to the United States was carefully contained in a manner that reached no further than dictated protocol, and thus offered little to no representation of American identity.

From here, we turn to a study of the 1992 Barcelona Summer Olympics. In these games, the organizers were committed to carefully depicting Catalan national identity instead of a Spanish state-centered identity. First, the creation myth set the entire tenor for these Opening Ceremonies. The creation myth, particularly the extension of Barcelona from the Iberian Peninsula into the broader socio-cultural and geographic unit of the Mediterranean, offers a quintessential example of regional demonstration. By drawing the audience's attention to the Mediterranean Sea, Catalonia attempted to set itself apart from the rest of Spain. We should remember that the identity of

Spain—including geographic setting—was never established beyond necessary Olympic protocol. The Catalanization of the Opening Ceremonies even permeated the Olympic Protocol that honored the state.

Let us reconsider Atlanta, Los Angeles, and Sydney for their uses of geography. Atlanta offered a geographic demonstration of the "South" by using the Mississippi River to help divide this region from the rest of the United States. Incorporating a very clear environmentalist display in the Summertime sequence further indicated a geographically and ecologically distinct area of the rest of the country. On the other hand, Los Angeles's opening sequence concluded with performers forming an outline of the continental United States. This geographical symbol provided the audience with a representational image of *American* identity. Finally, the variety of cultures and Australia's distinct cores and peripheries were merged, in a manner similar to the Los Angeles display, to form the outline of Australia. Granted, the similarities in these two ceremonies are due to the involvement of creative genius of Ric Birch (2004) in both productions.

II. FORGING REGION INTO NATION?

Geographical distinctiveness, while a key part of establishing regional identity in the Olympics, was just a starting point for Catalan organizers. The Opening Ceremonies opened with both the Spanish and Catalan anthems. Catalan flags were omnipresent throughout the ceremony whenever the Spanish flag was on display. Even the entrance of the color guard, which included the flags of Spain, Catalonia, and Barcelona, had Catalan music as its backdrop. The Catalan organizers particularly excelled at incorporating Catalan identity into the protocol elements of the opening ceremonies. The juxtaposition of the Catalan anthem beside its Spanish counterpart was quite brazen. The symbolism was even more deeply embedded by the fact that the Catalan anthem, *Els Segadors*, accompanied the entrance of the King of Spain. In contrast, the Atlanta organizers presented both the United States' national anthem and the Georgia state anthem, but separated the two in terms of their placement in the opening ceremonies. The U.S. anthem was a part of the official protocol of the Opening Ceremonies. The Georgia state anthem, on the other hand, was embedded in a cultural tribute to the City of Atlanta.

An even more impressive moment came from the official opening of the Barcelona Summer Olympics when King Juan Carlos I, Spain's reigning monarch, declared the games of the XXVth Olympiad open. Usually a simple piece of protocol, when the head of state simply states: "I declare open the Games of . . . (name of the host city) . . . celebrating the . . . (number of the Olympiad) . . . Olympiad of the modern era" (IOC 2004: 107). However, King Juan Carlos I made the now historic declaration in the Catalan language, instead of Castillian (Spanish). Both the use of the Catalan anthem for the king's entrance and his historic use of the Catalan language to open the games were both highly symbolic moments that support claims of Catalan cultural independence—a claim with considerable political implications.

It is important to remember that the Catalan language was legalized only after Franco's death. The Franco dictatorship (1939-1975) banned this language, in addition to prohibiting the country's other regional languages, as part of his regime's oppression of autonomist and separatist inclinations. To suddenly have Franco's successor use the Catalan language while acting as the Spanish Head of State, who had earlier acted personally to put down a revolution and who was popular in his own right, was significant to the people of Barcelona, as evidenced by the eruption of cheers from the crowd as the monarch spoke (COOB'92 1992b). Additionally, there was a second major challenge to Olympic Protocol. There was an unsuccessful move to incorporate Catalonia in the Parade of Nations by allowing Catalan athletes to enter as the last country, led by their own flag. Hargreaves (2000) noted that Catalan nationals wanted the same rights afforded the independent states of the Unified Team, a desire staunchly opposed by the IOC.

By the time the Barcelona Games started, the Soviet Union had collapsed into fifteen independent states. Three of them, Estonia, Latvia, and Lithuania, gained IOC recognition quickly and were present with their own teams. The other twelve, however, did not have separate National Olympic Committees. Instead, they marched together as the "Unified Team," using the Olympic Flag as their team entered the stadium. The Olympic Flag and Hymn were used for any athlete that won a medal. Right behind the placard bearer and flag bearer, however, were flag bearers representing the 15 independent states, many of which were using new national flags[3].

Once this privilege was afforded to the former Soviet Republics, Angel Colom, head of the main Catalan separatist party, the Esquerre Republicana de Catalunya (Republican Left of Catalonia), wanted the same treatment for Spain and Catalonia—Catalan Athletes within a Unified Spanish Team, marching with their own flag, while all of Spain would use Olympic symbols for medal ceremonies and other "official" representation (Hargreaves 2000: 66). The request was denied by the IOC, since Spain entered as the final state in the Parade of Nations as a unified entity under the Spanish Flag.[4] While there was a very powerful local movement for recognizing a Catalan Olympic Committee, attempts on the part of Catalan independence movements failed to convince the IOC (Hargreaves 2000: 70-75, 140), thus limiting Catalonia to a non-official, but still a clearly recognizable, status—a status that did not include governmental authority.

While Catalonia could not use its national symbols where Olympic protocol dictated the use of national symbols, the Barcelona Organizers successfully inserted the concept of Catalan in several of these locations. Although

Catalonia and Spain could not hold a perfectly equal place in the games, there was a concerted effort to guarantee that Catalonia had the same privileges as Spain whenever possible. The following comparisons can be made about the displays of Catalonia and Spain:

1. Both polities were afforded a place in the Color Guard entrance.[5] His majesty, King Juan Carlos I, entered to the tune of the Catalan, and not the Spanish anthem.
2. Both the Catalan and Spanish languages were used in the Parade of Nations. Disagreement over which language would be used to alphabetically order the entering nations resulted in a compromise—using French instead of Spanish or Catalan. Therefore, four languages appeared on the placards: French and English, (the official languages of the Olympic Movement), Spanish (the host state's national language) and Catalan (the host city's official language).
3. Spain retained the honors afforded the host state, appearing last in the Parade of Nations, declaring the games open, etc. Catalonia was displayed in most of these events, mainly through the use of the Catalan Flag and language.

So far, we have discussed both the Catalan creation myth and the presence of Catalan identity in Olympic protocols for the Opening Ceremonies. The analysis now turns to the aspects of the pageant that involved artistic or cultural elements. The cultural segment began with a depiction of the Rambla de les Flors, "one of the most charismatic streets in the city" (Cuyas 1993b: 53). The use of this boulevard was an excellent choice because it allowed the organizers to literally parade Catalan culture around the stadium. A mix of bright colors, costumes, puppets, acrobatics, and musical instruments depicted Catalonia as a vibrant, passionate, and living culture. The sequence moved the performance into a spectacle of Catalan culture.

After the official welcome by the city of Barcelona, twelve musicians of the *Cobla*—a traditional Catalan Band—began playing the *Sardana*. The *Sardana*, according to both the broadcasters and the Final report (COOB'92 1992b; Cuyas 1993b: 54), is a typical Catalan dance. The dancers slowly formed the Olympic rings, symbolically merging Catalan and Olympic symbolism, accompanied by the singing of two Barcelona-born Opera singers: José Carreras and Montserrat Caballé, along with the Olympic Chorus. In both cases, the music was either newly composed for these ceremonies or was based on Catalan folk-tunes or songs.

The Catalan Cultural sequence was followed by "Land of Passion," which was a brief tribute to Spain. Containing no historical reference, as had the Catalan creation myth, nor as many bright colors and flashy exhibitions, the Spanish demonstration was both brief and simple. This segment involved the arrival of hundreds of drummers, including drummers from Catalonia, and Bajo Aragon, who then formed a large circle. "Flamenco Dancers formed a poetic half-moon which entered the great circle" (Cuyas 1993b: 55). The passions of the Flamenco filled the stadium and provided the main demonstration of Spanish national culture as well as to remind Catalan and other audience members of the distinct Andalusian minority in Catalonia. Following the Flamenco performance, the Spanish tenor Alfredo Kraus sang a traditional Spanish love-song to conclude the segment.

While there was a "Spanish" demonstration at the Games, the "core" representation of Spain was performed almost entirely with peripheral elements. The two opera singers[6] in the Catalan section, Montserrat Caballé and José Carreras, are both natives of Barcelona. The opera singer who performed during the Land of Passion sequence, Alfredo Kraus, is from Gran Canarie in the Canary Islands—a Spanish autonomous region lying off the coast of Northwest Africa. The Flamenco dance, which is popularly viewed as a Spanish icon, was actually borrowed from Andalusia, the southern most region of Spain. The bands from the Land of Passion sequence were identified as coming from Catalonia, the Levant, the southeast coast of Spain, and Bajo Aragon, the part of Aragon just west of Catalonia.

The organizers subtly constructed a Spanish identity limited to the regions bordering the Mediterranean Sea. Without exception, the segment intended to depict a Spain devoid of formal elements from Spain's core—Madrid, Spain's capital, or any Spanish region that did not border the Mediterranean. In fact, during the entire Opening Ceremonies, only three elements came specifically from Spain's core: first, the necessary official iconography connected to the state (the flag and national anthem); second, the presence of the King of Spain, his wife, and the President of Spain, in accordance with Olympic Protocol;[7] and third, the opera singers Teresa Berganza and Placido Domingo, both from Madrid, were among the singers invited to sing during the European/Mediterranean Sea segment. In addition to only very specific segments being purely Spanish, the limitation of Spanish identity, in favor of Catalan, was accentuated by the stark simplicity of Spanish demonstrations compared to the Catalan Spectacle.

The European segment is more pertinent for other parts of this study, but the source of the performers is worthy of note here. Embedded in the distinctly "pro-European" sequence of the Opening Ceremonies was a unique performance of famous operatic arias, performed by "six of the finest opera singers in the world" (Cuyas 1993b: 72). This tribute to great opera music of the Mediterranean, which, as the Final Report calls it, was "music for the universe" (Cuyas 1993b: 72), was more strongly integrated with Mediterranean culture than Spanish national identity. The performers were Jaume Aragall, Teresa Berganza, Montserrat Caballé, José Carreras, Placido Domingo, and Juan Pons. Aragall, Caballé, and Carreras are from Barcelona. Pons is from the Balearic Islands. Berganza and Domingo are from Madrid.

Another part of the "pro-European" segment included a demonstration of the highly symbolic *castieres*, a Catalan tradition of building human towers. First, during the Opening Ceremonies, performers built twelve towers, one representing each member-state in the European Union. Second, is the construction of the towers themselves. The towers are traditionally constructed by men climbing onto each other's shoulders, forming a new base, and then having more men climb even higher. During the games, the towers were erected to a height of six-men and were topped by a child who waved to the crowd. Watching the ascent of these towers and the mutual support of Catalan individuals holds a good deal of symbolism as some Catalans strive for independence. Having the tower topped by a child adds even more symbolism as youth are, in the Olympics especially, often depicted as the future of any society.[8]

In every case in the Barcelona Olympics where Spain was given any significance, there was a very obvious and deliberate attempt at bolstering the periphery. The only exception to this trend occurred during the Parade of Nations, which, as Hargreaves (2000) has demonstrated, was a battle for equal display that the Catalan Olympic Committee fought very passionately, but eventually lost.

III. Interweaving Regional, Native, and National Identities

Lastly, we should consider the Calgary Winter Olympics of 1988 because of how they combined an exaltation of their regional identity together with a noteworthy Native/Immigrant element. The Calgary organizers, opting to fully cover all elements of its varied identities, had to consider incorporating a regional identity, Western Canada; a native identity, Canada's "First Nations"; immigrants to the host city, state and country; and finally the concept of Canada, including English and French Canada.

First, the Calgary Opening Ceremonies were comparatively short, running roughly two hours. In that span of time the organizers followed all Olympic protocols for the Opening Ceremonies and managed a pageant that covered the many facets of Calgary's identity. The Calgary Organizers opted to intertwine the various elements while still creating moments that were distinctly focused on just one identity. The ceremonies also alternated the pageantry with the official ceremony required by IOC protocol, further stratifying the Opening Ceremonies. As a result, there were moments during the Calgary Games that felt distinctly Canadian or Western Canadian, those that possessed elements of both, and periods in which protocol took center stage and host identity was minimized or absent. A valuable example, which the Final Report proudly notes, rests in the musical arrangements for the entire show.

According to the report, all thirty pieces of music required for the ceremonies were composed, performed, and recorded in Calgary utilizing only local musicians (OCO'88 1988c: 293). The music provided a constant Western-Canadian atmosphere, which was predominantly used as accompaniment to most parts of the pageant. It is interesting that every element of the Opening Ceremonies was in one way or another permeated with a sense of Calgarian-Albertan-Western Canadian identity. While many segments are intended to portray a specific part of Canada not directly taken from the regional identity of the host, these segments are either short or laced with the host's regional concept.

The opening sequences of the pageantry encompassed an adoration of the Canadian West. It began with a two part musical performance by the World Chorus (a choir made up of singers from all the nations competing in the games) and the Calgary Stampede Show band. The Show band began a demonstration of the Canadian West as different from all other "old west" cultures. The broadcasters called the first half of this segment "the Sophisticated West" which was depicted through the formal presentation of Mounties on horseback,[9] and backed in song with lyrics that praise the beauty and majesty of the Canadian west (OCO'88 1988b).

The second distinguishing factor was chuck wagon racing. A group of chuck wagon teams rode onto the field while the announcer explained that these races were the distinguishing feature between the Calgary Stampede and all other rodeos (OCO'88 1988b). A celebration of the Old West and the rodeo through trick riding, lasso artists, and other facets of this regional cultural phenomenon then followed this establishment of the Canadian West.

Embedded within this segment of the pageantry were two critical ethnic or native demonstrations. First, the ceremonies emphasized Canada's peaceful resolution with the Native Americans in western Canada. What are now known as the Tribes of Treaty 7 (OCO'88 1988b) rode onto the field in full dress and bearing their national flags. By placing this display within a showcase of the Canadian version of the old west, the organizers established that Canada's indigenous people are a part of that identity, and that Canadian conquest of the West was far more peaceful than other European/Native American interactions. This presence of native culture within the concept of western Canada recurred several times in the Opening Ceremonies.

At the end of the initial portion of the pageant native Calgarians, dressed in the ethnic costumes of their homelands, entered as part of a demonstration of the diversity of Canada, as well as a multi-national method of welcoming the world to Calgary. At this point, the festivities turned to the official element, which by IOC protocol represented Canada and Great Britain. Interestingly enough, the first taste of the state of Canada in the Opening Ceremonies was actually the arrival of Governor General Jeanne Sauvé, the representative of the Queen of England, Canada's official head of state.

At this point, the Governor General, with her full honor guard, the Vice Regal Salute, which is the first 8 bars of the British National Anthem, *God Save the Queen*, and the first 8 bars of the Canadian National Anthem, *O Canada,* and the Mountie Musical Ride, a formal horseback performance of the Mounties to music, were the only direct presentation of Canada. The limited presentation of the national identity quickly ended and was followed by the Parade of Nations. However, the best indication thus far of the exaltation of the periphery came, not in the austerity of the Canadian authority, but in the Parade of Nations. The Canadian team, which was afforded the right to enter in the parade as the final team, was dressed in the same costumes as the Calgary Stampede Show Band. Instead of the presentation of the host team as a celebration of the host state, it reinforced traits demonstrated as part of western Canadian culture.

The process of elevating regional identity above national, just as in Atlanta and Barcelona, continued after the Parade of Nations in the second pageantry segment. The second segment contained more celebration of Western Canadian culture, but this time specifically through dance and song. The sequence started with the Kalucco, a contemporary Western two-step dance that is unique to Calgary (OCO'88 1988b; 1988c: 297). Two Canadian artists, singing *Four Strong Winds* and *Alberta Bound*, accompanied the 360 local dancers that performed the regional dance step (*Ibid.*).

The sequence was quickly followed by more Olympic Protocol and an acultural celebration of the Olympic competitions. During this phase, the *World Chorus*, instead of a Canadian group, had the honor of performing the Olympic Hymn for the flag raising. The torch relay into the stadium was also presented with little attention to the national. Native American drummers heralded its arrival and provided the only backdrop for the cauldron lighting. Interestingly enough, the three most important elements of the protocols: The Olympic Flag and Hymn, the Cauldron Lighting, and the official declaration that opens the games were all completed without representatives of the national government. An international choir accompanied the Hymn, Canadian Aboriginal Music complemented the Cauldron Lighting, and the national anthem of Canada was initially sung in an aboriginal language. Even the official opening by the head of state was international, although that was due to the fact that Canada's head of state is the Queen of England.

From this highly restricted national privilege within IOC protocol, the ceremonies turned to the third segment of the pageantry, which was a tribute to Canada titled "*Mon Pays*" (My Country, in French). Two ballet companies handled the entire breadth of Canadian identity: one from Montreal, the other Albertan. The Montreal troupe performed a French Canadian folk dance while the Alberta troupe performed an English folk dance. At no point were the two separate demonstrations ever joined or in any way brought together to indicate a unified concept of Canada. Even the Final report indicates division, describing this segment as "a celebration of the Canadian English and French cultural mosaic," which is a cultural trademark of Canada (OCO'88 1988c: 297).

The *Mon Pays* segment transitioned back to a celebration of the regional identity in a manner that is still unique among Opening Ceremonies. The last required Olympic protocol remaining was the performance of the host's national anthem. The anthem was performed in two segments: the first, Daniel Tlen, a Tsuu T'ina Native American, sang in his native language, Southern Tsuu T'ina; the second segment was performed in English with a French echo. This was also clearly a legitimization of native culture as equal to English-Canadian.

During the ceremony, the French elements of national Canada, were only limitedly displayed. It is surprising that the Canadian national anthem was performed in an indigenous language and then one national language, as opposed to the two official state languages. French was relegated to an "echo" of the English performance. Officially, Canada's official federal languages are English and French, although from this performance it appears that Western Canada's national languages are Southern Tsuu T'ina and English, with French present only incidental or to satisfy the Olympic movement. The Opening Ceremonies then concluded with a western Square Dance and a performance of *Can't You Feel It*—the official song of the 1988 Winter Olympics.

The limitation of the presentation of French Canadian, while establishing a very strong sense of native Canadian, is a process of lifting the indigenous people of Canada onto a more even playing field with English and French Canada. Arguably, the opening ceremonies could be seen as taking what has been a relatively weak indigenous Canadian community and strategically repositioning it to challenge a stronger French Quebecois identity. Therefore one possible objective of the Calgary organizers may have been to promote a sense of Canadian multiculturalism as a rebuke to French Canadian ascendancy.

The opening sequence the 1988 Ceremonies involved a celebration of Alberta, which featured a series of cultural groups representing the diversity of Alberta. This included English Canada, ethnic nationals, and aboriginal tribes in full dress and with their own flags. From this point onward, the Ceremonies alternated between this overall Western (regional) identity of Calgary and all other elements of the Opening Ceremonies. During the two hour show, Central Canada was relegated almost to non-existence. Therefore, in the opening ceremonies the international community and the domestic audience gained a full understanding only of Albertan, Calgarian, and Western-English Canada.

This near dismissal of Canadian national identity persisted through the Closing Ceremonies as well. The Closing Ceremonies contained two key elements. First, the ceremony that took place entirely on ice featured a tribute to athleticism and winter sport through a figure skating exhibition featuring amateur and legendary Olympic skaters. The sequence was only faintly story-driven, featuring a brief look into Canada's history. The story revolved around a skater's waltz, with ice dancers dressed in period costumes, which could have demonstrated either Western Canadian or pan-Canadian identities; however, the color commentating and stadium announcements did not describe these elements as possessing that meaning.

The tribute to the past was heavily sports-oriented; the "story" described a day at a frozen pond where families would ice skate, ski, and go curling. Within this period, several "old heroes," including Canadians, Americans and British, "returned to the ice" (OCO'88 1988b). Along with these skaters, a main theme of the sequence was family. The games included sleigh riders and a family of skaters, depicting the love of sport that existed within Canadian culture. In many ways, it is easier to see this as a celebration of Canadian sport rather than Canadian culture, although claiming the display was a subtle hint to a thematic of family values is possible.

In addition to the Canadian love of sports, the Closing Ceremonies featured a reminder of the Canadian West: a game of "cops and robbers" on ice. The cops and robbers segment was nothing more than mere entertainment as the commentators and announcers noted (OCO'88 1988b). While the purpose of this was spectacle, nevertheless a few interesting points can be observed. First, there was nothing within the fight on ice that suggested Canada's national identity. Although the "cops" were dressed as Canadian Mounties, this represented a story-driven decision rather than an attempt at depicting national Canada, since the Mounties did not have flags and were "riding" toy ponies. The whimsical nature of this show strongly suggests that the lack of an "official" concept of Canada, or even Western Canadian regionalism, is probably best attributed to the organizers utilizing this segment only for old-fashioned fun.

All three examples presented in the chapter offer a consistent effort towards presenting a regional identity in lieu of an identity associated with the central government. Every example took well-established elements of the peripheral identity and focused its display around entrenching these aspects of the periphery, the result of which was a broader sense of the region rather than the state identity. In addition to a regional concept, the Calgary games augmented this demonstration by interweaving a depiction of it native heritage. By granting space to Canadian aboriginal communities within the official protocols of the Opening Ceremonies, the organizers legitimized the presence of Native Culture and in so doing raised their status as equal to English Canada. One could argue that this was an attempt to challenge

French Canadian cultural hegemony by suggesting a native replacement for it. However, it is less complicated to presume the presentation sought to take a state with a bi-polar sense of identity and make it a tri-polar one.

In the Barcelona example, the organizers raised the demonstration or exposition of Catalan identity to a level at least equal to (if not greater than) Spanish national identity. The bloodshed of the Spanish Civil War complicated the process, however, and made such bold statements as having a national anthem sung in the Catalan language impossible to interpret as legitimizing moments. The main problem of the display was that it was seen simultaneously as a challenge to Spanish authority and a sign of Catalan resilience in the Civil War and post civil war period.

Beyond the establishment of the regional identity, all three Olympics share three commonalities. First, they represented an attempt to further legitimize a regional or native identity by raising it to or above the state's officially sanctioned identity. Calgary presents both as it raises Western Canada to the predominant concept in Alberta, but not in equilibrium with a Central Canadian identity, and further elevates Native Culture as equal to English and French Culture within Canada. Second, all three sought to objectify the concept of their regional and ethnic identities.

During these opening and closing ceremonies, the pageantry and the official protocol were all laced with the symbols, meaning, and traits of a non-state-centered national identity. In all three cases, the same aspects of the central state's national identity were circumstantial, vaguely established, or outright dismissed. What we see then is the exact same process as the first goal of exalting the core but with a complete role reversal.

NOTES

1. Of course the irony in this "Southern" presentation is that the most recognizeable performer, Celine Dion, is not Southern, or American; she is Canadian.

2. The symbolism is especially poignant when one compares the menacing nature of the Thunderbird to the commonplace name of the Civil War in the south: The War of Northern Aggression.

3. All but one former Soviet republic (Tajikistan) had new national flags in time for the Opening Ceremonies. Such efforts on behalf of states to select symbols in time for these ceremonies further supports evidence that these events are indeed used by state actors to "parade" their nations.

4. The most logical explanation for why Catalonia was denied a separate recognition, along similar lines to the states within the Unified Team, was because Catalan athletes were part of an officially recognized NOC and the IOC refused to recognize a separate Catalan NOC.

5. The Spanish Flag was the center flag, flanked by the flags of Catalonia and Barcelona.

6. Biographical information on these Opera singers came from two websites: an Italian site, OperaWeb (http://archivio.opera.it/) and from Grandi Tenori (www.grandi-tenori.com). Biographical information on Juan Pons came from his official website (http://andypons.eresmas.net).

7. Protocol does not expressly require the presence of the Head of State to open the games, but it is generally expected.

8. Recall, Seoul's use of children born in the year that city won the Games, the arrival of children at the end of the Creation sequence in Barcelona, and the use of children as symbols of progress and change in opening ceremonies in Moscow, Atlanta, and Nagano.

9. The Mounties are an icon of Canada. Formally, the Royal Canadian Mounted Police, they play an official and symbolic role at many Canadian festivities. The Musical ride is a formal performance of precision riding.

CHAPTER 10
PROCESSES AND STRATEGIES: NEW UNDERSTANDINGS OF CULTURAL PERFORMANCE

I. MANIFESTATIONS OF NATIONALISM: PROCESS, STRATEGIES, AND THEIR OUTCOMES.

Three processes, defined in terms of goals, and a strategy that contains elements of the prior two sets, present avenues of cultural performance for actors constructing a nationalistic demonstration. This demonstration is designed to present to an audience audible and visual experience of national identity through the medium of cultural performance. Utilizing a complex arsenal of traits and icons, including music, dance, literature, history, religion, etc., organizers of the opening and closing ceremonies of the Olympic Games have constructed a living example of their identity as they choose to define that identity.

The effort in these games is a deliberate calculation. Organizers have a structural framework through which they have a limited window of opportunity to conduct their nationalistic goals. In that space, actors have highly regulated protocol elements around which they can carefully depict their identity, in addition to the open space of the pageantry section whose content is mostly at the discretion of the host. The tools discussed in this study are essentially a collection of options from which organizers can select the best processes and strategies to achieve their goals. Because the topics in this examination can be seen as a collection of tools, many possible combinations are visible. Therefore, the breadth of possibilities is suitably large to accommodate the needs of many different actors with many different goals.

From the Atlanta, Barcelona, and Calgary examples, the processes necessary to successfully revise historically, create, indoctrinate, or assimilate were shown to be part of a larger strategy to construct a presentation of a core or a periphery. Calgary used elements of its western and native cultural icons to construct a regional identity. Atlanta used historical revision to replace the destruction of Southern independence and identity with, in a manner of speaking, a temporary cessation in hostilities, thus establishing continuity within its identity that flows backwards in time well past the Civil War. In these three examples, processes were merged with a Core/Periphery strategy to present a specific concept of their national identity.

Combinations of two or more processes are also a potential plan for the organizers to attain their goals. As Los Angeles, Seoul, Salt Lake City, Lillehammer, and Athens demonstrated, these processes can also be the main feature or aspect of the goal instead of supplementing a different goal. In other words, the process of indoctrination, for example, can either support a broader goal, such as a core/periphery relationship, or can simply be the goal, as in indoctrinating skiing in Lillehammer. Even within the processes of indoctrination, assimilation, and revising/creating, there are opportunities for overlap and attainment of mutual or exclusive goals. Salt Lake City presented the indoctrination of ideology through a story of a boy triumphing over adversity (a storm). Los Angeles used the same processes to present the United States as possessing a musical and entertainment culture. Athens used the processes of custodianship to further establish their claims to the assimilated icons of Alexander the Great. In each of these, the process was the expression of the goal itself and not a path to attaining another goal. Keeping this in mind, these processes can also be used to attain the same or tangential objective.

Each of these processes represents microcosms of the display that can be either presented in isolation, or in conjunction with others consecutively or concurrently. Lillehammer provided an excellent example of a scenario in which historical revision and custodianship of culture were combined to suggest Norwegian hegemonic control over the winter Olympics. The Seoul Olympics provides an example where indoctrination and historical revision were used to present South Korea as a modernizing state that could exist harmoniously with the Soviet bloc in general, North Korea specifically, and still maintain good relations with the West.

Another possible example occurs in the 1988 Calgary games, in which there was a presentation of English and French Canada. Beyond presenting a regional/native western Canadian element, there was also a dual element of English and French Canada. As the focus of the Calgary games was on its regional and native elements, the English/French dichotomy was presented incidentally in a short and, supposedly, balanced performance. Therefore, the Calgary games also present a potential example of a combination of the "Stage for All" and regional/peripheral strategies. Several of the processes discussed in this study are examples in and of themselves, while others are supporting processes for a different aim. This fact is strengthened by the fact that the first three processes, which can be manifested as either the goal or as assisting a separate purpose, occurred in most host city performances. Furthermore, there does not appear to be a correlation between specific processes and specific strategies.

It is unwise to presume that strategies are tied to specific goals. It is equally unwise to expect that specific combinations of manifestations are required. Remember that Sydney's use of five categories woven together shows that the breadth of possibilities is limited only by structural concerns of time and regulations and the objectives of the actor. The lack of any definitive relationship between specific manifestations is a symptom of their purpose. It is best to interpret these elements as tools that can be adapted to suit any purpose.

The variety of combinations and the range of manifestations utilized by some hosts reinforce statements that organizers who design cultural performances at the opening and closing ceremonies are strategic actors who assess their options in terms of preset goals they desire to attain. When interpreting the contents of a presentation, it becomes evident that the processes and strategies used are selected because of their ability to express the actor's concept of his own identity to both a domestic and an international audience.

II. COMMON OBSERVATIONS

Given the range of diverse forms of national performance, let us focus on their commonalities. First, all of the examples analyzed in this study share a common thread of being simultaneously informative and entertaining. The Atlanta final report's statement that their goal was to present a "new perspective of the South" (Watkins 1997a: 352) reinforces the emphasis on information dissemination and Jean-Claude Killy's hope that the Albertville ceremonies would maintain a playful, albeit rather cerebral, mood among the audience (COJO 1992c) validates assertions of an inherent effort towards entertainment.

Much in the manner that museums, documentaries, and other institutions educate through entertainment, the Olympics represent a concerted effort at *infotainment*. While different societies have different definitions of what constitutes "entertainment," all of the preceding examples present adequate

material to justify the statement that every example in this study had some
element that was, in addition to promoting a specific nationalistic agenda,
designed to entertain the audience. In fact, most of the examples involved
presentations whose complexity was a direct result of the need for spectacle
to help convey the founding principles of a national identity to the audience.

The use of entertainment does not, however, preclude the presence of
nationalism in non-entertainment segments. Several examples in this study
covered the presentation of identity through protocol moments that focus
more on ceremony than spectacle. We find that presentations of identity in
the Olympics may be more common through spectacle and pageantry, but
that the presentation can actually appear in almost any moment of the games
over which the organizers have some control. The design of the Lillehammer
speed skating venue, made to look like the hull of a Viking ship and 'The
Hall of the Mountain King' subterranean ice hockey arena, is a stark testa-
ment to the possible avenues of identity presentation.

Beyond its entertainment aspect, there are several other qualities that
permeate every example presented in this study. What we find is that presentations of identity at the opening and closing ceremonies are half structured and half unstructured. The choices of organizers are partially under
their total control and partially controlled by the International Olympic
Committee. While the IOC maintains some general oversight over even the
pageantry segments, the IOC's charter specifically dictates the protocol elements of the ceremonies. Therefore, in every example, there is a careful
balance in maintaining the dignity and austerity of Olympic protocol while
also continuing their presentations of identity both within and outside of the
pageantry elements of the show.

The commonality of structuring the balance of these elements exists in
every example in this study; it should not be assumed that the method is also
the same in each ceremony. The actual order of events is not consistent with
each example. However, if the nationalistic elements are contained completely under the definition of "pageantry," then we can state without hesita-
tion that where the ordering may be different, the overall list of events remains consistent due to IOC protocol.

Likely the single most important observation on commonalities of display is vested in the actual process of the formation of a display in general.
Every outcome in the opening and closing ceremonies is governed by two
factors: structure and choice. The aforementioned list of events can easily
be seen as representing the structural factor. In short, the Olympic Charter,
the executive board of the International Olympic Committee, and the international venue of the event create a structure, through which the hosts may
conduct a display of identity. On the domestic side, the structure and regulations of the national Olympic committee, the government of the host city and

national government (provincial government, if applicable) all present other structural constraints on the choices of actors.

Taken together, the list of international and domestic structures presents a series of interacting regimes through which the choices of the organizers of the ceremonies are directed. This does not, however, preclude the authority of individual elites to make a choice. From the data presented in this study, it would be incorrect to assume that the hosts were denied the opportunity of being rational actors. This is, in fact, the common thread that weaves together all manifestations of performed identity. Each manifestation, whether process or strategy, is formed as a unique result of goals set by actors who are aware of the structures through which they are working. It is this latter statement that requires consideration, because it is incorrect to dismiss either choice or structure. Therefore, while the focus of this study is on the choices that actors have made, it is only correctly handled if this statement includes a reiteration of the fact that forces outside their immediate control influence the actors' choices.

An interesting and previously unexamined result of this study focuses on both the value and challenges of cultural performance at international festivals. Where many studies have established the success of staging cultural performance in a domestic festival or venue, one of this study's conclusions is that the same is true for international events. While there are distinct problems with an international stage, notably that establishing an identity requires an otherwise unnecessary duality, the benefits clearly outweigh these drawbacks. From the evaluations in this study, a few points are worth noting.

To the degree that one establishes an identity as a unique vis-à-vis "them," a distinct national identity gains credibility. By performing this dichotomy at an international forum, while simultaneously establishing the host identity as unique when compared to both the collection of international identities and to those present within the host state, its legitimacy at both domestic and international levels of analysis is validated. Beyond these factors, the concept of cultural performance remains relatively the same regardless of type of venue. Therefore, its definition as an artistic display of the elements of a national identity, through culture, icons, and narrative, remains valid and previous notions of cultural performance and nationalism are strengthened by this study.

Cultural performance and nationalism are both influenced by the process through which they are presented. Structural matters underscore how choices of actors are affected by the irreplaceable opportunity to display their identity at such a prestigious venue. Objectification is an avenue of establishing or altering identity, which is nothing more than a process that can be used on its own or as part of a larger effort at identity reformation. The Olympics represent a venue for such efforts. But, more than just a venue, the Olympics can be seen as a vehicle for identity formation and ref-ormation on a scale unmatched in any mere domestic manifestation.

As a vehicle for nationalism, the Olympics have within them a series of structures and factors, most of which are similar to cultural performance, and identity construction, which affect these processes. Each pathway to creating a definition of nationalism focuses on tangible elements, which can be per-ceived by the community of individuals whose identity is being defined. These presentations of identity always involve a collection of traits. As the presentation is an establishment of the concept of an identity, this display also includes a definition of that display as the vehicle for ensuring the "audience" receives the traits within the proper context. Because the collec-tion of traits and the context within which they are vested will be different for each objectifier, the relationship of national and the Olympics is clearly conducted in different ways.

The possible avenues for this display are all defined by both the struc-tural realities of the identity performed (meaning the actual factors of that identity which establish how a display must appear) and the nationalistic goals that the actor seeks to attain. These definitions are equally valid for cultural performance, and objectificationat the domestic level. The fact that we are primarily dealing with a process that is both deliberate and a result of decision-processes opens the possibility to see the entire concept of national-ism in the Olympics as an objective reality. As such, the emphasis of this study lies on the processes of that reality and not on the validity of what is displayed through it or on the degree of success of those displays.

To what extent the choices of individual actors designing their pageants were optimal is outside the scope of this study; however, we can conclude that, in a truly Machiavellian spirit, the decisions of what to display were a direct result of a decision process that intended on maintaining elite author-ity. As stated earlier in this study, degrees of success and failure were not the focus of this study, which focused on the simple notion that the Olym-pics, specifically the opening and closing ceremonies, were deliberately used to accomplish some selected nationalistic goals.

By establishing that displays of nationalism are deliberate, constrained through structures, and designed for both a domestic and an international audience, the choice of focusing on the different techniques in which cul-tural performance is manifested is justified as it avoided questions of what may or may not have influenced actor's choices. The manifestations, which were simultaneously strategies in terms of a broad notion of a goal (i.e., core vs. periphery) and processes through which identity demonstration is con-ducted, become formulas for effective nationalism displays. Noting that the term *effective* indicates only the ability to establish, define, and then objec-tify audio and visual material into a coherent presentation of identity and does not indicate a degree of success of that presentation, this study's research design is justified for its ability to establish the breadth of cultural performance in an international event.

The archaic notion perceiving the relationship of nationalism and the Olympics as containing an inherent moral ascription is clearly false. If cultural performance occurs through manifestations that are processes (tools) and are strategies (governed by choices), then the process has no inherent moral alignment. Without making accusations against or in favor of any state, the use of the games for "good" or "evil," admittedly controversial and subjective terms, is a result, not of an inherent quality in the relationship of nationalism and the Olympics, but instead is a symptom of "good" or "evil" goals of actors hosting the games.

All things considered, the relationship between nationalism and an international festival is merely a process through which identity formation and re-formation may be conducted. As a process, it can be used for multiple objectives and therefore has a versatility that is as equally capable as other current trends in the study of nationalism and cultural performance. While this study is focused specifically on the Olympics, we can project the results of this study onto international festivals in general, realizing that certain structural facts will be different dependent on which festival is the venue for cultural performance and nationalism.

III. FINAL CONSIDERATIONS AND NEW DIRECTIONS

The value of a study on nationalism in the Olympics is due to the consideration of a traditionally domestic process as an international process. As such, the focus of this study has been to define this process and in so doing, to dismiss several older notions about nationalism and the Olympics and cultural performance that are no longer tenable. What was initially dismissed as the framework for this study is now the new emphasis. Since this study has established processes within a framework that necessarily focused on the elements of process instead of the elements of choice, then the next step is to refocus the questions raised in this study to consider individual examples.

For all its potential value, this study has not been intended to draw meaningful conclusions on whether this relationship has a higher degree of success or failure, or if the process is reasonably balanced to provide either. It is my conclusion, based on the presumption that the process will be somewhat balanced, that focusing on the choices and ability of the actor as a determinant for the degree of success of a single example.

If this is correct, then the study of nationalism as performed through an international festival has opened a new avenue of research into nationalist identity formation. Studies that have been intrinsically state-centric can now focus on the study of nationalist formation with an international perspective as well as a domestic one. In a world that features increasing violence between states and ethnic groups, many cases of which transcend current legal international borders, the study of identity formation on an international scale is becoming increasingly relevant. Finding processes for peaceful and non-peaceful expressions of that identity and its meaning therefore has ramifications on domestic, international, and potentially global state policy.

In terms of cultural performance, if the concepts of this study prove valid on a theoretical and methodological level, it results in a noteworthy and likely effective path of identity construction and objectification. The duality that these events project, as identity constructors and as patriotic state building enterprises, requires a clearer understanding of both of these elements. This study establishes the terms of the former while accepting the reality of the latter. In doing so, it gives a sense of breadth to cultural performance as a process and establishes its many facets.

As part of this, we have reiterated the statement that nationalism and cultural performance, in any vein, but specifically the Olympics is a process. We have found that through different examples, the processes are themselves divested of an inherent moral quality. Even the process of historical revision, which can easily be manipulated for less auspicious purposes, is implemented for all types of outcomes. What has, therefore, regularly been seen as a negative relationship is clearly neither positive nor negative.

The focus in this study has been on the processes elites use, not on a specific identity or its realities. The actual content or situation of any given identity only influenced the handling or selection of which processes to use and how to handle their implementation. Because the elements of identity are not a factor in the potential use of these processes, then the type of identity being presented is not restricted to one fitting the definition of nationalism. Therefore, this study is valid for presentations of both nationalistic and tautopolic identities. The potential of this relationship is very important to the study of identity. Should tautopolic identities be governed by the same rules as nationalistic identities in cultural performance, then it is a reasonable extrapolation that these identities are constructed, objectified, and legitimized in the same manner as nationalistic.

This study hopes to draw the attention of the Political Science discipline towards the benefits of nationalistic display at the international level and establishing new avenues of research in the study of identity formation, while also suggesting the use of the term *Tautopolism* within studies of nationalism and ethnic identity.. By the use of this term, we find a productive method of studying identity formation, the resulting consolidation of political entities, and the interests and objectives of elites who govern these matters regardless of their time period and traits. In short, current logical limitations on the use of the term *nationalism* can be avoided while allowing for some of its theories and methodologies to see broader use in the discipline.

Originally, the political science discipline lacked a strong theoretical basis to study and then explain, for example, the choice to expend city-state resources on fielding a sports team in the ancient Olympics and why their success was considered a metaphor for success of the city-state as well. There are also no theoretical restrictions on tautopolic manifestations in the modern era. Present within the concept of identity is, therefore, an option beyond a strict definition of nationalism.

I conclude this study in the hope that it has accomplished several things. First, it was originally designed to broaden our understanding of the reason states compete in and host events such as the Olympics. In doing so, the value of the study of the Olympics is broadened to include examination of the concepts of identity formation and promotion. Second, it emphasized cultural performance and elite manipulations of national identity, the outcome of which can result in a broader understanding of nationalism, identity, and the socio-political ramifications of these concepts. Third, the introduction of the concept of tautopolism offers a step towards a broader understanding of identity.

It is the hope of this author that tautopolism may be used to establish an understanding of identity, without temporal restrictions, that can have two beneficial outcomes: first, that it can be used to synthesize a better understanding of the politics of identity in areas that nationalism is currently unable to explain; and second, that by broadening the study of identity to include definitions that fall within the concept of tautopolism, new understandings of nationalism can be discovered through the comparison of these two concepts.

APPENDIX A
CHRONOLOGY OF HOST CITIES

1980 Winter Olympics: Lake Placid, United States
1980 Summer Olympics: Moscow, Soviet Union

1984 Winter Olympics: Sarajevo, Yugoslavia
1984 Summer Olympics: Los Angeles, United States

1988 Winter Olympics: Calgary, Canada
1988 Summer Olympics: Seoul, South Korea

1992 Winter Olympics: Albertville, France
1992 Summer Olympics: Barcelona, Spain

1994 Winter Olympics: Lillehammer, Norway

1996 Summer Olympics: Atlanta, United States

1998 Winter Olympics: Nagano, Japan

2000 Summer Olympics: Sydney, Australia

2002 Winter Olympics: Salt Lake City, United States

2004 Summer Olympics: Athens, Greece

2006 Winter Olympics: Turino, Italy

2008 Summer Olympics: Beijing, China

BIBLIOGRAPHY

"A Magical Moment: XVIth Olympic Winter Games." 1992, April. *Olympic Review* 294: 159-161.

ACOG. 1996a. "Closing Ceremonies of the 1996 Atlanta Summer Olympics." New York: NBC News, 4 August.

————. 1996b. "Opening Ceremonies of the 1996 Atlanta Summer Olympics." New York: NBC News, 19 July.

Almond, Gabriel & Sidney Verba. 1980. *The Civic Culture Revisited.* Boston: Little, Brown & Company.

Amateur Athletics Foundation of Los Angeles Homepage. http://www.aafla.org/.

Anderson, Benedict. 1983. *Imagined Communities: Reflections on the Origin and Spread of Nationalism.* London: Verso.

Aristotle. 1934. *Aristotle in 23 Volumes, Volume 19.* Trans. H. Rackham. Cambridge, MA: Harvard University Press. Found In Crane, Gregory R., ed. 2005. *Perseus Digital Library Project.* Medford, MA: Tufts University. http://www.perseus.tufts.edu/cgi-bin/ptext?lookup=Aristot.+Nic.+Eth.+1161b+1 (Accessed Sept. 17, 2005)

Athens 2004 Organizing Committee for the Olympic Games. 2005. "Official Website of the Athens 2004 Olympics. http://www.athens2004.com/en/BoxingHistory (Accessed Sept. 20, 2005).

————. 2004a. "Closing Ceremonies of the 2004 Athens Summer Olympics." New York: NBC News, 29 August.

————. 2004b. "Opening Ceremonies of the 2004 Athens Summer Olympics." New York: NBC News, 13 August.

Bairner, Alan. 2001. *Sport, Nationalism, and Globalization: European and North American Perspectives.* Albany: State University of New York Press.

Ball, Donald W. and John W. Loy. ed. 1975. *Sport and Social Order: Contributions to the Sociology of Sport.* Reading, MA: Addison-Wesley Publishing Company.

Barreto, Amílcar A. 1998. *Language, Elites, and the State: Nationalism in Puerto Rico and Quebec.* Westport, CT: Praeger.

————. 2001a. "Constructing Identities; Ethnic Boundaries and Elite Preferences in Puerto Rico." *Nationalism and Ethnic Politics,* 7: 21-40.

————. 2001b. *The Politics of Language in Puerto Rico.* Gainesville: University Press of Florida.

Barth, Fredrik. 1969. *Ethnic Groups and Boundaries: The Social Organization of Culture Difference.* Boston: Little, Brown & Company.

Birch, Ric. 2004. *Maser of Ceremonies.* Crown Nest, New South Wales: Allen & Unwin.

Bostock, William. 1973. "The Cultural Explanation of Politics." *Political Science* 25 (July): 37-48.

British Olympic Association. http://www.olympics.org.uk/

Caldwell, Geoffrey. 1982. "International Sport and National Identity." *International Social Science Journal* 34(2): 173-183.

Chalip, Laurence & Arthur Johnson. 1996. "Sports Policy in the United States." In Laurence Chalip, Arthur Johnson, and Lisa Stachura, eds. *National Sports Policies.* Westport, CT: Greenwood Press. Pp. 370 – 403.

Chappelet, Jean-Loup. 1996. "Olympic Ceremonies From Moscow (1980) to Lillehammer (1994): Ceremonies and the Televised Spectacle." In Moragas, Miquel de, John MacAloon, and Montserrat Llinés, eds. 1996. *Olympic Ceremonies: Historical Continuity and Cultural Exchange.* Lausanne: International Olympic Committee. Pp. 147 - 152

Chase, Jeffrey Scott. 1973. "Politics and Nationalism in Sports: Soviet and American Government Involvement in Amateur Sport as an Aspect of the Cold War." Unpublished M.A. thesis: California State University, San Jose.

Chilcote, Ronald. 1984. *Theories of Comparative Politics: The Search for a Paradigm Reconsidered.* Boulder, CO: Westview Press.

COJO. 1992a. "Closing Ceremonies of the 1992 Albertville Winter Olympics." New York: CBS News, 23 February.

————. 1992b. *Official Report of the XVI Winter Games of Albertville and Savoie.* Albertville: Comite d'organization des XVIes Jeux Olympique d'hiver d'Albertville et de la Savoie (COJO).

————. 1992c. "Opening Ceremonies of the 1992 Albertville Winter Olympics." New York: CBS News, 8 February.

Comité National Olympique et Sportif Français.
http://www.comiteolympique.asso.fr/

COOB'92. 1992a. "Closing Ceremonies of the 1992 Barcelona Summer Olympics." New York: NBC News, 8 August.

————. 1992b. "Opening Ceremonies of the 1992 Barcelona Summer Olympics." New York: NBC News, 25 July.

Cook, Theodore Andrea. 1908 *The Fourth Olympiad.* London: British Olympic Committee.

Cooper, Christopher and H. Gibbs Knotts. 2010. "Declining Dixie: Regional Identification in the Modern American South." *Social Forces* 88(3), 1083-1101.

Cousineau, Phil. 2003. *The Olympic Odyssey: Rekindling the True Spirit of the Great Games.* Wheton, IL: Quest Books.

Cox, Cathy. 2005. "Georgia State Song." Office of the Secretary of State, State of Georgia.

http://www.sos.state.ga.us/state_capitol/education_corner/state_song.html (Accessed Sept. 26, 2005).

Crane, Gregory R. 2005. *Perseus Digital Library Project.* Medford, MA: Tufts University. http://www.perseus.tufts.edu (Accessed Sept. 17, 2005)

Cronin, Michael and David Mayall. ed. 1998. *Sporting Nationalisms: Identity, Ethnicity, Immigration, and Assimilation.* London: Routledge.

Cuyas, Roma. ed. 1993a. *Official Report of the Games of the XXV Olympiad Barcelona 1992 Vol. 3.* Barcelona: COOB'92.

————. 1993b. *Official Report of the Games of the XXV Olympiad Barcelona 1992 Vol. 4.* Barcelona: COOB'92.

Danforth, Loring M. 1997. *The Macedonian Conflict: Ethnic Nationalism in a Transnational World.* Princeton, NJ: Princeton University Press.

Dilling, Marnie. 1996. "Music in Atlanta.*" Olympic Review* 10: August-September, Pp. 49-52.

"Disputed History Text Approved: Outcry expected from Asia as Nanjing Massacre glossed over." *Japan Times:* 4 April 2001, p. 15.

Ducey, Kimberley Anne. 2000. *Nationalism and the Break-up of the Big Red Machine: A Study of the Importance of Olympic Sport in the Domestic and International Ideological and Symbolic Legitimization of the USSR.* Kingston, Ontario: Queens University at Kingston.

Dyreson, Mark. 1998. *Making the American Team: Sports, Culture, and the Olympic Experience.* Chicago: University of Chicago Press.

Eriksen, Thomas. 1993. *Ethnicity & Nationalism: Anthropological Perspectives.* London: Pluto.

Espy, Richard. 1988. "The Olympic Games: Mirror of the World." In Segrave, Jeffrey, and Donald Chu. eds. 1988. *Olympic Games in Transition.* Champaign, Il: Human Kinetics. Pp. 407 – 418.

Evaluation Commission. 2001. *Report of the IOC Evaluation Commission for the Games of the XXIX Olympiad in 2008.* Lausanne: Comité International Olympique, 3 April.

Fédération Internationale de Football Association, Official Site. http://www.fifa.com/

Flere, Sergej. 1992. "Cognitive Adequacy of Sociological Theories in Explaining Ethnic Antagonism in Yugoslavia." In Rupesinghe, Kumar, Peter King, and Olga Vorkunova. 1992. *Ethnicity and Conflict in a Post-Communist World: The Soviet Union, Eastern Europe, and China.* New York: St. Martin's Press. Pp. 251 – 270.

Geary, Patrick J. 2002. *The Myth of Nations: The Medieval Origins of Europe.* Princeton, NJ: Princeton University Press.

Gellner, Ernest. 1983. *Nations and Nationalism.* Ithaca, NY: Cornell University Press.

Glenny, Misha. 1993. *The Fall of Yugoslavia: The Third Balkan War.* New York: Penguin.

Gori, Gigliola. 1997 "Sports Festivals in Italy Between the 19th and 20th Centuries: A Kind of National Olympic Games." In Naul, Roland, ed. *Contemporary Studies in the National Olympic Games Movement.* New York: Frankfurt am Main. Pp. 19 – 54.

Gramsci, Antonio. 1971. *Selections from the Prison Notebooks.* New York: International Publishers.

Guerra, Lillian. 1998. *Popular Expression and National Identity in Puerto Rico: The Struggle for Self, Community, and Nation.* Gainesville: University Press of Florida.

Guss, David. 2000. *The Festive State: Race, Ethnicity, and Nationalism as Cultural Performance.* Berkeley: University of California Press.

Guttmann, Allen. 1994a. *Games and Empires: Modern Sports and Cultural Imperialism.* New York: Columbia University Press.

———. 1994b. *The Olympics: A History of the Modern Games.* Chicago: University of Illinois Press.

Hall, Stuart. 1997a. "Local and the Global: Globalization & Ethnicity." In Anthony D. King, ed. *Culture, Globalization, and the World System.* Minneapolis: University of Minnesota Press. Pp. 19 – 40.

———. 1997b. "Old and New Identities, Old and New Ethnicities." In Anthony D. King, ed. *Culture, Globalization, and the World System.* Minneapolis: University of Minnesota Press. Pp. 41 – 68.

Handelman, Don. 1990. *Models and Mirrors: Towards an Anthropology of Public Events.* Cambridge: Cambridge University Press.

Handler, Richard. 1984. "On Sociocultural Discontinuity: Nationalism and Cultural Objectification in Quebec." *Current Anthropology,* 25: 55-71.

Hargreave, John. 2000. *Freedom for Catalonia: Catalan Nationalism, Spanish Identity, and the Barcelona Olympic Games.* Cambridge: Cambridge University Press.

Harris, C. M. 1999. "Washington's Gamble, L'Enfant's Dream: Politics, Design, and the Founding of the National Capital." *The William and Mary Quarterly,* Third Series. 56(3): 527-564.

Hay, Roy. 1998. "Croatia: Community, Conflict, and Culture: The Role of Soccer Clubs in Migrant Identity." In Cronin, Michael and David Mayall. ed. 1998. *Sporting Nationalisms: Identity, Ethnicity, Immigration, and Assimilation.* London: Routledge.

Herodotus. 1998. *The Histories.* Trans., Robin Waterfield. London: Oxford University Press.

Higashi, Sumiko. 1995. "Walker and Mississippi Burning: Postmodernism Versus Illusionist Narrative." In Rosenstone, Robert A. 1995. *Revisioning History: Film and the Construction of a New Past.* Princeton: Princetion University Press. Pp. 188 – 202.

Hill, Christopher. 1997. *Olympic Politics: Athens to Atlanta.* Manchester, UK: Manchester University Press.

Hobsbawm, Eric. 1983. "Introduction: Inventing Traditions." In Hobsbawm, Eric & Terrence Ranger. eds. 1983. *The Invention of Tradition.* Cambridge: Cambridge University Press. Pp. 1 – 15.

Hodgson, Marshall G.S. 1996. *Rethinking World History.* Cambridge: University of Cambridge Press.

Holton, R.J. 1998. *Globalization and the Nation-State.* New York: St. Martin's Press.

Houlihan, Barrie. 1996. "Sport in the United Kingdom." In Laurence Chalip, Arthur Johnson, and Lisa Stachura, eds. *National Sports Policies.* Westport, CT : Greenwood Press. Pp. 370 – 403.

Ilmarinen, Maaret, ed. 1984. *Sport and International Understanding: Proceedings of the Congress Held in Helsinki, Finland, July 7-10, 1982.* Berlin: Springer-Verlag.

International Olympic Committee. 2005. "National Olympic Committee: Czech Olympic Committee." IOC. www.olympic.org/uk/organisation/noc/noc_uk.asp?noc_initials=CZE (Accessed Sept. 15, 2005)

———. 2004. *The Olympic Charter.* Lausanne: International Olympic Committee.

International Olympic Committee, Official Website http://www.olympic.org/uk/organisation

Katznelson, Ira. 1999. "Structure and Configuration in Comparative Politics." In Lichbach, Mark Irving, and Alan S. Zuckerman. 1999. *Comparative Politics: Rationality, Culture, and Structure.* Cambridge: Cambridge University Press. Pp. 81 – 112.

Killanin, Lord. 1974. "Minutes of the 75th Session of the International Olympic Committee." Vienna: Comité International Olympique, 21-24 October.

———. 1978. "Minutes of the 80th Session of the International Olympic Committee." Athens: Comité International Olympique, 17-20 May.

King, Anthony 1997a. "Introduction: Spaces of Culture, Spaces of Knowledge." In *Culture, Globalization, and the World System.* Minneapolis: University of Minnesota Press.

———. 1997b. "The Local and The Global: Globalization and Ethnicity." In Anthony D. King, ed. *Culture, Globalization, and the World System.* Minneapolis: University of Minnesota Press. Pp.

Klausen, Arne Martin. 1999a. ed. *Olympic Games as Performance and Public Event: The Case of the XVII Winter Olympic Games of Norway.* New York: Berghahn Books.

———. 1999b. "The Torch Relay: Reinvention of Tradition and Conflict with the Greeks." In Klausen, Arne Martin. 1999. ed. *Olympic Games as Performance and Public Event: The Case of the XVII Winter Olympic Games of Norway.* New York: Berghahn Books. Pp. 75 – 96.

Korporaal, Glenda. 2000. "Opening Ceremonies of the Sydney Games (Sydney 2000)" *Olympic Review* 35: October-November, Pp. 6-13.

Kossl, Kiri. 1988. *Czechoslovakia and the International Olympic Movement.* Prague: Orbis Press Agency.

Krotee, March L. 1988. "An Organizational Analysis of the International Olympic Committee." In Segrave, Jeffrey, and Donald Chu. eds. 1988. *Olympic Games in Transition.* Champaign, Il: Human Kinetics.

Krüger, Arnd and James Riordan. 1999. *The International Politics of Sport in the 20th Century.* London: E & FN Spon.

Krüger, Arnd. 1999. "Strength Through Joy: The Culture of Consent Under fascism, Nazism, and Francoism." In *The International Politics of Sport in the 20th Century.* London: E & FN Spon. Pp. 67 – 89.

LAOOC. 1984a. "Closing Ceremonies of the 1984 Los Angeles Summer Olympics."
       New York: ABC News, 12 August.
———. 1984b. "Opening Ceremonies of the 1984 Los Angeles Summer Olympics."
       New York: ABC News, 28 July.
Lapchick, Richard E. 1986. *Fractured Focus: Sport as a Reflection of Society.* DC:
       Lexington Books.
Lee, Jong-Young. 1990. *"Sport Nationalism in the Modern Olympics."* Unpublished
       Ph.D. diss., University of Northern Colorado.
Lefebvre, Georges. 1979. *The Coming of the French Revolution,* Princeton, NJ:
       Princeton University Press.
Leiper, Jean M. 1988. "Politics and Nationalism in the Olympic Games." In Segrave,
       Jeffrey, and Donald Chu. eds. 1988. *Olympic Games in Transition.* Champaign,
       Il: Human Kinetics. Pp. 329 – 344.
Lensky, Helen. 2000. *Inside the Olympic Industry: Power, Politics, and Activism.*
       Albany: State University of New York Press.
Levi, Margaret. 1999. "A Model, A Method, and a Map: Rational Choice in
       Comparative and Historical Analysis." In Lichbach, Mark Irving, and Alan S.
       Zuckerman. 1999a. *Comparative Politics: Rationality, Culture, and Structure.*
       Cambridge: Cambridge University Press. Pp. 19 – 41.
Lewis, Martin W. and Karen E. Wigen. 1997. *Myth Of Continents.* Berkeley:
       University of California Press.
Lichbach, Mark. 1999. "Research Traditions and Theory in Comparative Politics:
       An Introduction." In Lichbach, Mark Irving, and Alan S. Zuckerman. 1999a.
       Comparative Politics: Rationality, Culture, and Structure. Cambridge:
       Cambridge University Press. Pp. 3 – 16.
Lipset, Seymour. 1990 *Continental Divide: The Values and Institutions of the United
       States and Canada.* London: Routledge,
Llinés, Montserrat. 1996. "The History of Olympic Ceremonies: From Athens
       (1896) to Los Angels (1984), An Overview." In Moragas, Miquel de, John
       MacAloon, and Montserrat Llinés, eds. 1996. *Olympic Ceremonies: Historical
       Continuity and Cultural Exchange.* Lausanne: International Olympic
       Committee. Pp. 63 – 79.
LOOC. 1994a. "Closing Ceremonies of the 1994 Lillehammer Winter Olympics."
       New York: CBS News, 27 February.
———. 1994b. "Opening Ceremonies of the 1994 Lillehammer Winter Olympics."
       New York: CBS News, 12 February.
———. 1994c. *Untitled Final Report of the 1994 Lillehammer Winter Olympics.
       Vol. 4.* Lillehammer: LOOC.
Lowe, Benjamin. 1978. "Educational Objectives for International Sports Studies." In
       Lowe, Benjamin, David B.Kanin, and Andrew Strenk, eds. *Sport and
       International Relations,* Champaign, Il: Stipes Publishing Company. Pp. 572 –
       586.
Luke, Timothy. 2002. *Museum Politics: Power Plays as the Exhibition.*
       Minneapolis: University of Minnesota Press.
MacAloon, John J. 1996. "Olympic Ceremonies as a Setting for Intercultural
       Exchange." In Moragas, Miquel de, John MacAloon, and Montserrat Llinés,

eds. *Olympic Ceremonies: Historical Continuity and Cultural Exchange.* Lausanne: International Olympic Committee. Pp. 29 – 43.

Machiavelli, Niccolo. 1992. *The Prince.* Trans. W. K. Marriott. New York: Everyman's Library.

Macleod, Iain. 1998. "The Opening Ceremony: Nagano." *Olympic Review* 20: April-May, Pp. 20-22, 24.

Maguire, Joseph. 1999. *Global Sport: Identities, Societies, Civilizations.* Cambridge, U.K.: Blackwell Publishers.

Mallon, Florencia. 1995. *Peasants and Nation: The Making of Post Colonial Mexico and Peru.* Berkeley: University of California Press.

Marx, Anthony. 1996. "Race-making and the Nation State." *World Politics,* 48(2): 180-208.

Michels, Robert. 1959. *Political Parties.* New York: Dover Press.

Moore, Katharine. 1997. "Love of Fair Play: The Ambivalent Response to the Olympic Movement in England, 1891-1914." In Naul, Roland, ed. *Contemporary Studies in the National Olympic Games Movement.* New York: Frankfurt am Main. Pp. 71 – 92.

Moragas Spà, Miquel de, Nancy K. Rivenburgh, and Nuria Garcia. 1995. "Television and the Construction of Identity: Barcelona, Olympic Host." In Morages Spà, Miquel de, and Miquel Botella, eds. 1995. *The Keys of Success: The Social, Sporting, Economic, and Communications Impact of Barcelona '92.* Bellaterra: Servei de Publicacions de la Universitat Autonoma de Barcelona. Pp. 76 – 107.

Morgan, Prys. 1983. "From a Death to a View: The Hunt for the Welsh Past in the Romantic Period." In Hobsbawm, Eric & Terrence Ranger. 1983. *The Invention of Tradition.* Cambridge: Cambridge University Press. Pp. 43 – 100.

Mosse, George. 1975. *The Nationalization of the Masses: Political Symbolism and Mass Movements in Germany from the Napoleonic Wars through the Third Reich.* Ithica, NY: Cornell University Press.

Mraz, John. 1995. "Memories of Underdevelopment." In Rosenstone, Robert A. 1995. *Revisioning History: Film and the Construction of a New Past.* Princeton: Princetion University Press. Pp. 102 – 114.

NAOC. 1998a. "Closing Ceremonies of the 1998 Nagano Winter Olympics." New York: CBS News, 22 February.

———. 1998b. "Opening Ceremonies of the 1998 Nagano Winter Olympics." New York: CBS News, 7 February.

———. 1998c. *The XVIII Olympic Winter Games Official Report. Vol. 2.* Nagano: Organizing Committee for the XVIII Olympic Winter Games (NAOC).

Naul, Roland, ed. 1997. *Contemporary Studies in the National Olympic Games Movement.* New York: Frankfurt am Main.

Novikov, I.T. ed. 1981. *Games of the XXII Olympiad Moscow 1980: Official Report of the Organizing Committee of the Games of the XXII Olympiad, Moscow, 1980* Vol. 2. Moscow: OCOG-80.

OCO'88. 1988a. "Closing Ceremonies of the 1988 Calgary Winter Olympics." New York: ABC News, 28 February.

———. 1988b. "Opening Ceremonies of the 1988 Calgary Winter Olympics." New York: ABC News, 13 February.

———. 1988c. *XV: Olympic Winter Games Official Report.* Calgary: XV Olympic Winter Games Organizing Committee (OCO'88).

OCOG-80. 1980a. "Closing Ceremonies of the 1980 Moscow Summer Olympics." New York: NBC News, 3 August.

———. 1980b. "Opening Ceremonies of the 1980 Moscow Summer Olympics." Lausanne: International Olympic Committee, 19 July.

Official Site of the International Olympic Committee. http://www.olympic.org/

Ogilvie, John. 1884. *The Imperial Dictionary of the English Language.* London: The Century Company.

Olympic Games: Athens 1896 - Sydney 2000. London : Dorling Kindersley, 2000.

Olympic Museum. http://www.museum.olympic.org/

Organizing Committee of the XIVth Olympic Winter Games. 1984a. "Closing Ceremonies of the 1984 Sarajevo Winter Olympics," New York: ABC News, 19 February.

———. 1984b. "Opening Ceremonies of the 1984 Sarajevo Winter Olympics." New York: ABC News, 7 February.

———. 1984c. *Final Report.* Sarajevo: The Committee.

Parsons, Talcott. 1951. *The Social System.* New York: Free Press.

———. 1961. "An Outline of the Social System." In Parsons, Talcott, Edward A. Shils, Kaspar Naegele, and Jesse R. Pitts, eds. *Theories of Society.* New York: Free Press. Pp. 30 – 84.

Peppard, Victor and James Riordan. 1993. *Playing Politics: Soviet Sport Diplomacy to 1992.* Greenwich, CT: JAI Press.

Perelman, Richard. B., ed. 1985a. *Official Report of the Games of the XXIIIrd Olympiad Los Angeles, 1984 Vol. 1.* Los Angeles: Los Angeles Olympic Organizing Committee (LAOOC).

———. 1985b. *Official Report of the Games of the XXIIIrd Olympiad Los Angeles, 1984 Vol. 2.* Los Angeles: Los Angeles Olympic Organizing Committee (LAOOC).

Perrottet, Tony. 2004. *The Naked Olympics.* New York: Random House.

Petrie, Brian. 1975. "Sport and Politics." In Ball, Donald W. and John W. Loy. ed. 1975. *Sport and Social Order: Contributions to the Sociology of Sport.* Reading, MA: Addison-Wesley Publishing Company. Pp. 185 – 237.

Pindar. 1961. *The Odes of Pindar, including the Principal Fragments.* Trans., Sir John Sandys, Cambridge: Harvard University Press.

Pope, S.W. 1997. *Patriotic Games: Sporting Traditions in the American Imagination, 1876 – 1926.* New York: Oxford University Press.

Popkin, Jeremy D. 1990. *Revolutionary News: The Press in France, 1789-1799.* Durham, NC: Duke University Press.

Pound, Richard W. 1994. *Five Rings Over Korea.* Boston: Little Brown Company.

———. 2005 Personal Correspondences. November 9 - 27. Montreal, Canada.

Puijk, Roel 1999 "Producing Norwegian Culture for Domestic and Foreign Gazes: The Lillehammer Olympic Opening Ceremony." In Klausen, Arne Martin, ed. *Olympic Games as Performance and Public Event: The Case of the XVII Winter Olympic Games of Norway.* New York: Berghahn Books. Pp. 97 – 136.

Reed, John Shelton. 1976. "The Heart of Dixie: An Essay in Folk Geography." *Social Forces* 54(4): 925-39.

Reich, Kenneth. 1986. *Making It Happen: Peter Ueberroth and the 1984 Olympics.* Santa Barbara, CA: Capra Press.

Riordan, James. 1996. "Communist Sports Policy: The End of an Era." In Laurence Chalip, Arthur Johnson, and Lisa Stachura, eds. *National Sports Policies.* Westport, CT: Greenwood Press. Pp. 89 - 115

Riordan, James. 1996. "Olympic Ceremonies in History (1980 –1994): A Pilgrimage to the Past and a Gesture of Faith in the Future." In Moragas, Miquel de, John MacAloon, and Montserrat Llinés, eds. *Olympic Ceremonies: Historical Continuity and Cultural Exchange.* Lausanne: International Olympic Committee. Pp. 153 – 156.

Rivenburgh, Nancy. 1996. "Television and the Construction of Identity: Barcelona and Catalonia as Olympic Host." In Moragas, Miquel de, John MacAloon, and Montserrat Llinés, eds. *Olympic Ceremonies: Historical Continuity and Cultural Exchange.* Lausanne: International Olympic Committee. Pp. 222 – 342.

Roche, Lisa Riley. 2003. "Salt Lake Mulls Another Olympic Bid." *Deseret Morning New.* 21 July.

Roche, Maurice. 2000. *Mega-events and Modernity: Olympics and Expos in the Growth of Global Culture.* London: Routledge.

La Rochefoucauld. 1959. *Maxims.* Trans, Leonard Tancock. London: Penguin Classics.

Roosens, Eugeen E. 1989. *Creating Ethnicity: The Process of Ethnogenesis.* Newbury Park, CA: Sage Publications.

Rosenstone, Robert A. 1995. "Walker: The Dramatic Film as (Postmodern) History." In Rosenstone, Robert A. 1995. *Revisioning History: Film and the Construction of a New Past.* Princeton: Princetion University Press. Pp. 202 – 215.

Ross, Marc Howard. 1999. "Culture and Identity in Comparative Political Analysis." In Lichbach, Mark Irving, and Alan S. Zuckerman. *Comparative Politics: Rationality, Culture, and Structure.* Cambridge: Cambridge University Press. Pp. 42 – 80.

Schantz, Otto. 1996. "From Rome (1960) to Montreal (1976): From Rite to Spectacle." In Moragas, Miquel de, John MacAloon, and Montserrat Llinés, eds. *Olympic Ceremonies: Historical Continuity and Cultural Exchange.* Lausanne: International Olympic Committee. Pp. 131 – 139.

Sekulic, Dusko, Garth Massey and Randy Hodson. 1994, February. "Who Were the Yugoslavs? Failed Sources of a Common Identity in the Former Yugoslavia" *American Sociological Review*, 59(1): 83-97.

Segrave, Jeffrey, and Donald Chu. eds. 1988. *Olympic Games in Transition.* Champaign, Il: Human Kinetics.

Senn, Alfred. 1999. *Power Politics and the Olympic Games.* Champaign, Il: Human Kinetics.

Shinnick, Phillip K. 1978. "Sport and Cultural Hegemony." In Lowe, Benjamin, David B.Kanin, and Andrew Strenk, eds. *Sport and International Relations,* Champaign, Il: Stipes Publishing Company. Pp. 95 – 107.

Shinnick, P.K. 1982. "Progressive Resistance to Nationalism and the 1980 Boycott of the Moscow Games." *Journal of Sport and Social Issues* 6(20): 13-15.

Sinn, Ulrich. 2000. *Olympia: Cult, Sport, and Ancient Festival.* Princeton: Marcus Wiener Publisher.

SLOC. 2002a. "Closing Ceremonies of the 2002 Salt Lake City Winter Olympics." New York: NBC News, 24 February

———. 2002b. *Official Report of the XIX Olympic Winter Games. Vol. 1.* Salt Lake City: Salt Lake Organizing Committee (SLOC).

———. 2002c. *Official Report of the XIX Olympic Winter Games. Vol. 2.* Salt Lake City: Salt Lake Organizing Committee (SLOC).

———. 2002d. "Opening Ceremonies of the 2002 Salt Lake City Winter Olympics," New York: NBC News, 8 February.

Smith, Anthony D. 1999. *The Ethnic Origins of Nations.* Oxford: Blackwell Publishers Ltd.

Sobolev, S. 1951. *Letter to IOC*, Moscow, April 1951, in Avery Brundage Collection, No. 149, USOA NOC, 1947-69, p. 2.

SOCOG. 2000a. "Closing Ceremonies of the 2000 Sydney Summer Olympics." New York: NBC News, 1 October.

———. 2000b. "Opening Ceremonies of the 2000 Sydney Summer Olympics." New York: NBC News, 15 September.

———. 2001. *Official Report of the XXVII Olympiad. Vol. 2.* Sydney: Sydney Organizing Committee for the Games (SOCOG).

SLOOC. 1988a. "Closing Ceremonies of the 1988 Seoul Summer Olympics." New York: NBC News, 2 October.

———. 1988b. "Opening Ceremonies of the 1988 Seoul Summer Olympics." New York: NBC News, 17 September.

———. 1989a. *Official Report: Games of the XIVth Olympiad Seoul 1988. Vol. 1* Seoul: Seoul Olympic Organizing Committee (SLOOC)

———. 1989b. *Official Report: Games of the XIVth Olympiad Seoul 1988. Vol. 2* Seoul: Seoul Olympic Organizing Committee (SLOOC)

Spier, Fred. 1996. *The Structure of Big History: From the Big Band Until Today.* Amsterdam: Amsterdam University Press.

Spivey, Nigel. 2004. *The Ancient Olympics: A History.* New York: Oxford University Press.

Stam, Robert and Louise Spence. 1999. "Colonialism, Racism, and Representation.". In Braudy, Leo and Marchal Coen. eds. 1999. *Film Theory and Criticism: Introductory Readings.* New York: Oxford University Press. Pp. 235 – 250.

Stanton, Richard. 2001. *The Forgotten Olympic Art Competitions – The Story of the Olympic Art Competitions of the 20th Century.* Victoria, Australia: Trafford Publishing.

Steinberg, Stephen. 1981. *The Ethnic Myth: Race, Ethnicity and Class in America.* New York: Atheneum.

Strassler, Robert. B, ed. 1998. *The Landmark Thucydides: A Comprehensive Guide to the Peloponnesian War.* New York: Simon & Schuster.

Thelen, Kathleen, and Sven Steinmo. 1998. "Historical Institutionalism in Comparative Politics." In Steinmo, Sven, Kathleen Thelen, and Frank Longstreth, eds. 1998. *Structuring Politics: Historical Institutionalism in Comparative Analaysis.* Cambridge: Cambridge University Press. Pp. 1 – 32.

Thompson, William R. 1983. "Introduction: World System Analysis With and Without the Hyphen." In Thompson, William R., ed. *Contending Approaches to World Systems Analysis*. Beverly Hills, CA: Sage Publications. Pp.7 – 24.

Thucydides. 1910. *History of the Peloponnesian Wars*. Trans. Richard Crawley. London: J.M Dent; New York, E.P. Dutton.

———. 1989. *The Peloponnesian War*. Trans., Thomas Hobbes. Ed., David Grene. Chicago: University of Chicago Press.

Tishkov, Valery A. 1992 "Inventions and Manifestation of Ethno-Nationalism in and after the Soviet Union." In Rupesinghe, Kumar, Peter King, and Olga Vorkunova, eds. *Ethnicity and Conflict in a Post-Communist World: The Soviet Union, Eastern Europe, and China*. New York: St. Martin's Press. Pp. 41 – 65.

Trevor-Roper, Hugh. 1983. "The Invention of Tradition: The Highland Tradition of Scotland." In Hobsbawm, Eric & Terrence Ranger. eds. *The Invention of Tradition*. Cambridge: Cambridge University Press. Pp. 15 –43.

Tsebelis, George. 1992. *Nested Games*. Berkeley: University of California Press.

UCLA Special Collections Finding Aid. http://www.oac.cdlib.org/dynaweb/ead/ucla

United States Olympic Committee. http://www.usoc.org/

Vinokur, Martin. 1988. *More Than a Game: Sports and Politics*. New York: Greenwood Press.

Wallace, Ruth A. and Alison Wolf. 1999. *Contemporary Sociological Theory: Expanding the Classical Tradition*. Upper Saddle River, NJ: Prentice Hall.

Watkins, Ginger T., ed. 1997a. *Official Report of the Centennial Olympic Games. Vol. 1*. Atlanta: Atlanta Committee for the Olympic Games (ACOG).

———. ed. 1997b. *Official Report of the Centennial Olympic Games. Vol. 2*. Atlanta: Atlanta Committee for the Olympic Games (ACOG).

Weber, Eugen. 1976. *Peasants into Frenchmen: The Modernization of Rural France 1870-1914*. Stanford, CA: Stanford University Press.

Webster, Noah. 1869. *A Dictionary of the English Language*. Springfield, MA: G & C Merriam.

Weir, Maraget. 1998. "Ideas and the Politics of Bounded Innovation." In Steinmo, Sven, Kathleen Thelen, and Frank Longstreth, eds. *Structuring Politics: Historical Institutionalism in Comparative Analaysis*. Cambridge: Cambridge University Press. Pp. 188 – 215.

Winston, Brian. 1995. *Claiming the Real*. British Film Institute Publishing.

Woodward, Susan. 1995. *Balkan Tragedy: Chaos and Dissolution After the Cold War*. Washington D.C.: The Brookings Institute.

Wolper, David. 1984. "The 1984 Ceremonies." *Olympic Review* 201: July August, Pp. 508-509.

"World Heaps Scorn on U.S. Atlanta Organizers Get Bad Reviews," *Toronto Star* (Toronto) , 24 July 1996.

Xiangjun, Cao & Susan Brownell. 1996. *"The People's Republic of China."* In Laurence Chalip, Arthur Johnson, and Lisa Stachura, eds. *National Sports Policies*. Westport, CT : Greenwood Press. Pp. 67 – 88.

Zagare, Frank. 1984. *Game Theory: Concepts and Applications*. London: Sage Publications.

———. 1987. *Dynamics of Deterrence*. Chicago: University of Chicago Press.

INDEX